# AGINCOURT

1 4 1 5

# AGINCOURT

## 1 4 1 5

### Henry V, Sir Thomas Erpingham and the triumph of the English archers

*Edited by Anne Curry*

TEMPUS

First published 2000

PUBLISHED IN THE UNITED KINGDOM BY:

Tempus Publishing Ltd
The Mill, Brimscombe Port
Stroud, Gloucestershire GL5 2QG

PUBLISHED IN THE UNITED STATES OF AMERICA BY:

Arcadia Publishing Inc.
A division of Tempus Publishing Inc.
2 Cumberland Street
Charleston, SC 29401
(Tel: 1-888-313-2665)

Tempus books are available in France, Germany and Belgium
from the following addresses:

| | | |
|---|---|---|
| Tempus Publishing Group | Tempus Publishing Group | Tempus Publishing Group |
| 21 Avenue de la République | Gustav-Adolf-Straße 3 | Place de L'Alma 4/5 |
| 37300 Joué-lès-Tours | 99084 Erfurt | 1200 Brussels |
| FRANCE | GERMANY | BELGIUM |

British Library Cataloguing in Publication Data.
A catalogue record for this book is available from the British Library.

ISBN 0 7524 1780 0

Typesetting and origination by Tempus Publishing.
PRINTED AND BOUND IN GREAT BRITAIN.

# Contents

# Foreword

In Norwich Cathedral in October 1996 there happened a remarkable event, a symposium organized by the Norfolk Heraldry Society on the subject of Henry V's marshal of the archers at Agincourt in 1415, Sir Thomas Erpingham. A Norfolk man, around 58 at the time of the battle, an unwavering supporter of the Lancastrian dynasty, Shakespeare's 'good old knight' who in the play *Henry V* lends the cloak as a disguise when Henry goes among the soldiers encamped the night before the battle; it was he who on the actual day organized the five thousand or so archers, and who rode out in front of the English lines and threw his baton in the air with the cry '*Nestroque*', as the French hear it – 'Now strike!' or 'Knee stretch!' as English commentators have interpreted it since. Often have I stood on that famous field, in fact and in imagination, and strained to hear that far cry, which unleashed the first deadly volleys into the packed mass of the French.

For half a century, Agincourt has been at the centre of my studies concerning British military archery, and though I feel I have gone about as far as anyone can into the contemporary accounts of this much documented battle, I also feel that if by some magic one suddenly awoke from a deep sleep into the middle of that October day and that fearsome engagement, it would all happen around one in a shockingly different fashion from any we have deduced and imagined. But the very best chance of being guided towards an understanding of what the lamenting French called 'the Picardy affair', when up to ten thousand of their countrymen perished, and the flower of their nobility was culled, was to be at the 1996 Norwich Heraldry Society meeting of some of the finest medieval historians in Britain or now to read this resulting volume.

Erpingham was at the core of the day's investigations, partly because the gathering was to celebrate the life and loyalty, the military and civil prowess of a local magnate, but, because of his position of influence in the Lancastrian cause, they also embraced the battle itself, the contemporary concepts of chivalry, the heraldry of the battle, its victor and Erpingham's master, Henry V, and importantly, Erpingham's command – which represented five-sixths of the total English and Welsh army – the longbowmen. None can be sure exactly how the English were deployed: the sources themselves offer differing suggestions. Matthew Bennett and I will perhaps forever disagree about archer positions, but none will dispute the salient and unarguable facts, that the archers were deployed to best advantage, that they destroyed the initial French cavalry attacks, made life hideous for the advancing masses of French infantry and, when the two armies crashed together, turned on the instant into men-at-arms and inflicted merciless destruction among the French at close quarters.

Here in this collection of the best of the talks delivered in Norwich Cathedral, supplemented by additional contributions by members of the Norfolk Heraldry Society and others, you may follow the most lucid and elegant of minds into the dark nightmare of that famous victory, illumined by some of the shining characters who were the cause and the centre of one of the greatest moments of our Island story.

Robert Hardy CBA, FSA, Hon. D.Litt. (Durham), Hon. D. Litt. (Reading)

# Acknowledgements

The first thanks must be to the Norfolk Heraldry Society who organised the Erpingham Symposium in 1996, and to the the Dean and Chapter of Norwich Cathedral for hosting the event within the Cathedral and Close. Thanks are due especially to Tony Sims for assistance as picture editor, and to the following who have generously allowed use of their pictorial materials: David Laven (figs 3-5); Paul Hitchin (plates 1-11, figs 10-13); Anne Curry (plate 12, figs 7-9, 31-2); Ken Mourin (plates 18-22, figs 26, 30); Tony Sims (figs 14, 15, 37-42, 44-5); Brian Kemp (figs 51-5); Simon Eager (fig. 56); Sarah Cocke (plate 13, fig. 27); Henry Paston-Bedingfeld (plate 23); Robert Hardy (plate 24). The contributors would also like to thank the staff of the Norfolk Record Office for assistance with sources; Simon Walker for advice on Erpingham's career; Joan Hurrell for advice on heraldry and ships; Monsieur Claude Songis for his help in connection with French coats of arms; Jonathan Reeve and Tempus Publishing for encouragement and support.

Plate 16 and figure 6 are reproduced by permission of the British Library; figs 16-22 and 25 by permission of the Public Record Office; plate 15 and figs 46-8 by permission of the Victoria and Albert Museum; plate 14 by the permission of the Burrell Collection, Glasgow; and figs. 33-5 by permission of the Eastern Daily Press. Figure 24: © Crown copyright 2000; reproduced by permission of the Public Record Office on behalf of the Controller of Her Majesty's Stationery Office.

# List of Illustrations

## Colour plates

# 1 Henry V: A Life and Reign

## Anne Curry

'Take him all round and he was, I think, the greatest man that ever ruled England.' So wrote K.B. McFarlane in 1954, and try as they might, subsequent commentators have not been able to discredit this image of greatness. In customary fashion, academics have whittled away at the king's reputation, accusing him of over-stretching English resources, of negotiating an unworkable peace treaty with the French at Troyes in 1420, and thus of sowing the seeds of defeat overseas and civil war at home – features which colour much of the remainder of the fifteenth century. Yet for every bad thing one can say about Henry V, there are dozens of good things to say in his defence. Perhaps his only real offence was to die too soon, leaving an heir only nine months old, but blame for this can hardly be placed at the king's door.

So Henry remains the golden boy of fifteenth century history – strong, decisive, athletic, energetic, pious, and above all successful. Of all the kings of the fifteenth century, Henry V is unique. Unlike his father, he did not usurp the English throne, nor did he usurp the French. He was not deposed like his son, and it is unlikely that he ever came anywhere near deposition even in the supposed plots against him early in his reign. Moreover, unlike the other kings of the century, he came to the throne when neither too young nor too old, experienced but still in his full prime.

So, a royal success story. And our continuing admiration has a long pedigree. A fair reflection of the reputation of a king is the number of biographies written in his lifetime or soon after. For Henry we have more such works than for any king of England since William the Conqueror, though perhaps the Black Prince might have made it into this first division had he outlived his father. The first biography, the *Gesta Henrici Quinti*, was compiled as early as 1417 and gives us a full account of the Agincourt campaign. A single quote will suffice as an illustration of this contemporary view of Henry. Here he is on his return to England three weeks after the battle:

> Nor do our older men remember any prince having commanded his people on the march with more effort, bravery, or consideration, or having, with his own hand, performed greater feats of strength in the field. Nor, indeed, is evidence to be found in the chronicles or annals of kings of which our long history makes mention, that any king of England ever achieved so much in so short a time and returned home with so great and so glorious a triumph.

This was surely God's work. The feeling that God had shown his favour for England through such a king permeates the whole of the *Gesta* as it does the other biographical work that was written within Henry's lifetime, the versified *Liber Metricus* of Thomas Elmham. The adulation continues in the biographies written in the next generation and into the sixteenth century with, in particular, the *First English Life* of 1513. Indeed Henry V is the only monarch to remain basically unscathed by the Tudor's derogatory treatment of their fifteenth-century predecessors.

Anyone interested in history knows, however, that one should never take evidence at face value, and that biographies written within or near the lifetime of their subject are only marginally less subjective than autobiographies. The narrative sources for the reign of Henry V are no exception to this rule. Like many medieval narrative writings they were interdependent, borrowing shamelessly from each other but without giving credit, and they embroidered the truth, particularly those which were composed furthest from Henry's own day. Any legend in his own lifetime easily lends itself to further embellishment. Just as the Gospel writers and later theologians may have sought to fill in the gaps in the life and personality of Christ, so the biographers of Henry flesh out the bare bones with anecdotes of his childhood and youth, and with flashes of human rather than kingly personality. So through the sixteenth-century writers come the features of Henry that we know and love so well in Shakespeare: the brave but boisterous youth spent in the Boar's Head Tavern, the reconciliation with his father and the conscious abandonment of his former wicked ways at his own accession, and the love and courtship of Catherine. But in defence, many of the myths have some root in actual, known events. The king undoubtedly did offer much personal encouragement 'calmly and heedless of danger' (*Gesta*) to his tired and worried troops on the eve of Agincourt; we can surely forgive Shakespeare and even the much lamented Sir Larry their 'little touch of Harry in the night.'

Of course Henry's biographers were biased. The *Gesta* may even have been a work of propaganda commissioned to show Henry in a good light in the international scene of the Council of Constance; a Church council held to settle the problem of papal schism and where the English were attempting to cement anti-French alliances with the Germans. A good son of the Church – such as Henry claimed to be – should not be causing so much bloodshed by war between Christian nations. The onus was therefore on him, or at least on his biographer who was probably a royal chaplain, to justify the war with France and in particular the king's decision to launch a new campaign of conquest in the summer of 1417. Not such a difficult matter, of course, for the very success of the war effort so far showed that God himself fully endorsed the English war aims and methods.

Moreover was not Henry the most christian of princes, a man of great personal piety and a founder of two monasteries and potentially a third, all for the new orders dedicated to a return to the pure and original character of the true religious life? The Carthusian house at Sheen (April 1415) and the Brigittine house at Syon (March 1415) were in fact the last monasteries to be founded in Pre-Reformation England. Most of all, had Henry not shown himself to be a valiant friend and supporter of orthodoxy in his firm repression of the English heretical sect, the Lollards, particularly at the time of their armed rebellion in 1414?

A man who had revealed himself as a true son of the true Church could not fail but to be treated well by the monastic writers who in the first quarter of the fifteenth century still dominated historical writing in England. For Thomas Walsingham, the last of the long tradition of Benedictine chroniclers at St. Albans, here was the 'athleta Christi', the active defender of the faith. Thomas Elmham, monk of Canterbury and author of the verse biography composed within Henry's lifetime, placed even greater emphasis on the king's religious stance. Having likely served Henry as his chaplain in 1414, and writing his complex Latin panegyric of the king for a clerical audience, the tone of his work is hardly surprising.

The nature of bias in later works is also easily identified. The *Vita* (Life) written by the Italian Titus Livius Frulovisi in the late 1430s was commissioned by Henry's last surviving brother, Humphrey duke of Gloucester, motivated not only by affectionate brotherly memory but also by a desire to remind the growing numbers of those who wished to call an end to the Anglo-French war of the rightness and glory of Henry's campaigns. How could the English contemplate a peace which would destroy all that Henry had ever fought for? Our other mid-fifteenth century life, the *Pseudo-Elmham*, was sponsored in its first recension by Walter Lord Hungerford, Henry's close associate in war and peace, steward of the household, diplomat and one of the leading captains in France. In its later version, it was commissioned by John Somerset, Henry VI's physician. Both Hungerford and Somerset were of the Gloucester way of thinking. Moreover both promoters had their own reminiscences of the late king, seen as much through rose-tinted spectacles as through the mists of uncertain memory. Our first English life, *c.*1513, even further removed in date, also relied upon the transmission of the memories of an ageing retainer and companion in arms, the earl of Ormonde.

Do we have any chance at all of seeing the real Henry? Our biographers are known to be biased and all that survives from the king's own hand are two rather inconsequential letters. Much other contemporary or near contemporary evidence is equally adulatory and the king himself was an adroit and conscious user of propaganda both in France and England. However, we must not suppose that because the sources are problematic the legend itself is erroneous. Henry was the subject of much writing, of all kinds and for all types of fifteenth-century audience, and the amount of coverage in the vernacular town chronicles is also worth a mention here. He captured the attention of these commentators primarily because he was such an impressive ruler, indeed an exemplary ruler, whose career was worth recording and embellishing. Henry met all the characteristics expected of a medieval king. He was a military hero in his lifetime, he was actively pious, he was renowned for justice and he was praised for ruling firmly but without oppression or partiality. All kings were feared, but Henry was admired and appreciated by his people as a whole, by his friends who knew him more intimately, and even by his enemies, for some French chroniclers admit his military genius, his chivalric behaviour and his wise rule of their country.

We may never fathom out the man himself. We can scarcely understand those living and close to us today, so what chance with a monarch who lived over five hundred years ago. But let us consider some of the principal features and characteristics of this remarkable reign.

The child maketh the man. How did Henry's early experiences affect him? Henry was born into the leading family in England on 16 September 1387. As the eldest child in a family of eventually four boys and two girls, he led a predictable aristocratic childhood until his father, Henry Bolingbroke, then duke of Hereford, was exiled by Richard II in 1397. The young Henry faced a very real dilemma of loyalty, a dilemma exacerbated by his father's return in 1399 to claim the throne. In the intervening two years Henry had been hostage at Richard's court for his father's good behaviour, but there is some evidence to suggest that the relationship between Richard and the young prince – particularly on the Irish trip of 1399, where Henry was knighted by the king – was amicable. This has fuelled speculation about the early origins of the later awkward relationship between Henry and his own father. Did Henry feel more for Richard than he did his own father?

We can know little of the young Henry's reaction to Richard II's deposition, although some later chroniclers claim that he departed from Richard with great sorrow and only when the latter ordered him to follow his filial duty. At the outset of his own reign, he arranged the reburial with full kingly ritual of the body of Richard II, which Henry IV had ordered to be buried without ceremony at Langley. Henry V had of course attended the funeral of his own father at Canterbury Cathedral earlier, but the odd way in which the chronicler Walsingham records his attendance ('at the feast of the Trinity the solemn exequies of Henry IV were celebrated at Canterbury, Henry the king's son and heir being present') implies that his presence was worth a notice, perhaps as being unexpected.

By 1413 Henry did not have a good relationship with his father; he even failed to carry out the wishes of his will. There is, however, a considerable danger in placing the break too far back. The reburial of Richard II in December 1413 was an act of conciliation and, as such, a political masterstroke aimed at establishing the Lancastrian dynasty once and for all. It belongs more properly to the policies of Henry V as king rather than as prince, as we shall see. Although several other things happened in the young Henry's maturity to effect the apparent breach with his father, what is more significant is that the events of 1399 suddenly changed the position of the young prince. Now no longer a potentially disinherited hostage, separated from the rest of his family, but heir to the kingdom itself, and in his own right prince of Wales, earl of Chester, duke of Cornwall, duke of Lancaster and duke of Aquitaine; no mean landed endowment. He thus stands as unique again amongst fifteenth century kings because of the length and significance of the 'apprenticeship' before his accession. Indeed to find a comparable example one has to look as far back as Edward I, for the Black Prince died without putting his long experience as prince of Wales into practice as king.

Henry of Monmouth was his royal father's heir for nearly fourteen years, between his first year of teenship and his accession as a man of twenty five. These were the formative years, initially years of uncertainty as his father contended with successive rebellions and faced the difficult choice between conciliation and repression. Henry gave his father full support in the suppression of the Percy rebellions and first distinguished himself at the battle of Shrewsbury in 1403: the arrow wound in his knee was more than proof of his courage. He gained nine years of military experience dealing with the Glendower rebellion in Wales, primarily very much under the tutelage of his father's trusted nominees, but subsequently taking full charge. It was here that he learnt valuable lessons about command, military finance and siege warfare, and not least how to deal with a rebellious but finally defeated people, experiences which clearly influenced his later strategies in Normandy. It was in Wales too that he came into contact with many of the men who were to form the basis of his later royal household and army.

The fall of Harlech in February 1409 released him from active service and led to his first central appearance in politics. By this time his father's state of health was causing intermittent crises in government, which the prince began to exploit despite his father's apparent resentment and obstruction. From early in 1410 to November 1411 the prince and his nominees dominated the royal council and royal policies, but at the king's recovery and apparently up to the end of the reign they appear to have gone into the political wilderness.

1. *Miniature from the Psalter of Humphrey, duke of Gloucester, believed to show his brother, the young Henry V, kneeling before the risen Christ.*

It is in these years that father and son are seen at their most distant. Differences over foreign policy are the most obvious manifestation. Such were the violently opposed policies of Henry and his father that the former sent an army in 1411 to assist the Burgundian party in France, whilst in 1412 the latter sent troops to fight against the Burgundians.

A phenomenon known to students of the eighteenth century as the 'reversionary interest' can be observed as a party built up around the prince, in apposition if not direct opposition to the king. The serious nature of the rift is revealed by a letter given in Walsingham, supposedly sent to his father by Henry on 17 June 1412. Rebutting charges that he was aiming to seize his father's crown (though there probably were some rumours, possibly even princely plans, concerning abdication), Henry claimed that there were others, 'certain sons of iniquity... sowers of wrath and instigators of discord who, with something like the guile of the serpent' (probably implying that they had the ear of the king) were attempting 'to disturb the line of succession'. We can see clearly that, in the last two years of his reign, Henry IV was much closer to his second son, Thomas, than to his heir, but surely no usurper would consider himself tampering with the rightful succession within his own dynasty. Perhaps the young Henry's accusations in 1412 were in effect a form of blackmail, an attempt to remind the king of his eldest son's rightful position and to restore him to it by bringing the king to his senses, for – as the prince implied in his letter – rumours and dissensions would only serve to damage the kingdom and its present king. Whatever the case, Henry was certainly outmanoeuvred by his father in 1411 and 1412.

Whether Henry was ever reconciled with his father or not – and in a way it is immaterial, for he succeeded unchallenged – there can be no doubt that the new reign began with a general feeling of optimism, quite to be expected for here was a young and dynamic ruler replacing a care-worn invalid. There can be no doubt that Henry was intelligent, even relatively bookish by the standards of the age, although it is unlikely that he went to Oxford as some have claimed. Was there a change in his character at his accession? The change noted by chroniclers may not have been merely one of lifestyle – drinking, whoring and the like – but of 'liberalism'. Like many young men whose fathers do not understand them, Henry may have had a slightly anti-establishment view, for instance over religion (for example the Lollards and Oldcastle) though he had shown himself a true son of the Church in the Badby case during his father's reign. Perhaps there is some degree of 'modernity' in his religious stance even as king: for example in his favouring of the new more reflective and mystical orders; in his acting upon criticisms of the Benedictine order, criticisms undoubtedly put forward to him by Carthusians; or in his own stress on personal prayer and humility.

All in all, hopes were high at his accession. 'Now spring had come to melt the winter snows', as Walsingham wrote, commenting on the significance of the late and unexpected snow which accompanied Henry's coronation on 8 April 1413. In response to parliamentary petitions, the new king made the right noises about reforming abuses, remedying the ills of the preceding years. Henry seems to have taken on the duties of kingship with ease, enthusiasm and – a virtue often lacking in medieval kings – tact. Indeed there are three aspects of his rule which first manifest themselves in these crucial early days and which appear fundamental to Henry's success as king. The first is his willingness to conciliate, to patch up old quarrels and wipe the slate clean, although as we shall see this was always on his terms, and this did not prevent him acting savagely when he was opposed. The second element was his stress on justice and 'good governance', and the third was the high degree of his personal involvement in government.

Henry knew the importance of conciliation. Fair enough, a king is in the happy position of being able to conciliate on his own terms, but I think it would be true to say that Henry was a good man-manager. There was no witch hunt against his father's advisors, although inevitably the former prince's associates were introduced to the principal offices of state; not surprisingly as these offices were still very much based on the personal household of the monarch. Henry recognized talent, and throughout the reign, offices both high and low in England and in France were filled by men of competence. He also rewarded loyalty, including the loyalty of men who had served the two previous generations of Lancastrians. He even gave Oldcastle chances to recant his Lollard views for the sake of friendship and past service.

He soon made moves to reinstate the heirs or survivors of those who had initially opposed the deposition of Richard II. But we must not forget that he moved slowly on this and that he rarely forgave without imposing conditions or without expecting much service and benefit to himself in return. For example, Salisbury was only restored to part of his inheritance in 1414 and not declared to be entitled to all his father's lands until after his service in Normandy in 1421; Huntingdon had his lands restored in 1416 after military service; Percy petitioned for the restoration of his estates in 1414 but this was not completed until 1416 when the earldom of Northumberland was in fact created anew. The estates of Cambridge, York and March were similarly carefully withheld by the king, while the restoration of the dukedoms of Norfolk to the Mowbrays did not occur until his son's reign. Like all successful kings, Henry kept tight personal control of patronage.

It is worth remembering that his peerage creations were extremely limited. Examples of life peerages were Cambridge, Bedford and Gloucester at the May 1414 parliament and Exeter in

1416. Those in receipt of royal annuities were expected to fight and the king was clearly unimpressed by the excuses put forward by those asked to give service in 1419. He kept the royal demesne largely intact at least until his marriage, as he needed all the money he could get and no doubt was aware of parliamentary criticism in his father's reign of the king's inability to live 'of his own'. Indeed one wonders whether a reputation for meanness may not have emerged for Henry V had it not been for the new found availability of land to grant out in Normandy.

Henry did reward but without being extravagant. He kept the nobility under control, but by personal connection and example rather than by flattery and purchase. He expected men to enrich themselves at the expense of others and not the crown. Moreover he could be cruel in the face of opposition: for example, the executions of Cambridge, Scrope and Heton; the killing of prisoners at Agincourt; the treatment of Henry Beaufort over the issue of his proposed cardinalcy in March 1418, excused only by a very large loan of £22,000. Note also Henry's treatment of the French towns of Harfleur and Caen (even their records were burnt), and his attitude to those thrown out of Rouen during the siege. But he was not vengeful.

This firmness without repression came from his strong sense of justice. Indeed 'justicia' even appears to have been his nickname amongst some of the legal fraternity. Complaints of a breakdown in law and order had mounted in the last years of Henry IV, with certain areas of the country (most notably Staffordshire and Shropshire) being marked out as particularly lawless. Although there had been earlier attempts to remedy the problem, the restoration of good order was largely due to the efforts of Henry V in the first two years of his reign. Special circuits were undertaken by Kings Bench – the principal criminal court normally based in Westminster – and other commissions combined investigations into local disorder with enquiries into Lollard activity. In addition, the Statute of Additions at the May 1413 parliament attempted to tighten up the wording of summonses whose earlier looseness had let many a suspect off the hook. The king himself presided over some cases but was prepared to be lenient where necessary. A particularly useful royal tool was the general pardon or amnesty issued in December 1414, for not only did it sweep the board clean but it also raised vital revenue, with the 5,000 or more takers paying for their pardon.

Henry's reign stands out as one of the few periods of comparatively good order in the generally disorderly fifteenth century, although certain problems – such as counterfeiting – were almost impossible to eradicate. Some earlier commentators have suggested that the renewal of the war with France did much to help public order, in particular by channelling magnate ambition into military activity abroad rather than political activity at home. This view is of course too simplistic: in some ways Henry's absence generated new problems, and we hear plenty of complaints about the excesses of departing and returning soldiers. But it is worth emphasizing Henry's stance on military discipline praised even by French chroniclers as part of his undoubted chivalric virtue. For all his campaigns he issued lengthy disciplinary ordinances, not decidedly innovatory but enforced as closely as possible. Shakespeare's reference to the summary execution of a soldier who stole a pyx is probably true, and we know of other cases where Henry acted swiftly and savagely to protect the civilian population in France against his soldier's excesses.

Henry was a hard task master who expected a high standard of behaviour from himself as well as from others. Fortunately he usually managed to instil such standards, but heaven help the transgressor. For example, Sir Hugh Annesley took wages to sail in the 1421 expedition but failed to cross and was thus put in the Tower by the king. Even Henry's brother Gloucester was penalized for shipping costs when his retinue fell two short. Henry had a strong sense of the contractual element in justice: so long as one kept one's side of the bargain then he was an active protector. But any transgression, particularly after the king had offered clemency or had laid down codes of behaviour, would most certainly lead to punishment. Hence the king offered full protection, pardon and restitution of rights to those French prepared to take an oath of obedience to himself and later to the Treaty of Troyes. Those who refused were traitors and could expect no clemency. 'Ruthless but fair' would perhaps best sum up the king's attitude to the behaviour of all of his subjects.

Mention of matters such as law and order raises an important question, that of the degree of Henry's personal involvement in government. When we look at medieval monarchs we have to be careful not to attribute everything that happened, even in the minutiae of government, to their hands directly. Already there was much in the conduct of government that was impersonal and bureaucratic. There were administrative systems which operated often surprisingly smoothly irrespective of the monarch. Henry was not one of those 'reforming' kings so beloved of constitutional historians. He had a trusted and competent council and team of administrators both in England and France. Moreover, he was absent from England for about half of his reign, for about three months in 1415 and then for three and a half years from July 1417 to February 1421, and again from July 1421 to August 1422.

He was, however, no mere cipher for he kept a close scrutiny over all aspects of government even in his absence. Evidence suggests that he was well informed about what was going on, that if he felt it necessary he could turn his attention to even routine matters. On one occasion he even appears to have checked through the accounts of the keeper of the wardrobe himself, adding marginal annotations requesting clarification and explanation of income and expenditure.

Whilst he did delegate to his brothers, who acted as Protectors of England in his absence, he never released the reins of government completely. He required all petitions to be sent to him, and warrants issued continued to need the king's approval. There was a steady stream of instructions sent back to England even when embroiled in intense military action. We can see his personal activity at its sharpest definition in the letters issued under the most intimate of seals: the king's signet. Two of these are in the king's own hand. The others were dictated by him and many are crouched in the king's distinctive style: abrupt, to the point, clear and unequivocal. There was a certain brusqueness about Henry which indicates a man who grasped the issues quickly, a man used to thinking on his feet, a man who didn't like wasting time. Henry offered decisive and clear-cut government. He was a king who led from the front.

Little has been mentioned about the main concern of Henry's reign and indeed the main aspect of his historical reputation: the war with France. However, it would seem that our understanding of Henry's military success is enriched by what we have gleaned so far about the nature of his government in general and about his personality.

*2. Royal portrait of Henry V.*

There can be no doubt that Henry was a man who enjoyed life on campaign, whose adrenalin only really started to flow in fighting and in preparing to fight. After all, he had spent most of his formative years on campaign in Wales and took a strong interest in proposed military involvement in France in his father's reign. Whilst many domestic matters occupied him in the first two years of his own reign, we must not forget that preparations for the 1415 expedition began long before, even whilst diplomatic negotiations were taking place. His 12,000 strong army (very large by medieval English standards) embarked in August 1415, and Henry led it throughout the siege of Harfleur, on the march northwards across the Somme to the fateful meeting with the French at Agincourt on 25 October (with Shrewsbury Henry's only experience of a pitched battle and fought essentially at the behest of the French), and then brought it back to England in victory in November, an absence on active military service of three months.

Over the next two years Henry remained in England, leaving the defence of Harfleur and the naval actions in the Channel to his uncle Exeter and middle brother, Bedford, whilst he himself pursued negotiations with the emperor and the French. But even in this period of truce, Henry's thoughts continued to concentrate on the next move against the French. The resulting campaign launched on 1 August 1417 was intended as a serious long-term venture quite different from the customary form of English campaigns in France. He and his army would spend the winter in the field instead of returning home at the end of the campaigning season. For the aim was to conquer territory systematically by gaining control of the defensive centres. We can only assume that right from the start Henry envisaged a lengthy personal absence from England (although what would have happened if he had met with less success in Normandy we cannot tell).

The military actions of this campaign lasted right up to the final negotiations which led to the signing of the treaty of Troyes on 21 May 1420. Whilst some military initiatives in this period were delegated to his leading captains (indeed various campaigns were being conducted at the same time) Henry remained in overall command of strategy and was himself present at many major sieges and assaults. After his marriage to Catherine on 2 June 1420, he cut short the celebrations to begin the siege of Montereau, only returning to England in February 1421, his absence now totalling three and a half years. Even after his return to France in July 1421, when he also had to see to his new role as Regent, he spent much of his time in the field. It was at the siege of Meaux that he contracted the dysentery which was to bring about his premature death at the château of Vincennes on 31 August 1422.

Henry was fortunate in having many able captains under his command, some – like him – with military experience gained in Wales, and others whose skills developed as the French campaign progressed. There is ample evidence that Henry frequently consulted his chiefs of staff and that charge of many military initiatives was delegated to others. We also know that, in preparing for war, the king deliberated with his council in England and successfully negotiated parliamentary approval and taxation: eleven parliaments were held in nine and a half years, granting more taxation than in any other reign, and well-managed in the king's interests. He also made considerable use of propaganda and the personal touch in the country as a whole through proclamations, royal pageants and in 1421, by the fifteenth century equivalent of the royal walkabout, a tour of the towns and religious shrines of the Midlands and North. Indeed, all the way through we can see attempts to involve the whole community in the war effort, partly for the sake of material requirements, money, men, shipping, but also for less tangible needs, such as prayers, political obedience, morale boosting and national unity. Through such widespread involvement, the nation was united behind its king by the war effort.

In all of this, whether on campaign or in preparation for war, Henry led from the front. He was the mastermind behind strategy. Indeed the actual destination of the expedition of 1415 may have remained a secret known only to the king and his closest advisors until disembarkation across the Channel. Henry was in full command at the siege of Harfleur and at Agincourt where he showed considerable tactical foresight in particular in the choice of the English position. The strategy of the Norman campaign was also of his devising, as too were the later sieges. Even if others saw to the routine administration, Henry took upon himself much of the responsibility for the deployment of manpower, the provision and use of artillery and ordnance, and disciplinary supervision. And of course he retained sole control over appointments to captaincies, over grants of lands in conquered territories, and over the important matter of relations with the native population. His active involvement in campaigning was paralleled by his personal oversight of diplomatic negotiations and his personal influence is seen clearly in many of the clauses of the final treaty.

Of his physical energies and mental capacity there can be no doubt. According to literary and portrait evidence, he looked the part: above average height – certainly taller than his father

– slim but sinewy, with a long, oval face, which was usually clean shaven (although evidence of the York chancel screen may suggest that he sported a small forked beard in 1421), and clear, expressive hazel eyes which were apparently dovelike when unmoved but which became fierce as a lion when roused. We learn too that he exposed himself to danger at several sieges and that in his lifetime he enjoyed a reputation – dating back to at least 1403 when he suffered an arrow in his face – for bravery and military prowess. This is a man who drove himself on in the last months; despite his illness and the wasting of his body he insisted on continuing to ride for as long as he possibly could and on being seen by his people.

What we seem to be building up here is the picture of a man who lived for military action, for war as an end in itself. A medieval Rambo? But surely this is not enough to explain his renewal of the war with France. Other factors are of clear importance. We cannot give this consideration full discussion here but we must remember that England and France had never properly ended the first stage of the Hundred Years War: Henry inherited a half-peace, initiated in the reign of Richard II. His own father had already begun a policy of military involvement, albeit tentatively. There can be no doubt that France was in a weak, divided condition in the first quarter of the fifteenth century. Both Henry IV and Henry V realized the potential which this offered the English, both in diplomatic and military terms. International relations were then as now very much a matter of opportunism.

Was Henry V ambitious? Did he want to be king of France as well as of England because of a personal power craving? All in all there is little evidence for this. A study of the diplomatic activity of the reign suggests that Henry followed the by now customary English line of using the claim to the French crown as a bargaining ploy. There are signs as late as the middle of 1419 that he was prepared to give up the title in return for an advantageous territorial settlement. But it is hard to know what Henry would have settled for. His demands tended to harden as he prepared for war, as he met with increasing military success and as his opponents were proved weaker and more divided. Whichever way one considers it, it was the murder of the duke of Burgundy, John the Fearless, by the Dauphin's supporters on 10 September 1419 which opened up the real possibility of achieving the crown and thus the best territorial settlement possible. Even so, Henry was magnanimous in victory. Arguably he could have seized the throne at this point for the French government was effectively leaderless after John's death and Paris lay at Henry's mercy. But instead he agreed to a pacific settlement and quite a strange one at that. The treaty of Troyes marks a complete break with the Anglo-French conflict of the last ninety years or so. By sealing it Henry recognized Charles VI as king of France for the first time and, at his own request, became not Charles usurper but his regent and heir (and son-in-law, although in fact it was the treaty and not the marriage to Catherine which gave Henry the inheritance of the French crown). All that was needed was for the mad Charles VI to die, then Henry and his successors would forever more be kings of a dual monarchy of France and England. The treaty in almost all its other clauses – and there are a lot of them – is testimony not to Henry's ambition but to his belief in justice and reconciliation. It shows too his realism, because surely the only way he could ever have been accepted as king was by a settlement which preserved French rights, including the rights of their existing king. Unworkable the treaty may have been, overbearing and oppressive it was not.

Were we able to ask Henry why he went to war, we would no doubt be given the same kind of explanation as the biographers and chroniclers relate. His war was above all a just war. He had legitimate claims in France arising out of the non-fulfilment of the terms of Edward III's Treaty of Brétigny of 1360 and indeed out of the ancient claims of English kings to the territory they had possessed until the reign of John. It was the French who were unjustly and rebelliously withholding these claims, just as at this time they were supporting a schismatic Pope and refusing overtures of peace. The reopening of the war was thus portrayed as a crusade, even a war to end all wars. As the Chancellor proclaimed at the opening of the parliament of 1416, 'we make war so that we may have peace, because the end of war is peace'. To us this may seem rather self-deluding, but this is what Henry believed. And in this respect he was a man of his age. War was seen as a way to peace, a way that has to be adopted when peace has failed. In the same context, anything which disturbed the right order of things, which usurped the power of God and his anointed had to be destroyed. It was the acknowledged duty of the Christian prince to protect his rights, his people and his Church, for all were God-given.

According to fifteenth-century standards, Henry was a success. He had restored good government in England and by all accounts had even started to do so in France. By war he had achieved peace in the treaty of Troyes. He had helped to extirpate heresy and to rejuvenate monasticism in England. He had elevated England to a prime place amongst the nations of Europe and had played a not inconsequential though largely indirect role in the settlement of the papal schism.

At the outset of this chapter it was implied that his main fault may be that he died too soon, but did he? Is he remembered favourably both in his own age and ours largely because he died whilst still on the crest of the wave? There are some who cast doubt on whether he could have continued the impetus of military action in France, whether he could have won the hearts of all the French people whilst also retaining those of the English. Already in 1420 and 1421 he had experienced difficulties in England over the voting of parliamentary taxation for the war and had had to increase his reliance on loans. We know too that there were some reservations in England over the prospect of a dual monarchy, for many feared a French take-over, or lamented the likely extension of the king's absence overseas which they already felt had been too long.

The treaty of Troyes had changed the nature of the war. Now it was not so much a case of English versus French as Henry – French king-elect – versus his rebellious French subjects. Would the English have continued to support such a war? The treaty also committed Henry to continue fighting until all France acknowledged his position as heir. Yet 1421 saw the first real setbacks: the defeat by a Franco-Scottish army at Baugé in March when his brother Clarence met his death; and the difficult siege of Meaux conducted by Henry himself at the end of the year. Were these a sign of things to come?

Yet Henry had already overcome many difficulties in his reign so we can never know how he would have coped with the new problems which the treaty of Troyes generated. Henry is often blamed for the disasters of his son's reign, but looked at from another angle, we can claim, as did some contemporary observers, that it was the legacy of Henry V which gave some measure of security and even success at least in the early days of Henry VI's minority. It took the French twenty-seven years to recover what Henry had taken in less than seven. With Henry V at the helm for longer, the course of English and French history might have been quite different.

# 2 The Battle

## Matthew Bennett

### The background to the campaign and battle

Few battles are as well known, superficially at least, as the memorable encounter fought thirty miles south of Calais, in an otherwise obscure corner of modern northern France. To a certain extent we have William Shakespeare to thank for ensuring that the event has become part of our national consciousness. More significantly, perhaps, for a twentieth-century audience, the films of Laurence Olivier and Kenneth Branagh have kept the battle in the popular imagination. Agincourt has been taken to symbolize the indomitable spirit of the British (as opposed to the English), as Shakespeare makes clear with his humorous emphasis on the multi-ethnic nature of Henry's army. This is what made the play such a perfect vehicle for Olivier's wartime propaganda. It also contrasts the pragmatic, no-nonsense attitude of the English army with the bombastic posturing of the aristocratic French.

It might almost seem that the result was a foregone conclusion but nothing could be further from the truth. Henry's sickly and starving forces were outnumbered by at least four to one in bare numbers, and in terms of men-at-arms – the fully-equipped fighting men of the day – by perhaps ten to one. So how did Henry pull off such an improbable triumph? Again, the story is almost too well known. It was his brave archers who overwhelmed the French and snatched victory from the jaws of defeat. Their success is so much celebrated as to sometimes overshadow the full story of the battle, in which plans, tactics, the hard fighting of the men-at-arms and the slaughter of the French prisoners fade into the background behind the archers' achievement. This was a result of the development of the 'English tactical system' (as the interdependence of archers and men-at-arms is described), and for which the French had devised a plan intended to defeat this deployment. That this did not occur on 25 October 1415 was due to a combination of factors, of which the superior leadership displayed by Henry V and the much greater cohesion displayed by his army were not the least.

First, it is necessary to sketch in some political and military background to the campaign and the battle. In 1399, King Richard II had been deposed, and replaced by Henry IV (Bolingbroke). As a usurper, Henry found himself involved in defending his crown at the battle of Shrewsbury, in 1403. His son, Prince Henry who was only 16 at the time, performed very bravely in the battle, continuing to fight in the front line despite being wounded in the eye by an arrow. This was only part of Henry V's military apprenticeship, for he was also involved in long campaigns, including extensive siege warfare against the Welsh rebellion of Owen Glendower. Richard II had sought peace with France, and it was not until 1411 that the English resumed a more aggressive policy. In fact, the times were much more propitious then, because the French king Charles VI was mentally ill, incapable of ruling, leaving power to be disputed between John the Fearless, duke of Burgundy, and the Armagnac lords. This political division, occasionally erupting into bouts of civil war, gave the ambitious Henry V new opportunities when he came to the throne in 1413. In 1414, a French army campaigned in exactly the region that was to be fought over in the following year. It resulted in a brutal sack of Soissons by the Armagnacs, and was remembered a year later, on the feast day of the city's patron saints, Crispin and Crispinian, when the battle of Agincourt took place. Many commentators saw the outcome as divine revenge for the outrage, but this was in the future. The peace of Arras made between the French factions that closed the year did little to rebuild trust among the divided French nobility. Perhaps it was this factor, rather than God's will, which was to lead to the downfall of French fortunes in 1415.

Henry spent the first two years of his reign preparing for an expedition during which he hoped to emulate or exceed the military successes of his illustrious great-grandfather, Edward III. In 1415, the plan adopted by Henry was quite similar to Edward III's in 1346. He chose to attack in Normandy, as an area that could be detached from the French crown. He may also have planned a grand *chevauchée* to Bordeaux (a grandiose development of Edward's scheme) which, in the event, was not possible. Henry's forces may have been twice as numerous as Edward's: some 20,000 men supposedly transported in '1,500 ships' (according to contemporary accounts, although this number of vessels is mostly likely to be an exaggeration by a factor of three at least). This 20,000 included many infantry, siege engineers and artillery men for the siege of Harfleur. The rest of the force was made up of about 2,500 men-at-arms and 8,000 archers, with some 10,000 horses for the rapid movement of *chevauchée*. *Chevauchée* (literally 'a ride through an enemy's territory') was a method of warfare by which the invader ravaged the lands of defender. Crops and property were destroyed, animals and the human population driven off, and the countryside set alight. The purpose of this activity was to undermine the political authority of the king of France, proving him unable to defend his subjects and so encouraging them to accept another lord. This policy had been very successful in the earlier part of the Hundred Years War (up to 1360), but had proved fallible when the French, under Charles V, developed a strategy of avoiding battle with the English armies, by shadowing their advance and preventing them from ravaging or sending out foraging parties effectively; and by reducing the invaders to starvation and neutralizing their damaging strategy. This was essentially the French plan for what became the Agincourt campaign.

Henry's siege of Harfleur, although well prepared, seriously undermined his plans. Either through sensible caution or confusion among the commanders, the French made no attempt to relieve the place. The marshal of France, Jean Le Maingre, called Boucicaut, commanded an observation force at the port of Honfleur, across the Seine; but neither he, nor Charles VI, nor the Dauphin Louis proved capable of intervention. The siege is an interesting military study in its own right, but this is not the place to discuss it. Although eventually successful after five weeks, it left too little of the campaign season for Henry to march to Bordeaux, or even to the closer objective of Paris. Water-borne diseases which had swept through the English ranks had killed over 2,000 men, including many nobles. Perhaps another 2,000 were injured and sent home, and 500 men-at-arms and 1,000

*3. The English march to Agincourt.*

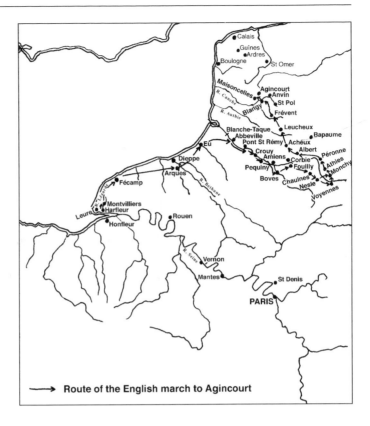

**Route of the English march to Agincourt**

archers were needed to garrison Harfleur. This left to Henry, according to the *Gesta*, some 900 men-at-arms and 5,000 archers with which to continue the campaign. Despite the advice of his counsellors he announced that he would march to Calais. This was a very risky strategy in the face of a much superior enemy. Why did he do it?

Probably, an important factor was the example of Edward III, whom Henry was eager to emulate and to surpass. So, when his small force set out with only a week's rations he had set himself a demanding task. He was shadowed by the French advance guard under the veteran Marshal Boucicaut, some 6,000 strong, while the French main body at Rouen numbered 14,000 men-at-arms with numerous other support troops. The French successfully blocked passage of the Somme, including the crucial ford at Blanchetacque, driving the English up-river away from Calais. Supplies ran out opposite Amiens, an unassailable city, and Henry led his sick and starving army further away from the coast. Attempts against the towns along the river proved equally unavailing. Then, by good luck, or, most probably, good judgement, he did manage to get his troops across the Somme before reaching its headwaters, and marched north again. Henry was able to do this by cutting across on a short route on his side of the river whilst the French were forced to take the long route around a great curve of the Somme. The crossing of the river by the fords at Voyennes and Bethéncourt was in many ways as heroic as the crossing at Blanchetacque fifty-nine years earlier. While it was true that Henry's crossing was not opposed, an advance guard under Sir Gilbert Umfraville and Sir John Cornwall did have to secure the bridgehead. Then there was a flurry of repairing the two causeways, but this

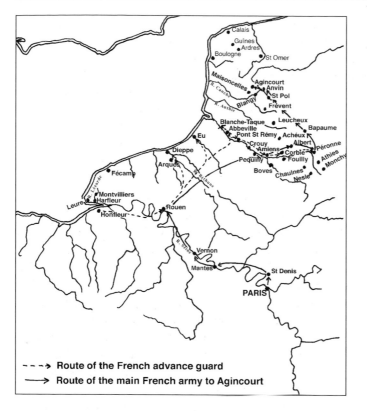

*4. The French march to Agincourt.*

still only allowed one horseman to cross at a time. Having commenced work at dawn, the army began crossing by midday and was safely over by about five o'clock and then advanced to camp at Péronne on the night of 19 October.

By this time, of course, the French main force had also crossed the river and was in a position to block his path. This was not at Péronne, as some historians state, but further north at Bapaume, blocking Henry's route to the north. Henry used 20 October as a rest day, then set out again on 21 October. There was now no possibility of avoiding the French host which marched parallel for three days, then directly in front of Henry blocking his route. This it did at Agincourt, two days march short of Calais.

## Sir Thomas Erpingham and the Archers at the Battle of Agincourt

> Some on the French side say that the king of England sent 200 archers towards the French and behind their army, secretly, so that they could not be seen, towards Tramecourt to a meadow close to where the vanguard of the French were positioned. The purpose of this was that when the French marched forward, the 200 archers could fire on them from the side. But I have heard said and certified as true by a man of honour who was there on that day in the company of the king of England that nothing like this happened... The king of England ordered a veteran knight, called Sir

Thomas Erpingham, to draw up his archers and to put them in the front in two wings. Sir Thomas exhorted everyone on behalf of the king of England to fight with vigour against the French. He rode with an escort in front of the battle of archers after he had carried out the deployment, and threw in the air a baton which he had been holding in his hand, crying 'Nestroque' which was the signal for attack. Then he dismounted and put himself in the battle of the king of England, which was also on foot, between his men and with his banner in front of him. Then the English began suddenly to advance uttering a great cry which much amazed the French.

This is how the subject of this study is pictured at the battle of Agincourt by a young man then aged 15 who was with the French army, Jean de Waurin, and who half a century later at the court of Philip the Good, duke of Burgundy, was to compose his *Chronicles of the Kingdoms of England and France*. Another young Frenchman, Jean Le Fèvre, sire de St Rémy, this time accompanying the English army and aged 19 or so, also records this story. (These accounts are discussed more fully later in this volume.) For the sixteenth-century writer Holinshed, Erpingham's 'throwing up his truncheon was a signal for the archers posted in the field at Tramecourt to commence the battle'. It must be said, however, that Waurin and Le Fèvre both refute the Tramecourt ambush story, saying 'a man of honour who was that day in the company of the king of England assured me that the report was not true', perhaps because it implied an unchivalric sneakiness with which the chroniclers felt uncomfortable?

The purpose of these introductory remarks is to make three initial points. First, that the role of Sir Thomas Erpingham in managing the archers was recorded by eye-witnesses; secondly that these archers required some kind of orders as to their positioning and a signal to commence action; and thirdly, that sources describing a battle are rarely clear and often contradictory. It is with the second point that we are most concerned today. How did medieval commanders deploy their archers and use them to best effect in battle? In attempting to answer these questions it will be necessary to look at how the archers were raised and commanded on campaign, how they were deployed in battle, and what evidence there is for a chain of command and what might be called 'fire orders'. For it will become apparent from the first extracts that such details are far from clear in contemporary sources.

The deployment of the archers has long been a matter for hot debate (perhaps surprisingly). Almost exactly a century ago, the pages of that distinguished journal, *The English Historical Review*, featured a long-running argument about how this was done during the Hundred Years War. The dispute was settled in favour of those authorities, chiefly J.E. Morris and Sir Charles Oman, who believed that an English battle-line was laid out in a particular way. All medieval armies used the tripartite division of van(guard), main body and rearguard. Each of these divisions was called a 'battle', from which we derive the modern word 'battalion'. These three 'battles' could then be deployed in a line, or one behind the other, or some other variant. It was usual to place missile men on the flanks of an army, and also possible to place them on the flanks of each 'battle' to give 'fire support' to its close-order, armoured men. By the later middle ages these hand-to-hand

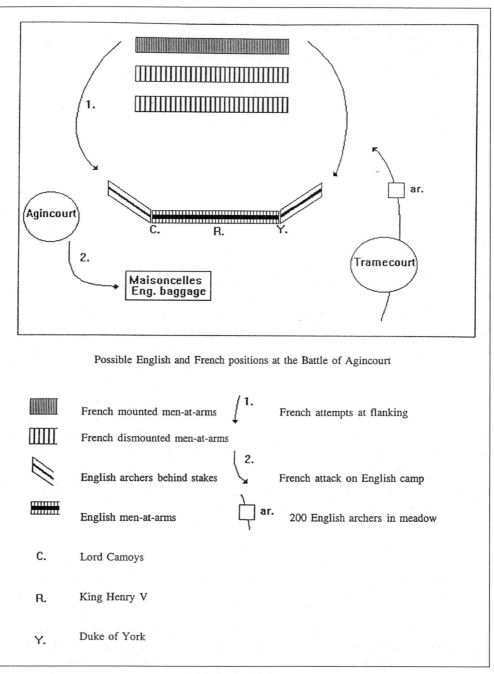

Possible English and French positions at the Battle of Agincourt

French mounted men-at-arms

French dismounted men-at-arms

English archers behind stakes

English men-at-arms

1. French attempts at flanking

2. French attack on English camp

ar. 200 English archers in meadow

C. Lord Camoys

R. King Henry V

Y. Duke of York

*5. The battle of Agincourt.*

combatants were usually known as men-at-arms, that is to say, warriors equipped in whatever counted as full armour for the day. In the 1340s, when the conflict usually called the Hundred Years' War began, men-at-arms were largely armoured in mail, although plate armour was being introduced. By the time of Agincourt, their descendants wore the complete harness of full plate. In the 1330s, the English, particularly, had developed the tactic of dismounting their men-at-arms rather than having them remain mounted as cavalry. This served to provide a solid infantry capable of defeating the chivalrous charges of the French. What won battles for the English was, though, the combination of archers and men-at-arms. As a result of the *English Historical Review* debate just mentioned, the normal English deployment was understood to be three 'battles' of men-at-arms, each with projecting wings of archers. Where these projections met they joined to form a hollow wedge. Any attacking force would then find itself funnelled between these projections and endure a cross-fire as it tried to come to grips with the men-at-arms. The projecting wedges were assumed to represent the formation described by the fourteenth-century chronicler Jean Froissart as employed by the English at Crécy, that is to say the *herce*: a kind of spiky formation (the word relates to other meanings such as 'hedge', 'harrow' or even 'hedgehog').

There the matter rested until 1985, when Jim Bradbury published a book entitled *The Medieval Archer*. In it, he pointed out that medieval chronicles are far from specific in identifying the herce formation as looking like twentieth-century representations of it. In fact, the sources stress the importance of keeping archers on the wings of the deployed army. Building on this idea, in my own book on Agincourt in 1991, I ventured to suggest that any reference to the harrow might relate to the way its interstices are set off against one another. In other words that it was not meant to represent the entire formation but how individual archers were deployed in ranks, allowing them to shoot past one another. In support of this interpretation, we have the *Gesta Henrici Quinti* (*The Deeds of Henry the Fifth*) – an eye-witness account by an English priest, quite possibly Thomas Elmham – of how the English archers deployed with their stakes at Agincourt:

> As a result of information divulged by some prisoners, a rumour went round the army that enemy commanders had assigned certain bodies of knights, many hundred strong and mounted on barded horses, to break the formation and resistance of our archers when they engaged us in battle. The king, therefore, ordered that every archer, throughout the army, was to prepare for himself a stake or staff, either square or round, but six feet long, of sufficient thickness and sharpened at both ends. And he commanded that whenever the French approached to give battle and break their ranks with such bodies of horsemen, all the archers were to drive their stakes in front of them in a line and some behind them and in between the positions of the front rank, one being driven into the ground pointing towards themselves, the other end pointing towards the enemy at waist-height. So that the cavalry, when their charge had brought them close and in sight of the stakes, would either withdraw in great fear or,

reckless of their own safety, run the risk of having both horses and riders impaled.

I have also followed Bradbury in asserting that the English archers were formed up on the wings of the army, and not on each battle, as the traditional view described it. This drew down upon me the wrath of Robert Hardy and resulted in a public debate at a study day held by the Battlefields Trust in February 1995. Hardy pointed out, quite rightly, that the *Gesta* states that Henry drew up three 'battles', *et intermisisset cuneos sagittariorum suorum cuilibet aciei*. This is usually taken to mean 'and he positioned wedges of his archers in between each battle', and therefore seems to support the traditional interpretation. But *cuneus* does not only mean wedge, it also means 'troop', 'unit', 'body of men', or even 'a mob'! The word is used just a few lines earlier in the *Gesta* where its translators render it as 'platoons' to describe units in the mounted, rear 'battle' of the French. So the Latin phrase could be rendered as 'and he mixed troops of archers in his battle lines'. Not the same thing at all.

I am unhappy with the idea of projecting wedges, because I believe that such a formation would have been vulnerable to attack by oncoming men-at-arms. If contacted at the apex, from where the archers would have fewer arrows directed at the enemy, they could not hope to sustain the attack of fully-armoured opponents. That wily veteran Jean de Bueil recognized this fact in his *Le Jouvencel* (*c*.1466) when he advised protecting archer formations with men-at-arms; this after the personal experience of a lifetime of war (and over a century of the French fighting the English). Why then this obsession with crossing-fire? The reason might lie in the tactics of the early twentieth century. In the period before and during the First World War, tacticians were much concerned with how to arrange cross-fire against an enemy. A diagram from a 1916 manual shows just how this could be done. Interestingly it even has a three-battalion front, just as A.H. Burne envisaged medieval battle lines! To be honest, the lines between myself and Robert Hardy were not so fiercely drawn as some of the newspaper accounts of the debate would have wished. Whilst we might differ on where the archers stood, we are agreed on how flexible a missile force they provided. They did not stand in bullied ranks like the Redcoats of the eighteenth and nineteenth centuries. They were not, in the words of J.E. Morris, mere 'animated dummies'. Nor were they a peasant levy but men of some social standing, as later chapters will exemplify. They were soldiers with a high degree of individual skill, proud of their craft (like guildsmen) and capable of independent action.

If we are to examine in a little more detail how the archers were best deployed, then we must turn to an Elizabethan commentator. Sir John Smythe had long experience in the wars, and was a determined exponent of the superiority of the bow over the gun. In 1590, he published a treatise justifying his claims, and his description of the array at Tilbury in 1588, in readiness for the Armada, is extremely informative as to how he thought archers should be best deployed:

> [The arrayers] placed certain ranks of archers in the midst of their
> squadrons of pikes, behind the ensigns, and seven ranks of archers they

placed upon the very back of the battle and the rest they reduced into sleeves close by the flanks of their three battles, of which sleeves some of them were five in a rank and some three in a rank. And because they should surely be guarded with shot they reduced sleeves, or rather squadrons of caliver shot, close to the ranks of the archers of which sleeves of caliver shot some were nine-and-twenty in a rank, others fifteen in a rank, which to all men of any judgement in matters military might be a wonderful scorn and mockery.

The problem with this formation is that it did not allow the 'shot' (that is to say the missile-weapons of all kinds) to employ their shooting to the best effect. This impediment bore most heavily upon the archers who needed to be deployed with a clear 'field of fire' against an approaching enemy. Smythe continues that, as an enemy drew closer, the pikemen should close up their formation to the front and in from the flanks: 'then the archers are to give their volleys of arrows at the enemy approaching within eight, nine, ten or eleven scores [between 160-220 yards/paces]. And to perform the same they might not have any other weapon placed before them that may anyways take away their sights to direct their arrows towards their enemies' faces.' Without a clear sight, their target obscured by smoke, other types of 'shot' in the way, or if standing behind ensigns (banners) or rows of pikes which caught the arrows as they flew, the archers could not be expected to perform properly.

According to Smythe, 'the ancient order of reducing archers into form [deploying them] was into hearses, that is broad in the front and narrow in the flank, as, for example, if there were twenty-five, thirty, thirty-five, or more or fewer archers in front, the flanks did consist but of seven or eight ranks at most. And the reason was this: that if they had placed any more ranks than seven or eight, the hinder ranks of archers should have lost a deal of ground in the volleys of their arrows at their enemies, considering the convenient and proportionate distinction betwixt rank and rank and the ranks before them, as also that the sight of the hinder ranks should have been taken away by so many former ranks from directing their volleys of arrows towards their enemies' faces.' He goes on to praise the old formations; 'our ancestors … placed their hearses of archers either before the front of their armed footmen or else wings upon the corners of the battle and sometimes both in front and wings.' He then cites 'Froissart and the French chronicles' who describe the French at Crécy as not being 'able to enter and break the archers although they had no pikes, stakes, banks nor trenches to guard them. But being the plain and open fields, the archers with their volleys of arrows did break both horsemen and footmen, wounding or killing both horses and men in such sort that the French king himself, being in great peril, had his horse with the shot of arrows slain under him.'

Smythe's admiration for the English archer is such that he asserts 'that archers being in great numbers and reduced into the form of herses or double herses as wings to a battle or squadron of pikes, that they may the more conveniently give their volleys of arrows, need not be guarded with pikes or staves [as some talk of the battle of Agincourt] but they themselves are most brave pikers'. To be honest, the importance of the close-fighting troops in order to support his polemic is most likely played down, but this should not be allowed to undermine the crucial point that medieval archers were deployed in the same way as sixteenth-century 'shot'. That is how missile men were used before the invention of the bayonet in the 1670s enabled musketeers to hold off cavalry unaided.

In order to understand how 'shot' – meaning, as we have seen, any kind of missile men – were used in the mid-sixteenth century, we can look at the advice given by a veteran of Henry VIII's wars to his son, Edward VI. Sir Thomas Audley drew upon his own experience and also sought to bring to the king's attention what might be learned from continental practice (he refers especially to the German manner of fighting). He clearly envisaged a 'clump' of pikes around which the 'shot' were to be deployed. He makes no distinction between bows or arquebuses: to him all were 'shot'. This is an important point because commentators have tended to emphasize the revolutionary nature of the impact of firearms in the sixteenth century. To an old soldier like Audley, the difference was that bows were reckoned to be more reliable in all weather conditions and to inflict more casualties on the enemy. Audley's advice is that the pikes and halberds (or bills) should be surrounded by shot. He expects there to be an equal split between archers and arquebusiers, but if there is an imbalance, then bows taking the slight majority is to be preferred. Interestingly, he recommends that if the commander has too many shot, then a proportion of them should be relieved of their weapons, to be re-equipped with hand-arms and incorporated into the pike-block. Audley actually refers to the armoured front-rankers of his main body ('corslettes') as being the direct descendent of the dismounted men-at-arms. He also provides some valuable insights as to where he thought that 'shot' should be best positioned. Essentially he describes four formations: first, on the flanks of the main body; second, all around that body; third, positioned forward of the main battle-line, again on the flanks; fourth, operating in front of the main body, possibly detached in what became known as bodies of 'commanded shot'.

The last part of my chapter returns to the issue of just how the archers knew when to shoot and at what target. As discussed elsewhere in this volume, they were raised for service overseas by a system known as indenture. That is to say, a 'captain', who might differ in rank from a simple squire to an earl, contracted with the king to provide a certain number of men-at-arms and archers. Over the period 1340 to 1475, that is between the French campaigns of Edward III and Edward IV, the proportion of archers in the force grew from about 2:1 to 7:1;(at the battle of Agincourt it was perhaps about four to one.) In addition, a larger proportion of the archers became mounted men. This was to enable them to keep up with the men-at-arms, especially on the ravaging campaigns known as *chevauchées*, at which the English became so expert when pursuing their wars in France. Although the close fighters and missile men were recruited together, they were brigaded apart on the battlefield, as we have seen. We do know that the archers were grouped in hundreds, under *centenars* and scores under *vintenars,* but we have no descriptions of any 'chain of command' and how it might have worked. Considering the issue for a moment highlights the problems of 'fire control'. We are frequently told that the English archer could shoot a dozen shafts a minute, with ease, in contrast to the laborious crossbow's once or twice. Undoubtedly this helped the archers to swamp the Genoese crossbowmen at Crécy. However, we cannot assume that such a rate of fire was sustainable for a long

6. *Letter of Henry V in his own hand, referring to the safe-keeping of prisoners captured at Agincourt, c.1419 (British Library Cotton MS, Vespasian F iii, folio 8).*

duration. Archers carrying as many as three or four dozen shafts in their arrow bags would have exhausted their supply quickly, even allowing for resupply from carts. (We know these were present in large numbers at Crécy, and there was certainly a supporting baggage and supply train in 1415, although for rapidity of movement this had been much reduced from its normal proportions.) In fact, commonsense suggests that they shot a few ranging and disrupting shots at, say three hundred yards, stepped up the rate a little at two hundred yards, but reserved the intensive arrow-barrage for the last one hundred yards, and shot most quickly over the last thirty yards. This accords with later musketry drill. It is worth remembering that even today, the most effective small-arms fire is delivered at less than one hundred yards.

So what was Sir Thomas Erpingham actually doing at Agincourt? First there is the problem of what his order, 'Nestroque' (or sometimes spelled as 'Nestrocq'), meant. It has been variously interpreted to mean 'knee stretch', or my preferred option, 'now strike!'. But how do we get from this to the 'Nestroque' of the chroniclers. Perhaps the reason lies in Sir Thomas's accent and the French writers' misunderstanding of it. A 'Norfolk bor' does not say 'now strike' in a cut-glass Home Counties accent but 'naow stroik!'. Any Frenchman hearing this had every right to be confused. One can imagine the discussion between author and scribe: 'Qu'est-ce qu'il a dit?' 'Je ne sais pas, il me semble qu'il a crié "nestroque".' 'C'est un mot de commandement anglais?' 'Bien sûr.' 'Mais qu'est-ce qu'il signifie?' (shrugs shoulders) 'Ecrivez-le.'

The trouble with Sir Thomas's order is that it only tells the archers when to commence shooting, not at what target or what rate of fire or for how long. This then must have been left up to the experience of archers on the ground and their commanders. Unfortunately, nothing exists in writing to tell us how this was managed. We do know, of course, that practice at the butts, regularly carried out, mixed with clout-shooting (that is, into the air in order to land on a piece of ground covered by a cloth), would have taught the archers everything they needed to know as individuals. However, these things are much more difficult to manage *en masse*. Given the great rareness of really big battles, there were most probably no opportunities for practising the necessary drills to ensure that shooting was directed to best effect. Even Sir Thomas Smythe does not tell us exactly how he would wish his 'hearses' of archers to be managed. This is simply taken for granted. Remember that even before gunpowder weapons obscured the battlefields of Europe in smoke, little is clear in a battle. The two hundred archers in Tramecourt woods – if we accept their presence – were left very much to their own devices after Sir Thomas had shouted his order and given his signal. Even in the relatively compact formation adopted by King Henry at Agincourt, and even assuming a system of runners or gallopers (nowhere mentioned in the sources), it would have taken minutes to get orders to the flanking archers to instruct them when and where to shoot or when to desist.

In fact, these kinds of decisions were most likely left up to the decision of the archers and their local commanders. This only goes to strengthen their reputation as individuals of great military worth. Unlike the dragooned musketeers of the sixteenth century onwards, they were expert players in the game of war. So much depended upon them judging it right. Their job was to so disrupt the enemy formations so that when they, like the French at Agincourt, reached the English main battle-line, the men-at-arms had an enormous superiority in cohesion and freshness in contrast to their battered and confused opponents. Whereas archers could probably not win a battle unsupported – Agincourt is proof enough of that, with the hard-fighting that saw Henry V struck, his brother wounded and his second cousin killed – but they did play a vital role in making that and other victories possible. So when Sir Thomas shouted 'now strike!', those in the enemy ranks knew what they were in for!

## The course of the battle

Agincourt has been dealt with in great detail by many authors, including myself, but it seems appropriate here to add a brief account of the battle itself. This will help to show how the tactics described actually worked on the battlefield. At about 11 o'clock on the morning of 25 October, Henry deployed his small forces just north of the village of Maisoncelles: some 900-1,000 men-at-arms in three 'battles', but effectively joined into one, with the much larger force of archers, 3,000 to 5,000 (numbers differ widely according to the sources used), divided equally on either flank. It seems that the archers planted their stakes in front of them, but when the French made no move to attack, Henry gave the order to advance, so they lifted them and carried them forward across the ploughed field. This was an extremely dangerous manoeuvre in the face of such overwhelming odds; but Henry had clearly taken the calculated risk that the French were too disorganized to launch an assault while the English army was on the move and so vulnerable.

The problem for the French seems to have been one of a divided command. The officials responsible for the management of the French host in the field (the word 'general' had not yet been invented) were the marshal, Boucicaut, and the constable, d'Albret. They had devised a plan for defeating the English with the vanguard of the army. This involved dismounting the main body of men-at-arms and supporting them

*7. A view of the battlefield of Agincourt.*

with missile men (bows and crossbows) on the flank and a little in front; essentially mimicking the English disposition. The trick, though, was to retain some men-at-arms on horseback, and support them with the lightly-armed servants of the rest mounted on their master's chargers. They were then to be divided into two cavalry wings and kept a little behind the main battle line. The intention was to occupy the attention of the English with a dismounted assault, leaving the way clear for a surprise attack on the archers on either flank. The right-hand cavalry wing was even to come around onto the English rear. With the archers driven off or neutralized, the French hoped to win the infantry battle in the centre.

The plan was a good one and it might have worked; but at Agincourt too many factors militated against it. The first was the nature of the ground. Once Henry had advanced his small force into the gap between the woods of Agincourt and Tramecourt, his flanks were protected and there was no room for an outflanking manoeuvre such as had been planned. Furthermore, the stakes protected the archers who were in the open field as securely as if they had been in broken ground or in the woods. From the French point of view, the failure of command was a result of the royal princes taking charge and deciding to launch an all-out attack on foot. The French missile men (over 5,000 strong) were not allowed to take their place in the front line and were bundled out of the way by nobles and knights eager to claim the full glory for the defeat of the English and the capture of their king. The flanking units of cavalry were supposed to number 1,600 on the left and 800 on the right; but a fraction of these forces actually lined up as the action commenced (about 150 on each side). The dismounted force in the middle apparently numbered 8,000 in the first 'battle', with a further 6,000 behind and a final mounted 'battle' of 8-10,000 men. Even if these numbers are exaggerated (which they certainly

*8 and 9. Monuments erected in the 1870s (left) and 1960s (above). The calvary probably marks the site of one of the grave pits from the battle.*

are, and we have no muster rolls to draw upon to check them) the odds were overwhelming. There were so many French noblemen in the front rank that their banners were flapping in everyone's faces, causing such a distraction that they had to be furled and taken away.

It might seem strange, considering the balance of the forces, that it was the English who started the action. Yet, when the archers first loosed their shafts (at Sir Thomas's orders), the intention was to disrupt the French and encourage them into an over-hasty assault. This plan worked perfectly. The cavalry charges were launched on either flank; but the difficulties of charging across the sodden ploughland, the effectiveness of the archers' shooting and their stake defences, shattered the French initiative. The mounted men-at-arms were driven back in confusion, straight into the mass of dismounted men advancing against the English line. The result was complete chaos as horses, riderless, maddened by arrow wounds or both, bundled over the men on foot. This meant that when the French main body eventually reached the English men-at-arms they were dazed, disorientated and wounded. The English archery, once turned on them, inflicted causalities even through the fine plate armour which they wore. French accounts speak with horror of arrows even penetrating the visors of their helmets. This was possible because of the 'bodkin' (needle-pointed) head fitted to certain arrows. It can be argued that this only occurred at fairly short range (thirty metres or less), but the dismounted men were not capable of moving quickly over the heavy ploughland, and they were effectively in a shooting gallery.

When the two lines clashed, the French weight advantage told, and the English men-at-arms were pushed back a distance. The hand-to-hand fighting was intense, especially around the banners of the three 'battles' which made up the English line. The commander of one of these, Edward, duke of York was killed, and King Henry himself had to fight for his life. A blow, landing on his helmet, struck the floret from a golden crown which encircled it and left a hefty dent. Henry himself is credited with saving the life of the duke of Gloucester, straddling his wounded body to defend him. Incredibly, and despite the weight of numbers, the English line held. This enabled the lightly-armed archers to issue out from behind their swathe of stakes and attack the French from the flanks. Normally, they would have not been a match for the well-armed and well-protected men-at-arms, but faced with opponents who were bemused and exhausted, the archers began to pick them off, attacking them with swords and axes and even the lead-tipped mallets which they used for driving in the stakes. Feeling themselves defeated, the first French ranks wished to fall back, but they were unable to because of the pressure of men still coming forward from behind. Even the greatest began to surrender, handing over their gauntlets as a sign and expecting to be taken for ransom. Generally this was possible and indeed desired by the English because of the enormous wealth a rich prisoner would bring, but in the confusion many great prizes were lost. The duke of Alençon, it was said, tried to surrender to Henry himself, but was killed by one of the king's bodyguards.

So within a couple of hours of the outset of the battle, the decision, unbelievably, favoured Henry. The drama was not yet quite over, though. The cry went up that the third French 'battle', still mounted, was renewing the assault. Although this is possible, it is more likely – since most of the cavalry in the French rear had seen the defeat inflicted upon the first two lines and ridden off to safety – that only a few men under the count of Fauquembergues launched an attack. This may have been because he was a local landowner and did not want it to appear that he failed to defend his own territory. At much the same time, news came of an attack on the English baggage train, which had followed the English battle-line as it advanced. Just who led this attack and who took part in it is now far from clear. Isambart d'Azincourt, also a local landowner, is blamed for it, supposedly at the head of '600 peasants'. It may be, though, that this was in fact part of the original out-flanking plan, with a local man chosen to lead men along the sunken road and onto the English left-flank. We shall never know for certain. The outcome is well-recorded, though. Henry, alarmed at being taken in front and at the rear, and still substantially out-numbered on the field, gave the orders that the many prisoners still milling around were to be killed. By modern standards of the Geneva Convention this appears a horrifying atrocity. Indeed, the men-at-arms refused to become involved in such a slaughter, partly, one supposes, through the companionship of arms, but also because of the huge loss of potential revenue in ransoms such an action predicted. Henry had to command a squire with fifty archers to begin the massacre. We cannot know how many died as a result of this action, but it is certain that the French attacks ceased. Interestingly, Henry was not condemned by contemporaries for his actions; they preferred to heap blame on the Frenchmen who renewed an action which they should have known was lost, and so behaved unchivalrously. The total losses to the defeated side may have been in the region of 6,000, with some 2,000 of them being princes, nobles and men-at-arms. This was a severe blow to the French royalist cause, and one from which it never really recovered. English losses were apparently trifling (although probably not as light as Henry's propaganda made out); apart from the duke of York and the young earl of Suffolk, a couple of knights and esquires, an unknown number of archers and those killed in the baggage train. Henry's victory was total. In achieving it the archers played a crucial, although far from solitary role. In our more egalitarian age, it is these 'ordinary' men who receive the praise rather than the king and his nobles, and who is to say that they do not deserve it.

# 3 The Bowman and the Bow

## Paul Hitchin

> What of the men?
> The men were bred in England,
> The bowmen, the yeomen,
> The lads of dale and fell.
> Here's to you and to you
> To the hearts that are true,
> And the land where the true hearts dwell.

Stirring words indeed, taken from 'The song of the bow' from Sir Arthur Conan-Doyle's historical epic *The White Company* (1890), and perhaps reflecting a long held ideal of the archers of England in the fourteenth and fifteenth centuries. A myth has grown around the bowmen of the Hundred Years War and particularly those of Agincourt. They have become ingrained in English tradition and folklore, supposedly becoming the predecessors of 'Tommy Atkins', and their place in history has been further enhanced by writers such as Conan-Doyle with his character Samkin Aylward, the hard, but honourable, consummate archer. There seems little harm in this tradition, but it is best to attempt to see more of the reality behind the myth. Herein lies the intention of this personal interpretation of the English bowman.

The question arises, who were these men who had such an effect on the battlefields of Western Europe for more than a century? What we seek is the reality behind the archetypal English archer though this in itself is a misnomer since many Welsh and even Gascons and other allies from the English-held lands fought in the so-called English army.

Firstly, as to his background. The idea of an archer being merely a common soldier may be disputed since the status of the archer rose progressively throughout the period of the Hundred Years War. This status appears to have risen with his increasingly winning contribution to the success of English arms. Admittedly the archer was not from the higher echelons of society but neither was he from the poorest. His social standing was below that of the gentry or merchant class, but he seems to have stemmed largely from that group of upper peasantry which came, by the mid fifteenth century, to be called the 'yeomen'. This word is actually the middle English version of the French 'valet' and the Latin 'valettus', meaning a servant, but one who offered close and often fairly honourable service. Richard II's 'valetti' who formed his special bodyguard were all archers, many from Cheshire. It is interesting to note that some of the muster rolls for the army, as it embarked from the Southampton area in the summer of 1415, use the term 'valetti' for the archers instead of the more usual 'sagittarii' or 'architenentes', calling the men-at-arms 'armigeri' (esquires) instead of the usual 'homines ad arma'. Archer and yeoman thus became synonymous over the course of the later fourteenth and fifteenth centuries, although by a process which no one has as yet elucidated fully. Obviously the status and origins of individual archers varied, but we can conclude that they came from a social grouping of fairly respectable citizens, landholders or artisans, in essence perhaps, the lower middle class: a grouping that had emerged more fully with the weakening of manorial lordship and the growth of wage earning as a result of the Black Death.

A good example here is Chaucer's Knight's Yeoman, seemingly a close retainer of his master. He is described as being well clad in a coat and hood of green, carrying a mighty bow and accompanying arrows, expensively fletched with peacock, with sword and dagger at his belt, together with other accoutrements and silver jewellery besides. He is obviously a man of at least some status and skill, and conceivably reflecting his master's satisfaction with him. Chaucer also describes him as a forester and this is one of the groups of men from which the bowmen of the king's armies were drawn: the honourable servant, the guild member, craftsman, freeholder, a respected member of medieval society, a man proud of himself, his skill and his possessions and not a down-trodden peasant.

Furthermore, military status implies at least some social standing, since the actual cost of going to war necessitates an element of wealth. Arms and military equipment cost money. The bowmen who formed such a large part of the armies of Edward III and Henry V were not pressed into service, but in many cases became almost a professional military elite making a living by war. Raised and indentured to serve in the retinue of an individual noble or captain or as a levy from the area in which they lived, all were contracted to serve for a set period. These men were no rabble, but trained and disciplined soldiers, subject to the statutes and ordinances of war which were set down at the start of each campaign, and which stipulated the rules and code of conduct of the army as was proven by the instance of the archer on the march to Agincourt, who was summarily hanged for looting from a church. By the time of Agincourt, bowmen were paid 6d a day and, considering that a skilled artisan might earn ten to fifteen shillings yearly (a shilling being 12d), this shows the esteem in which skilled archers were held since they could earn that sum in a month. In that respect, following the archer's trade could be a profitable occupation. Not only were the wages good in comparison to civilian occupations, but there were other ways in which wealth could be made and many men became far richer than they dreamed of as a direct consequence of participation in the wars against the French. Some archers at Agincourt certainly reaped rewards from ransoms, and later in the conquest of Normandy, they were given grants of houses and property in the duchy as well as benefiting from the capture of other war booty.

Few – if any – of the bowmen's lives have been chronicled. Their deeds were not those of knightly honour, but of professional skill and prowess with their chosen weapon. Nevertheless, in many areas even today, there are folk tales of how the men from a particular district left their homes, shouldered their bows and marched away to serve Henry V. As explained later in Chapter Four, muster lists survive in the Public Record Office giving the names of some of those serving in the Agincourt campaign. Supposedly the finest bowmen were provided by the midland or marcher counties, those of Cheshire and Flint being greatly prized. (The author's family originate from villages around Shrewsbury and were smallholders and blacksmiths, perhaps the very stock from whom the archers were drawn.) The Welsh also were important for the provision of archers, not least because the principality was held by the crown.

*10. The archer and his page.*

The bowmen of some areas were, in fact, sometimes exempted from service abroad. Those from counties north of the River Trent were expected to serve to counter the threat of the Scots in the North and those in the southern maritime counties to defend the coast against any French excursion. The Cheshiremen in their green and white livery were so sought after that they supposedly received higher wages, even forming a semi-official bodyguard for Edward III and Richard II. At the battle of Shrewsbury in 1403 they were initially so effective on the Percy side that they caused the royal archers to run and furthermore wounded Prince Henry. Ironically some of those same men may well have served that very prince twelve years later against the French as part of the army of Henry V. Cheshire, like Wales, was a good recruiting area as it too was held by the king (or prince of Wales) as earl of Chester.

Sadly, other than muster lists, little remains to tell of the archers' lives and, for the Agincourt period, hardly any contemporary illustrations of these men exist. The few surviving writings indicate that they were not unthinking automatons, but men of spirit and initiative such as the group of Cheshire archers, who, after the battle of Poitiers in 1356, 'found' upon the field a silver model of a ship, possibly a salt cellar, and promptly sold it to the Black Prince. Another good example, admittedly some fifty or so years before Agincourt, is that of John Dancaster who served as a bowman under Edward III. Dancaster may well have been some kind of officer, since, after being captured by the French, he was – unusually – offered ransom. However, he could not pay for his freedom and was put to work repairing the defences of the French castle at Guînes, just beyond the English-held march of Calais. Whilst working there he became somewhat involved with a laundress and by 'laying with her', learned of weaknesses in the defences. Not satisfied with that intelligence alone he then actually measured the defences and secretly passed the information to the garrison of Calais who then took Guînes by stealth and released all English prisoners. That was not enough for Dancaster who refused to hand over the keys to the castle until he could actually sell it to the king. This is an example presumably of an exceptional man who may reflect the resourceful nature of the English archer.

At this stage it may be worthwhile to take into account those facets which produced such men as Dancaster and the thousands of other archers that served in the armies of England, and for this the background of the bowmen must be considered. The Statute of Winchester of 1285 ordained that men of certain social standing should provide military service as part of the *posse comitatus* in whatever degree their wealth reflected. Men with lands or rents valued between forty and one hundred shillings were expected to provide themselves with bow, arrows, sword and dagger and serve as an archer in time of need. Later the system was adapted in that they did not have to serve themselves if they could provide an alternative archer to serve in their place. Thus, in theory, archers were raised from and supported by their peers in both rural and urban areas by this 'array' system which provided a pool of manpower and a ready source of archers for selection into the forces to serve with the king abroad.

It is known and recorded that archery practice was an important and regular feature of English life, both rural and urban. Constant practice was fundamental to the provision of a trained supply of bowmen for the king's wars. Youths and men between the ages of sixteen and sixty by law had to shoot upon the butts each Sunday and Holy day after mass. Even today certain towns have areas known as 'the Butts', reflecting the importance of these practice fields. Edward III even went as far as to ban distracting pastimes such as 'football, handball, bandyball, cambuck and cockfighting or any such vain plays' lest they come between the archer and his craft. Legislation even provided a defence for any archer who was absolved from manslaughter or murder should he accidentally shoot a man whilst at practice.

Thus archery became an integral part of English life, not only a legal requirement for a large proportion of the male population, but also a pastime for much of society. This perhaps explains the popularity of Robin Hood legends throughout England, possibly reflecting the status of the archer in society. Interestingly, the first mention of the ballads seems to be in William Langland's poem, *Piers Plowman,* of 1376-8, and the earliest texts of the ballads date to the mid fifteenth century. Competitions were encouraged, as were many different styles of shooting. There was the standard target archery at the butts, although the range of individual targets would differ between shooting at the wand – a stripped stick placed in the ground – and clout shooting, where the arrow is shot at great distance and high into the air to drop down on a target; a skill which some say was to train archers in the skills of shooting over walls in sieges. Other popular forms of shooting were the 'roving mark' and the 'popinjay'. Mark shooting was a form of archery when bowmen would shoot at a distant mark, possibly a wand, and then move on to another target, man-made or natural, selected by the man whose shaft either struck the mark or came closest to it. Shooting at the 'popinjay', a medieval term for the parrot, involved archers aiming at a bird-like form, generally suspended in a tree.

Tradition has it that men trained their sons in the use of the bow from around eight years of age and increased its power as the child's strength increased. (This is borne out by the fact that the author's son who is now twelve years of age shoots upon the butts on a Sunday using his fourth bow with a draw weight – that being the weight required to draw back the bow – of over 40lbs, his previous bows having become underpowered for him, though, sadly, he may be an exception in this day and age.) Certain authorities on the bow, notably Robert Hardy, believe that the archers of Henry V were a different breed to most modern Englishmen: more robust and well used to physical labour and easily brawny enough to manage bows exceeding 150lbs draw weight. This could well be true.

The use of the bow became commonplace. Nevertheless, this common usage did have obvious drawbacks since it put not only a lethal weapon, but a competence with that weapon, in the hands of the people. Such an arm could cause fearsome wounds as is shown in the murder of one Simon Skeffington who was shot and killed with an iron-tipped arrow head tipping an ash shaft of 33-34in in length, which was shot from a yew bow of around 5ft 7in in height. Master Skeffington's fatal wound was recorded as being three inches long, two inches wide and six inches deep, a truly horrific wound showing only too graphically the effectiveness of the bow as weapon. It should be said that, although there was a pool of potential killers, and court accounts do relate tales of the attempted settling of neighbours disputes by armed men, the relative freedom and prosperity of the English lower classes, compared to their European counterparts, saved England from anything like the horrors of the French peasants revolt of 1358: the 'Jacquerie'. The yeomen turned their skills against the king's enemies rather than on their own nobility.

Leaving aside the man, perhaps the time has come to discuss the weapon from which the bowman draws his name: the bow. Once more the words of Conan-Doyle from 'The song of the bow' can illustrate the traditional view of the weapon.

> What of the bow?
> The bow was made in England,
> Of true wood, of yew wood,
> The wood of English bows;
> For men who are free
> Love the old yew-tree
> And the land where the yew-tree grows.

Again, these are moving words, but contain perhaps a little less than the full truth of the source of the weapon, carried so effectively at Agincourt and the other battles of the Hundred Years War, and now called the 'longbow'.

Firstly, the weapon itself was not called the longbow during the period – that title was apparently adopted in the sixteenth century and until that date it was simply called the bow. The origin of the weapon has been a source of contention for many years. Certain histories suggest the weapon first appeared in Wales in the early medieval period and there are accounts of Welsh bowmen using great bows to good effect against Norman and Angevin expeditions. However, bows found in the late Roman period and Scandinavian sites are exceptionally similar in size and construction to those found on the *Mary Rose*, and the weapon found alongside the Neolithic 'iceman' found in the Alps would not have been out of place in the hand of an English bowman. In essence the longbow, in similar or even exact form, had been in existence for centuries but what changed in England was its adoption as the seemingly national weapon under Edward III and its continued usage as a specific tactic in the English successes of the subsequent Hundred Years War.

The bow of Agincourt was, simplistically, a bent stick. It was a self wood bow, meaning that the bowstave is made from a single piece of wood unlike the laminated recurve bows of Eastern Europe and Asia. As the song suggests, yew was the favourite timber (although other woods were frequently used such as elm and ash), since the heart wood and sap wood of the tree, when used together, provide the bow with both strength and natural elasticity. The best and strongest bows would have been made from the trunk of the tree, but 'boughstave' bows cut from suitable branches were also used. Woods other than yew do not have the same properties (as the author has recently found to his cost when two elm bowstaves being prepared on his behalf by a professional bowyer broke during production.) Elm, after seasoning appears to become rather brittle and unable to take the shock of repetitive drawing and it could well be that the numerous elm bows used in the Middle Ages were created from wood that was still green, so providing the requisite flexibility. Ash on the other hand appears to be a fairly stable wood although after regular use an ash bow begins to 'follow the string', with the bow maintaining a bend and not fully returning to the undrawn position after unstringing.

Perhaps it is worthwhile at this stage to provide an exceptionally brief description of the production of the bow. It is created from a basic billet of seasoned yew, as straight grained as possible. This is then split and any of the 'pins' within the billet carefully removed if feasible. The stave is then cut to perhaps two inches square with ideally an even layer of the lighter coloured sapwood on the outside. In a perfect bow this sapwood should now be left alone and the rest of the bow making takes place around it since otherwise the grain may be disturbed and cause splintering. The stave is then worked on with a drawknife and spokeshave to slim and taper each limb until they are reduced to the desired dimensions. The bowyer will follow the grain of the wood so the bow may not appear smooth and even but may have a few raised areas where knotted wood is left proud.

The limbs are not quite symmetrical, the lower being slightly shorter and marginally stronger. The cross section of the bow should ideally be D-shaped, with the sapwood on the flat 'back' of the bow and the heart wood on the rounded 'belly'; oddly, these parts of the bow are seemingly reversed and the 'belly' is the rear of the bow and the 'back' of the bow is actually the front. Once the bow has taken shape it must be tillered. A 'tiller' is a device fixed to a wall which will hold the bow firm by the grip section while the string is then drawn to a series of measured notches as it is drawn, commencing few inches to a final full draw length which should be dependent upon what length of arrows it is intended to shoot. Once it is tillered to the desired draw length the bow is then finished, the horn nocks which take the string are glued in place and shaped and the weapon then has a final protective coating. In the Middle Ages this would be layers of wax or oil to protect the bow from hard usage and the elements. So, even after all the bowyer's skill, the bow remains little more than a bent stick.

There is little doubt that yew bows were the favourite weapon of the bowmen (as the song suggests), but had English yew been used alone then there is doubt that the weapon could have been so effective. Sadly, for the 'men who are free' to love the 'land where the yew-tree grows', they would have to look further afield than the shores of England. English yew is far from the best quality due to the rather changeable and temperate weather found in the British

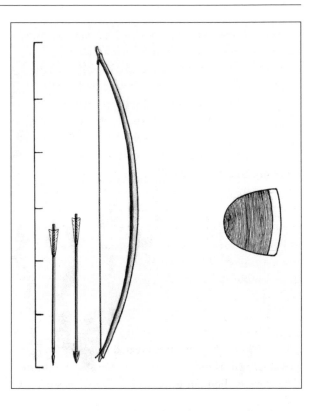

*The bow. On the left we see a scale sketch of a yew bow strung for use. Also shown are a 'flight' arrow and heavier bodkin arrow, drawn to the same scale. On the right is a cross-section showing both the heartwood and sapwood of a yew bow.*

Isles. The climate does not produce the right sort of growth within the tree, sadly, due to wind's twisting and the tree's natural tendency to turn, and it is seldom straight-grained enough for an appropriate amount of the heart and sap wood to be available to the bowyer. Furthermore the grain tends to be more open than wood grown either in the warmer south or the cold of Scandinavia, and so, in general, the wood is inferior for bowmaking than its European equivalent. Trees were tended in an effort to produce straighter growth; nevertheless, during the later medieval period numerous bowstaves were imported, particularly from Spain. In fact merchants were expected to bring a quota of yew staves into the country as a form of taxation with many being imported from Spain with shipments of wine.

Very few ancient longbows still exist, and the best examples, albeit from over a century after Agincourt, survive from the wreck of Henry VIII's ship, the *Mary Rose*. It can be assumed that they little differed from those carried in the footsteps of Henry V on the march from Harfleur in 1415. Their study gives an insight into the archer's weapon. The bow varied in size, supposedly according to the height of the man intending to use it, in that its length, when unstrung, should match the man's height. However some of those found on the *Mary Rose* appear to have dwarfed many of their apparent users, being well over 6ft in length. The quality of the bows appears also to have varied; some were classed as 'white' and others were painted as shown by their costs of one shilling and sixpence and two shillings respectively. This may reflect the different type of wood used or even how seasoned they were. Existing examples from the wreck show that some bows were roughly formed whilst many others featured nocks carved from horn or antler for taking the string. None of the *Mary Rose* bows have these nocks still *in situ* due to the effect of sea water on the animal matter, but the bows bear the marks of where they had been fixed and one nock has been recovered, amazingly, from within the skeleton of one of the archers under whom it had lain for centuries. It does not appear that the bows had the handgrips found on modern longbows; rather the grip was marked by a maker's mark, various different ones being illustrated on those found in the wreck. An archer would most likely equip himself with the best bow available to him. The bow was not only the tool of his trade but could also reflect his status. Obviously replacements on campaign would not necessarily be of the same quality and there is little doubt that the rigours of the march and military action would lead to breakages since, after all, what is the bow but a bent piece of wood. Certainly royal accounts for Agincourt and other medieval campaigns show central provision of replacement bowstaves, strings, arrows etc.

Bowstrings were created from wound strands of thread, the fibres of hemp generally being used, although other natural fibres such as linen were utilized, even silk or sometimes thread made from nettles was put to use. Strings were kept waxed against rain and to give some small added protection against use. The English expression 'keep it under your hat' is said to have derived from the archer's practise of placing their bowstrings under their hats or helmets at the onset of a shower in order to keep them dry. Thousands of spare strings must have been carried by the army on campaign, together with numerous spare bows and hundreds of thousands of arrows. The bowmen must have been adept at the various necessary skills to maintain and repair their weapons, though bowyers and fletchers were attached to the army for the duration of the campaign, as they were to garrisons established by the English in France.

The power of individual bows differed dependent upon the strength of the man using them. It can be assumed that the war bow of the archers of Henry V was a mighty weapon with a draw weight of a minimum of 80lbs, with many bows exceeding 100lbs and some above 150lbs. There are not many men today robust enough to regularly and repeatedly shoot such a weapon. (A notable exception is Simon Stanley, a farmer and blacksmith from Staffordshire, who has been an archer for many years and has shot replica war bows with seeming ease and often hosts longbow competitions featuring the 'military arrow'.)

The bow would have, at maximum elevation, a range of perhaps three hundred and fifty to four hundred yards. Its effective range could be considered from around two hundred and twenty yards downwards. In skilled hands it would be lethal from a closing range of around eighty yards, and from that distance an archer would be able to actively target the weak spots in armour for best penetration. Hence the demise of Henry 'Hotspur' Percy at Shrewsbury in 1403 when he opened his visor for better vision or a breath of air. This action proved to be his last, since an unknown archer killed him with an arrow through his open visor. The rate of discharge during battle was considerable with easily twelve aimed shots in a minute and possibly fifteen to twenty shots under certain circumstances. An archer who could not shoot ten aimed arrows a minute was not considered fit for selection for the army. Even with at least fifteen years experience with the bow the most the author has ever managed in a minute has been seventeen arrows and, to be truthful, with some of those the aim was far from true. Considering that Henry V had perhaps some 5,000 archers upon the field of Agincourt on that October morning it is easy to envisage the sky actually darkening beneath the arrow storm with potentially between ten and fifteen thousand arrows in the air at one time. An awesome and devastating rain of death and destruction. The English soldier did not have a similar 'rate of fire' until the adoption of the bolt action rifle by the British Army at the end of the nineteenth century.

The arrows so effectively loosed by the bowmen of Agincourt came in two types. Firstly, there were arrows for the softer targets, with heavier shorter shafts specifically for piercing armour. Several woods were utilized in their production, ash being the favourite, although most of the arrows recovered from the *Mary Rose* are poplar, that being a less dense and consequently lighter wood. Commonly they were fletched with goose feathers, but some of the most favoured archers appear to have carried arrows feathered with peacock. Millions of goose feathers must have been used in the production of arrows and the counties throughout England were expected to supply them in the huge numbers required. The fletchings, of whatever feather used, were normally fixed to the shaft with some sort of plant or animal based adhesive or pitch (a glue made from bluebell sap has been referred to for this use). They were then, generally, bound in place with thread. Often slivers of bone or horn were inserted into the arrow shaft to reinforce it at the nock, where the arrow fits on the bowstring.

The second type of arrow was for longer flight, and was thus used at a greater range. They were generally over thirty inches long, although some sources indicate that they were the traditional 'ell' or clothyard, being thirty-nine inches in length. Modern archers would consider that an exceedingly long shaft. Illustrations do indicate that bowmen of the period drew the arrow back to the ear as opposed to the cheek so possibly the different technique could discount some doubts. However, the majority of arrows found on the *Mary Rose* average at around thirty inches in length so the idea of the 'cloth yard shaft' is possibly, in reality, another misconception.

Arrows are shot using either two or three fingers, one above the arrow and either the other, or two, below it. Both arms and the upper body are used to draw back the bow with one arm pulling and the other pushing until the bow is fully bent and the string drawn back. Then, after aiming, the string is released and the arrow discharged. The two-fingered release supposedly gave rise to the possibly apocryphal story of the origin of the distinctly English two-fingered gesture. It is said that the French swore to mutilate any captured archer by severing his drawing fingers and, in return, after the battle the English bowmen reciprocated by gesturing that they still had the necessary digits.

The lighter arrows would be fitted with leaf shaped or barbed arrowheads, forged in iron. These arrowheads vary in design and size from small, almost lozenge shapes to far larger swallow-tailed heads that could cause the fearsome wounds described earlier on unarmoured targets. These arrows would be loosed in volleys at long range, perhaps up to and over three hundred yards and would be frighteningly effective against soft targets such as unarmoured men and horses as sheets of arrows rained from the sky. The intent would be to harry, disorganize and cause losses to an enemy as they advanced. As the range decreased so would the trajectory and dual-purpose arrows, such as the type 16 head from the Museum of London would come into play. This is a compact arrowhead, of basic leaf shape but with laid back barbs which as the range lessened would possibly begin to pierce through fabric armour and likely through some mail. Once the range was suitable, perhaps from 150 yards and less,

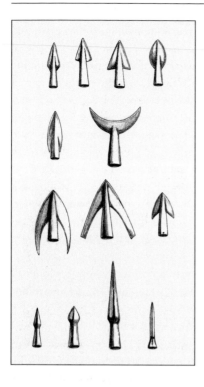

*Contemporary arrow heads taken from surviving examples, many of which are from those in the collection of the Museum of London. At the top we have 'flight' arrowheads, for general use at longer ranges and against soft targets. In the second row are shown 'type 16' from the Museum of London, a multi-purpose head, believed to be the most commonly used arrowhead. In the third row is the crescent head: it has been said that its function was to 'hamstring horses or shred sails or rigging', but it could be for birding. At the bottom we see two broadheads (the kind of arrow responsible for the wound of Simon Skeffington mentioned in the text), and two armour-piercing 'bodkin' heads, short and long, for the penetration of armour.*

the heavier, shorter armour-piercing arrows would be brought into use. These shafts, thirty inches long or less, were tipped with hardened 'bodkin' heads. These were narrow, almost chisel pointed and were designed purely for the penetration of armour and come in a range of styles and lengths. They were extremely effective and by the Agincourt period these arrows are recorded as punching through even the thickened steel of the helmets of the archers' unfortunate foes. From viewing modern experiments with such arrows, it would appear that the initial punch of the blow commences the penetration, but then the shaft of the arrow driven forward by the force flexes and deepens the incision. From personal experience the author can vouch that at close range, around twenty to thirty yards, poplar shafted arrows fitted with forged bodkin heads easily punched through a combination of thin plate, mail and fabric. Consider then what devastation could have been wreaked by more expert archers armed with heavier war bows.

There is another type of arrowhead that has been found. It has a crescent shape and some authorities have said that it was used for 'hamstringing', cutting the tendons on horses; others have stated that its use was for the cutting of rigging in a sea battle. In both instances this can be disputed. Firstly, to hamstring a horse it must be travelling away from a bowman, so why even shoot at it? Secondly, arrows shot at rigging, even in volleys, are likely to glance off tarred and taut ropes. Possibly these arrows were used *en masse* in an attempt to shred the sails of enemy ships. In the author's opinion, these particular arrowheads were used for the hunting of birds since the crescent head increased the chances of hitting a target and, in effect, acted like the spreading pellets of a shotgun cartridge.

Arrows were supplied bundled into 'sheaves' of twenty-four. Each archer would carry a ready supply of arrows (at the time of Agincourt quivers do not appear to have been carried).

Canvas arrow bags, sometimes lined with grass and possibly with a wicker framework and leather spacers carried around two sheaves of arrows. An immediately available supply of perhaps a dozen or twenty-four were carried in the belt and at critical times the whole supply could have been discharged in no more than five minutes. Considering the potential rate of discharge of arrows, a vast number must have been carried in the army's baggage, and boys and supply staff from the camp would keep up the supply of arrows to the battle line since a failure in replenishment could have dire results against a determined enemy. In one (admittedly later) instance at the battle of Towton in 1461 during the Wars of the Roses, can be found an effective way of saving ammunition. Unusually, the battle was fought in a snowstorm and during the confusion the Yorkist archers shot a volley and then fell back slightly before their Lancastrian counterparts could reply. The Lancastrian volley is supposed to have fallen short, and the Yorkist bowmen then are said to have advanced once more, and to have picked up the wasted Lancastrian arrows and shot them back, thus using the enemy's own arrows to bring about their downfall. Ironic, but effective.

The bowman's main weapons have now been examined and at this time the archer's personal equipment should be mentioned. The archer of Henry V was potentially far better armed and equipped than his predecessor under Edward III. The standard of archers' accoutrements rose throughout the period of the Hundred Years War. Obviously the standard and quality of clothing, arms and armour varied amongst individuals, but it seems apparent that each man would equip himself to the best of his capabilities, and gear could be enhanced by the easy expedient of retrieval upon a victorious battle field. Due to his style of fighting, by necessity an archer should be relatively lightly armed, he must be manoeuvrable to be effective since, in essence, he is a light infantryman. The following section will describe the clothing and armour that might have been found on any typical archer of Henry V.

There was no uniform as such, beyond perhaps the issue of some form of livery coat the bowmen would wear beneath any military gear, the civilian dress of their class. By the second decade of the fifteenth century, they wore a linen shirt, reaching well down the thigh, and linen 'braies', these being underwear of various different styles, some resembling a draw string waisted boxer short whilst others almost like a nappy or loincloth. Above the shirt and underwear were worn hose and doublet of wool often lined with linen or calico and no doubt very infrequently washed or cleaned. The hose which covered the legs were single legged and tied to the doublet or to a sleeveless pourpoint, a garment somewhat resembling a waistcoat. Doublets came in varied styles, some just below waist length and some to the thigh and others featuring detachable sleeves. Very few had buttons; most were fastened together with points, that is, they laced together. With the hose having no crotch the nether regions were covered merely by the braies and the shirt tails. On the march from Harfleur and at Agincourt itself quite a number of the archers suffered from a 'flux' of the bowels, presumably some form of dysentery, and many are described as fighting in an almost naked state to appease their frequent bowel movements. With single leg hose such problems can be facilitated by rolling down the hose to the knee and appearing 'bare shanked'. They can be worn in a similar manner in warm weather. In less clement atmospheric conditions, a woollen coat or overgown would often be worn over the doublet. With personal hygiene being less of a concern than today, and the warm and heavy, and frequently damp, woollen clothing, animal infestation must have been a frequent feature of the bowmen's lives to say nothing of their potentially interesting aroma.

Hats of various sorts were always worn – the wearing of some form of headgear appears to have been the norm – and to appear bareheaded was not common. Tight fitting linen coifs with strings that tied beneath the chin were sometimes featured and hoods with caped shoulders were popular. These hoods were sometimes issued to the archers by their captains as an item of uniform, featuring the livery colours of their respective lords and sometimes with a representation of the livery badge sewn or pinned to them. The dangling tail or liripipe of the hood was sometimes used in place of a purse for the keeping of any valuables. Footwear for the archers varied with many styles being worn, including shoes of below ankle height which appear to slip on to the foot, to ankle boots of diverse designs, some buckled and others with laces. Others were made with excess leather in the uppers which then was wrapped across and buckled. All shoes were generally of the turned type, being made inside out and then soaked and turned the right way round. This method of production was utilized to help protect the stitching. However, as the campaign continued, footwear would suffer accordingly and deteriorate until some who fought at Agincourt may well have been lacking any shoes at all or making do with whatever was available. Since an increasingly large proportion of archers were by this time mounted, boots of some form or other were often worn, knee length or, for the most well-to-do, reaching to the thigh and with ties which suspended them from a belt to keep them from slipping down the leg.

All soldiers on campaign require the 'necessities' of life and the archers of Agincourt would have been no different. Personal items such as spare clothes, eating and drinking utensils and firelighting equipment would obviously have been carried. Most of this personal kit would have been carried on the horse of those fortunate to have one or perhaps with the baggage wagons. There was a considerable amount of equipment to be carried and the baggage train must have been an integral part of the army, as shown in later illustrations from the fifteenth century. There are no contemporary images of archers carrying much personal gear, so it could be the case that the individual contingents carried most of their chattels on wagons, these being marked in some way for identification, perhaps with a pennon. On the Agincourt campaign, since the King's march from Harfleur was a *chevauchée* or mounted raid, it is believed that all heavy gear was left at Harfleur and packhorses were used since speed was of the essence.

However, in times of need all personal belongings had to be carried by the archer himself, most probably in a 'snap sack' of some sort, believed to be the forerunner of the knapsacks of today. Similarly, it should be assumed that some sort of flask may have been carried for any drink that could be obtained. It should be perhaps remembered that, certainly in English armies of the following century, part of the rations was eight pints of beer per man per day, so some utensil seems likely. Flasks could have been of leather, ceramic, caulked wood or even gourds. A piece of equipment specific to all archers would be a bracer, the guard of leather or horn worn on the bowman's forearm to protect it from the bowstring. A shooting glove of some sort or possibly a leather tab may have been used to protect the drawing fingers from the pull of the string, but there is a good chance that these bowmen were so accustomed to the bow that their fingers had become hardened from its frequent usage. From the archer's belt would hang a purse of some sort for money or other valuables the bowman possessed and often a knife or dagger was also worn. A common feature would be the wearing or carrying of a rosary since, although the English had quite a healthy disregard for much of the authority of the Church, they were still sufficiently religious and superstitious to be recorded as kneeling and praying before battle and even taking earth into their mouths as a sign of whence all men would end. It is also said that for some reason the English were very devout prior to heavy drinking.

Having discussed the personal clothing and kit of the archer, now his military equipment will be considered. As previously stated, the archer should be thought of as a light infantryman and in fact heavy armour could well be a hindrance to his role, although some form of protection would have been considered necessary. Fabric body armours known variously as *jacks*, *gambesons* and *hacketons* were a popular form of body defence. Their construction and style varied; some were made up of layer upon layer of linen whilst others were stuffed with diverse fillings such as rags, tow, sheep's wool or even grass and then quilted making a light but effective body defence. Some were sleeveless whilst others bore half or full length sleeves also padded though less heavily than the body of the garment. Other jacks were given the extra defensive feature of having horn or iron plates sewn or tied inside them. Some of these body armours were covered in coloured cloth and had decorative rivet heads whilst others were left in their undyed linen colour, and some were fashioned from leather in place of fabric.

Body defences of mail were also worn – the combination of mail and fabric making a composite armour with very effective protection. The mail body armour could consist of complete mail shirts (in general short sleeved and thigh length), mail skirts for the nether region, mail standards or collars to cover the neck or gussets or strips of mail attached to the jack, particularly to the sleeves. Sometimes, metal discs were tied or stitched to the sleeves of a jack, but plate armour for archers was not common. There are some illustrations, albeit somewhat later than the Agincourt period, which show bowmen with plate arm defences. However, the wearing of plate does not facilitate the shooting of the bow and that, after all, was the prime function of the archer. Certain better off or favoured bowmen may have worn plate leg armour or *poleyns* to protect the knee, though it should be remembered that for a light infantry missile-armed soldier, mobility is of great importance and anything hampering that mobility reduces the man's effectiveness as a soldier.

One piece of armour of paramount importance to the bowman was a helmet. If no other armour is possessed, the wearing of some form of helmet gives a feeling of security, whether this is actually merited or otherwise. Henry V's archers could be considered at least a semi-professional body and so it is easy to believe that each man had at least some form of head protection. Helmets were many and varied. Some were as simple as a leather or even wicker cap reinforced with bands of iron or a basin-shaped skull of iron, others differed very little from those worn by the knights or men at arms. By the time of Agincourt there were two main types of helmet being worn, albeit in different forms, these being the bascinet and the kettle hat.

The kettle hat was, by 1415, a style of helmet well over a hundred years old, but still much used and supposedly taking its name from the fact that if it is turned upside down it resembles or even can be utilized as a cooking pot. It is a brimmed helmet with a skull that can be either domed or with straight sides. Some were hammered from a single piece of metal while others were constructed in pieces and riveted together, some were plain and others banded across the skull. The British army helmet of 1916 is supposedly derived from this style of headgear and it does offer good protection, particularly from missiles or blows from above.

The bascinet is a close fitting, almost nut-shaped helmet which follows the contours of the head far more than the kettle hat. It had developed in the middle years of the fourteenth century. By the period of Agincourt the helmet had become rather deeper and featured a skull with the point to the rear of the centre. Earlier models had been more rounded and somewhat shallower. A common feature of the bascinet was a hanging mail collar or aventail which hung from lugs fixed around the lower part of the skull of the helmet, affording good protection to the chin, neck and shoulders. For the knightly class these helmets were visored, but since an archer needs good visibility for the best use of his bow then it is unlikely that bowmen would wear the visored patterns, favouring the better view provided by open-faced helmets.

Both styles of helmet were commonly worn; in what degree it is impossible to say. (The author favours the bascinet since it is easier to shoot a bow whilst wearing a close-fitting helmet since it lacks the brim of the kettle hat which could potentially hinder the drawing of the bow slightly more than the brimless bascinet). It is common sense that each man would equip himself to the best of his ability, choosing whatever style he preferred. After battle there could often be newer and better helmets to be had for the taking by the mere expedient of removing them from previous owners who no longer had a use for them.

Beyond his bow and supply of arrows, each archer carried some form of sidearm for personal protection. The Statute of Winchester even specified sword and dagger. Accordingly, at the start of a campaign each man would equip himself corresponding to his taste and the depth of his purse, and during that campaign plunder could easily upgrade the standard of the arms carried. Most of the archers of Henry V carried swords, but it is unlikely that many of them were trained swordsmen and so used their sidearms as weapons of last resort, such as at Agincourt when the French attack reached the English line and the fighting became hand to hand. The swords carried would most likely have been double-edged dual purpose slashing and stabbing swords, slightly shorter, perhaps, than those carried by the men-at-arms and nobles. Falchions appear to have been quite popular. These are heavy-bladed, single-edged, cleaver-shaped swords, used for slashing, possibly the sort of weapon favoured by a brawny but unskilled swordsman. Normally used in conjunction with the sword was the buckler, a small circular shield, rarely more than a foot in diameter and made of wood reinforced with iron and with a central iron boss or completely of iron and either convex or concave in shape. Bucklers were used to parry blows at arms length or even as a form of offensive weapon to punch an opponent in the face; rather brutal, but highly effective and carried by many archers.

Daggers or knives were also commonplace, in assorted styles, suspended from the belt or sometimes tucked behind the purse. There were rondel daggers with discs at either end of the grip, baselards with T- or Y-shaped hilts, and the 'bollock' dagger, so called for the distinctly phallic hilt, later called the 'kidney' dagger by less broad-minded people. Some were single edged like a knife, or broad bladed, and others were long, tapering and with diamond section or even cruciform blades for punching through mail, rather ironically called 'misericordes', since their usage was to give a none too merciful end to an enemy's life. Hatchets, axes and billhooks were carried for foraging, cutting firewood and for the cutting of the stakes, and were 'the height of a man and the breadth of a forearm and pointed at both

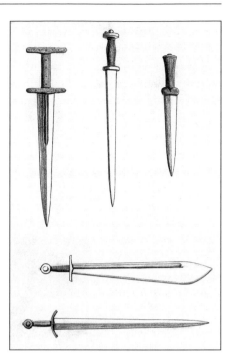

*A selection of sidearms. At the top from left to right we have a baselard, a rondel (so called after discs on the dagger's hilt), and the 'kidney', or 'bollock' dagger, showing the somewhat phallic shape of the grip. At the bottom are two swords, the heavy, broad-bladed falchion, a cleaver-like weapon effective in the hands of a strong man perhaps not too skilled at sword play, and a dual purpose cut and thrust sword, not too dissimilar but possibly slightly shorter than that carried by the king and his men-at-arms.*

ends', which King Henry ordered his archers to carry and plant before them as a defence against cavalry. Another item carried by many archers was the maul or mallet used for hammering in stakes; a long-shafted, wooden hammer, reinforced with metal or leaden-headed, and capable of being used as an effective weapon to bludgeon an enemy. Understandably, in time of dire need – such as in the hand-to-hand fighting at Agincourt – anything would be used and was. The chroniclers state that at that time the archers armed themselves with spears, hatchets and mallets to fall upon the exhausted French and proved themselves more than a match for their heavily-armoured and increasingly exhausted opponents.

The man and his arms and weapons have been covered, but what of his methods of fighting and the tactics deployed by those commanding him? The specific tactics of Agincourt were addressed in Chapter Two, so perhaps a more general overview may be of assistance. There is no doubt whatsoever that the archer of Agincourt was an eminently capable soldier; commanders using such troops dominated the battlefields of France and beyond for the best part of a century. However, it should also be stated that he was not the super soldier of myth and was only successful when his commanders fully exploited his skills and put him in a position and on ground where he could be most of use combined with the other arms of the English army. In many cases their best actions were in defensive positions with features both natural and man-made creating broken ground to impede an enemy advance. This had been the case both at Crécy and Poitiers. At Agincourt the field is narrowed by the presence of woods on each flank so causing the French attack to be funnelled. The actual positioning of the archers, 'in the manner of a herce', is subject to debate. It is sufficient to say that the archers were placed behind their stakes as a defence against mounted attack, and in the best position that Henry V considered would break the French attack with their missiles, and support the men-at-arms. The choosing of the field and the use of the stakes provided both natural and man-made features which assisted in the utilization of the bowmen. In fact the use of stakes assisted in other English victories at Valmont, Cravant and Verneuil, and stakes appear to have become a standard part of the archer's equipment. In the earlier battles mentioned, potholes and hedges had been used to provide broken ground and later, at Rouvray, a wagon laager produced a fort from within which the English held off a superior French force, giving one of the few successes during the siege of Orléans.

Archers were not limited to standing in defensive lines. Bowmen were light infantrymen, who, *en masse*, had a missile power that could be used in a variety of situations. For example, on the march from Harfleur at the crossing of the Somme, a body of archers advanced and their arrows gave cover to attacks which pushed back the defenders of the river line. The mobility of the archer allowed him to be used as a skirmisher: bowmen advancing and pouring arrows into an enemy could gall sufficiently to push forward an ill-prepared attack. The two hundred archers ordered forward on the flank of the battlefield at Agincourt shooting into the French line may well have caused them to attack too early. By Agincourt the majority of archers were mounted, the horses of retainers and indentured men being supplied or paid for by their employers and those of the levy archers by their county or city. The use of the horse gave the archer an added flexibility; he rode to battle but then dismounted to fight. This increased mobility must have enhanced their tactical use and given them a similar function to later dragoon regiments, and at Agincourt mounted archers took an active part in the pursuit of the beaten French. There are a few illustrations of the longbow being shot from horseback, but these are most likely due to artistic licence since the English military archer was essentially a footsoldier.

Finally, in conclusion, what was it that gained the English archers such a formidable and deserved reputation? In the right hands a simple bent stick was the decisive factor in the success of English armies for a century or more. The bowmen, when used tactically on chosen ground and in conjunction with men at arms were, without doubt, the decisive factor in English victories of the Hundred Years War, and Agincourt can be said to be the zenith of their attainment. Massed archers provided the king's army with execution equivalent of a modern day creeping artillery barrage, machine gun fire, or the destruction of selected targets by trained snipers. Their skill, gained by the training that was an integral part of their way of life in England was undoubtedly essential, as was their tradition of victory and confidence in their commanders. Yet, there may conceivably be further influences to reflect on; those of nationalism and the English temperament. By 1415 in England there had developed a national identity and the archer of Henry V considered himself to be the finest man in the finest army of the finest king of the finest land in Christendom and that was a spirit that found defeat hard to contemplate. Furthermore, at Agincourt there was another national trait that could have influenced Henry's beleaguered army, the 'bloody-mindedness' so endemic to the English character. If they were to fall at the hands of the French then they would ensure that they would take some of the enemy with them and this they proved with alacrity. All these factors made the 'Goddam with his crooked stick' what he was, and they have left a legacy that remains even today.

# 4 Sir Thomas Erpingham

## A Life in Arms
Anne Curry

The archers were a distinctive and crucial element of the English army and of its success at Agincourt. Since the late thirteenth century at least, archers had formed an important part of the recruitment strategy of the English crown. In the first half of the fourteenth century there was no fixed proportion of archers. Armies crossing to France between 1369 and 1389, however, were raised on the basis of one archer to every man-at-arms, so that the two groups were balanced in size. By this period, too, archers were regularly mounted so that the whole army was mobile. In the Welsh wars of the reign of Henry IV, in which Henry of Monmouth – the future Henry V – had been much involved, an optimum ratio of three archers to every man-at-arms seems to have developed, and this ratio remained the norm in the campaigns against France from 1415 to 1450. The army of 1415 was raised with this basic ratio in mind, although there were additional companies of archers which boosted the proportion of archers above 75%. This is testimony to the perceived value of archers in all kinds of military activities. They were as useful in sieges as men-at-arms, and so long as they were mounted (which most of the mixed retinue archers were in 1415), they were as mobile on the *chevauchée*. Their value in pitched battle had already been seen in the fourteenth-century campaigns; as Agincourt was to show, they were useful as artillery to soften up and disorientate an enemy, but also had the flexibility and freedom of movement to go in for the kill in close combat, especially against an already weakened foe. Moreover, they were easier to recruit than men-at-arms, requiring less training and cheaper equipment. And they cost half as much in pay as men-at-arms. So if Henry wanted to take a sizeable but not too expensive army in 1415 – which we can be certain he did – recruiting archers to form over three-quarters of his army was a sensible move.

Some French chronicles imply that Sir Thomas Erpingham was the commander of the English archers at the battle, and this notion has come down into popular tradition. There are some reservations on this point, as will be revealed. Whether it is true or not, however, the experiences of Sir Thomas, a Norfolk knight, provide a useful point of entry into the subject as a whole. As we shall see, plenty of material on his service in the Agincourt campaign survives in the administrative records of the English crown, now housed in the Public Record Office at Kew. This material can be used to shed light on the general issues of how the army was raised and organized. But Erpingham's experiences can also tell us more. Even if he was not commander of the archers, he was undoubtedly an important member of the army and of Henry V's inner circle. The battle was just one incident in what was, as we shall discover, a very full life. His was mainly a soldier's life but it was not lacking in other experiences at local and central level. The survival of a wide range of sources – documents, artefacts and buildings – offers a very vibrant impression of the kind of man who was instrumental in Henry V's political and military successes.

This chapter is thus divided into four sections. The first gives an account of Sir Thomas's life and then shows how the sources for his service in 1415 can be used to shed light on the English army and battle. The second section looks at him in the local context of his home county, Norfolk, revealing not only his wealth and local prominence but also his largesse and religious patronage. The third section focuses specifically on the Erpingham gate – one of the entrances to Norwich Cathedral Close – which was constructed at his behest, and which again shows much about his piety and family concerns through its religious and heraldic decoration. These features are also revealed in another surviving artefact, the Erpingham chasuble, a richly embroidered ecclesiastical vestment bearing his arms which is now preserved in the Victoria and Albert Museum.

Sir Thomas was probably one of the oldest participants at the battle of Agincourt. Born in 1357, he was, on that eventful day of 25 October 1415, either fifty-seven or fifty-eight. We must give the two possibilities because we do not know when his birthday fell. By the time of the battle he had served three generations of Lancastrians. He was, like many others at Agincourt, a tried and trusted supporter of this dynasty which had held the crown since Henry Bolingbroke (subsequently Henry IV) had deposed Richard II in 1399, an event in which Erpingham played a major part. He did not participate in full military service again after 1415, but he continued to fulfil central and local administrative duties for the rest of the reign of Henry V and into the reign of the fourth generation of his Lancastrian masters, Henry VI. Sir Thomas died on 27 June 1428 – a mere eleven months before Joan of Arc raised the siege of Orléans and set in motion the decline of English interests in France.

His career is striking and worthy of reconstruction. It is essentially a life in arms, but we would be doing Sir Thomas and his knightly contemporaries a disservice if we did not stress other aspects of their existence. Service to the crown or to a prince embraced a wide range of functions: companion, counsellor, military adviser, administrator, local government officer, diplomat. Sir Thomas is a good example for us to take because his experience was broad as well as lengthy. There are plenty of source materials on which to draw within the records of central and local government. There are also some letters written by him, and he features in that great collection of fifteenth-century England, the *Paston Letters*. Such sources, as well as architectural and artistic remains, can tell us much about the knightly existence and lifestyle in the later Middle Ages. In some ways, his life was that of a perfect knight given that it combined service and loyalty to the ruler, local pre-eminence, military prowess and religious piety and generosity. It can thus serve as a model, although we must also remember that each knight has his own story to tell, and that although careers show similar broad patterns, it is the individual experience which proves the most fascinating. That is not to say, of course, that we can arrive at an idea of what Sir Thomas was *really* like: the historian can reconstruct events, but alas, not personalities. On that readers must make up their own opinion, as too on Sir Thomas's physical appearance. Even if the figure on the Erpingham gate came originally from his tomb, we cannot assume that it is a likeness, and no other contemporary portrayal is known. Sir Thomas's character can only be guessed at from a study of his background and his actions. Who was he? What did he do?

The first question must be answered by looking at his family background. His ancestors had probably lived at Erpingham long before they began to use the place name as their own surname. The latter situation arose, it seems, in the early thirteenth century when they came to be holders of the manor. The social milieu into which Sir Thomas was born is best described as 'local gentry', small-scale landholders – sometimes knights, sometimes esquires – whose main significance was in the local context but who appeared on the national scene from time to time. Tracing his immediate ancestry, however, is slightly problematic. In his history of Norfolk, Francis Blomefield suggested (and this line has been followed by many others) that Thomas was the son of a Robert Erpingham who died in 1370, and the younger brother of a Sir John who died later in the same year, on 1 August according to a brass in Erpingham church. The first problem is distinguishing between generations. Various Robert Erpinghams are known from the records of the royal government over the course of the fourteenth century. One was MP for Norfolk in the 1330s and 40s. There are also references to men of that name serving as an arrayer of troops and on commissions of oyer and terminer in Norfolk from the 1330s to 1360. Some are knights, others apparently not, although the printed Chancery records, such as the Calendars of the Patent rolls, are not always consistent in recording this kind of thing. A Robert Erpingham is known to have served in the Weardale campaign of 1327, in Scotland in 1335, on Edward III's first expedition to France, in the Sluys/Tournai campaign of 1340, and at the battle of Crécy. But is this the career history of the same person or are we seeing two generations?

The second problem is establishing Sir Thomas's relationship with Sir John. In 1846 Thomas Stapleton drew attention to a document of 8 March 1370 which refers to a Robert de Erpingham and his son, John. This Stapleton took to prove that John and Thomas were indeed brothers and that both were the sons of Robert and his wife, Agnes. Yet an entry in the Patent rolls for November 1372 speaks of Sir John and his *son* Thomas – not very flatteringly, incidentally, as the document concerns an assault they had launched on a monk of St Benet Holme Abbey. The date of 1372 causes further – and as yet unresolved – problems concerning the dating of Sir John's death, which his brass puts as 1 August 1370, although it is possible that the entry in the Patent rolls was dealing with an event which had occurred earlier. A John Erpingham had served Edward III in Brittany in 1342-3, had been on the Crécy campaign, and was on a commission of oyer and terminer in Norfolk in 1354. If this John was indeed Sir Thomas's elder brother then he must have been elder by many years, for as we saw, Thomas was not born until 1357. More likely the Brittany John was his father, and Robert his grandfather, both dying in 1370, with Sir John – described on his brass as 'lord of this vill' – enjoying the family possessions only briefly. Indeed, one of the Harley Charters in the British Library has Sir Thomas describe himself as the son and heir of *John* Erpingham. It is difficult to place in the family tree the William Erpingham who described himself as sixty or more when he gave evidence in August 1386 at the Austin Friars, Norwich, in the court of chivalry case between Lord Lovel and Lord Morley. Here he said that he had served on expeditions to France in 1345, at the battle of Crécy and the siege of Calais, and in the Black Prince's *chevauchée* of 1355. Family reconstitution for this period is more problematic than one might expect and is certainly not helped by the fact that families often drew on a relatively small pool of first names.

*14. The brass of Sir John Erpingham, Erpingham Church (Norfolk).*

Moreover, there is certainly at least one other Erpingham line in the county in his period, probably based in the city of Norwich.

About four things, however, we can be confident. The first is that Sir Thomas came to be sole inheritor of the family holdings, although we cannot know exactly when. If it was 1370, then he would have been a minor of thirteen or so, and we would have expected to find some documentation concerning this (because heirs under twenty-one were placed under wardship). The second certainty is that Sir Thomas was the last of the Erpinghams of his line for he had no children by either of his marriages. His first wife was Joan, daughter of Sir William Clopton of Clopton, Suffolk, and sister of Sir Walter Clopton. The marriage occurred sometime before 1389, with Joan dying in 1404. He married his second wife, another Joan and daughter of Sir Richard Walton, sometime after the death (1409-10) of her first husband, Sir John Howard. This Joan also predeceased her husband, dying on 13 December 1423. The lack of heirs adds an extra piquancy to Sir Thomas's commissioning of a window in 1419 in the Austin Friars to commemorate those lords, barons, bannerets and knights of Norfolk and Suffolk who had died without male issue since the coronation of Edward III. At his own death in 1428, therefore, his property was inherited by his nephew, the son of his sister Juliana by her husband, Sir William Phelip.

(Some authors incorrectly have this nephew as the son of Sir Thomas's supposed brother, John.) Sir Thomas's sister's son was also called Sir William Phelip, and was born in 1383. Both he and his younger brother, Sir John Phelip, served on the Agincourt campaign. Sir John died at Harfleur but William was present at Agincourt and on later campaigns, and subsequently became treasurer of the household of Henry V, also serving Henry VI as a privy councillor and chamberlain. William married the daughter and co-heiress of Thomas, Lord Bardolf, and thus from 1437 is commonly called Lord Bardolf. He died in 1441. It was no doubt partly through the royal links of his uncle, Sir Thomas Erpingham, that he himself became so prominent at court.

The third matter of which we can be confident is that Sir Thomas's immediate ancestors, however we ought to arrange them on the family tree, had, akin to many families of knightly and squirarchial status, a tradition of royal service, most notably in the military sphere. We must assume that Thomas received training in arms befitting his station, and that he knew French. It is not surprising, then, that our Sir Thomas should follow in their footsteps. The fourth area of certainty is that the extent of his rise to a prominence on the national stage was totally unprecedented within his family circle.

Most of the discussion of his career will relate to his role in affairs at the centre. As will be shown, his activities took him well outside Norfolk, even perhaps as far as the Holy Land, yet the local context remained central to his life, and, as can be demonstrated through his religious patronage, his death. As he rose to ever increasing prominence in the service of the Lancastrians, he gained access to ducal, and subsequently, royal patronage, and advanced in both wealth and influence. To the Erpingham family lands he added others in the county of his birth, both by grant and purchase. He also gained temporary acquisitions in the area and beyond – in 1399, for example, the custody of the inheritance of Thomas Mowbray, erstwhile duke of Norfolk, which included the control of Framlingham, and in 1413 the keeping of the temporalities of the bishopric of Norwich during an episcopal vacancy. Moreover, Sir Thomas frequently acted as feoffee for other knights and esquires in the county, a good indication not only of his network of friends but also of the fact that he was seen as a man of importance whose support was useful. He did come to hold properties outside Norfolk but the principal focus of his landholding always lay in the county. When not in Lancastrian service elsewhere or at his London house, he seems to have resided in Norwich and in Erpingham itself. Towards the end of his life he lived almost wholly in Norfolk. He never served as an MP for the county but this is more a reflection of his importance on the national stage than of his lack of local prominence. He was involved in several local issues, as the next section will reveal. He was a justice of the peace in Norfolk on several occasions in the reigns of Henry IV, V and VI, but as warden of the Cinque Ports in the first half of Henry IV's reign he was also, and sometimes simultaneously, appointed to the Kent bench. One can never be entirely certain whether or when he sat in person on either bench in the early years of the fifteenth century, but in later years we can be certain of his personal involvement. After his retirement from the national scene in the late 1410s, he continued to loom large in the county of his birth. In 1420 we find him writing from Erpingham to the bishop of Durham concerning the feud between Sir John Howard and Sir Thomas Kerdeston, and

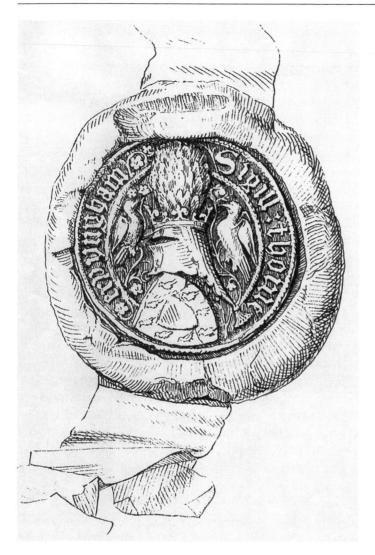

*15. The seal of Sir Thomas Erpingham.*

warning of likely problems. His words here, written when sixty-three years old, are worth quoting in full as an insight into his character:

for as moche as I am an agid man evermore willyng and desiryng the good pees, rest and tranquillite of this reaume and specially as in this contre where my symple dwellyng ys, likith unto youre wurshipful estat to accepte my symple relacion as of a matter the which I suppose is not unknown unto youre honorable person.

Erpingham's concern for local law and order, and the manner whereby he executed the office of justice of the peace in the mid 1420s, is also revealed in the Paston Letters, although it must be admitted that his actions and decisions were not entirely pleasing to William Paston. He emerges from these materials as a firm, perhaps slightly over-zealous, magistrate. So, even if he saw himself as an 'agid man' in 1420, he was still fully involved in administrative activity for at least another six, if not seven, years, almost to the time of his death in 1428.

It is in his death that further evidence of his commitment to local interests can be seen. His will was made at Norwich on 2 February 1428, about four and a half months before his death, and was proved at the Prerogative Court of Canterbury, hence being enrolled in the register of Archbishop Chichele. This reveals bequests to the church, both the mother church of his diocese and the parish churches of the county with which he had a personal link, to monastic institutions, to the poor, the sick and needy, to prisoners, and to recluses. Sir Thomas also seems to have made further bequests closer to death. We know from a reference in the will of his nephew and heir, Sir William Phelip, of December 1438 which is also in Chichele's register, that Sir Thomas again requested pensions to be given to the poor of the manor of Erpingham. Sir Thomas's will expressed his wish to be buried in the cathedral of Norwich 'beforn the cross cleped (called) the brown rode (rood) where my sepulture (tomb) is made and ordeyned'. Alas, thanks to the effects of the Reformation, this tomb no longer survives, although its possible location in the cathedral is now commemorated by a banner bearing Sir Thomas's arms, and, as noted earlier, it could well be that the kneeling figure of Sir Thomas on the Erpingham gate may have come from the tomb. In his will he added the following instructions concerning his funeral; 'I wole and assigne that myn armure and harnoise of werre to my propre persone apertenyng be offered up to the Holy Trinite in Norwich (i.e. the cathedral) the day of myn enterment in the manner and forme as I shal devyse and ordeigne in my last will'. This reminds us of the custom, which continued for several centuries to come, whereby knights and gentry had military accoutrements placed in churches after their death. Many examples from later centuries survive, and for the later fourteenth century we have the splendid example of the Black Prince's achievements which were placed above his tomb in Canterbury Cathedral. Unfortunately, we do not have any pieces of Erpingham's armour extant.

Sir Thomas Erpingham was undoubtedly a generous patron during his lifetime of the cathedral of Norwich as well as of the churches of the city, of his manor of Erpingham and of elsewhere in the county. Although documentary proof of this remains disappointingly elusive, there is ample iconographic evidence, as later sections of this chapter will indicate. Finally, many within the circle of Sir Thomas's friends and acquaintances were from the county, and, as we shall see, the core of his men-at-arms at Agincourt can be shown to hail from the area. For men like Erpingham there was no great divide between national and local. Prominence on the national stage increased his standing in the county but things could work in the other direction. As Trevor John has pointed out, it was through Erpingham that Henry IV managed to gain acceptance of his regime in Norfolk. And, vice-versa, it was through Erpingham that the Norfolk gentry could make their loyalty known to the Lancastrians. He was particularly important, for instance, in conciliating and winning over men such as Sir Simon Felbrigg, who had been Richard II's standard bearer and who was also one of the 'veterans' serving at Agincourt.

What, then, did Erpingham do? As we have seen, an early documentary reference to him dated 1372 is apparently about his involvement, at the age of fifteen or thereabouts, in an assault on a monk, but let us pass on to more salubrious matters and see how he developed his military career and his connections with the house of Lancaster. In 1368 he probably crossed to Aquitaine with his father when the latter was in the company of the Black Prince. Four years later, he was serving in a naval expedition under William Ufford, earl of Suffolk, with whom he also crossed to France in 1373. In 1379 he crossed with the earl of Salisvbury to garrison Calais. In the following year, aged twenty-three or so, he became a retainer of John of Gaunt, duke of Lancaster, third surviving son of Edward III, and one of the most powerful and, if the activities of those peasants and others who revolted in 1381 are anything to go by, one of the most unpopular men in England. Gaunt's connections with East Anglia stemmed from an exchange of lands in 1372 whereby he came to hold the hundreds and the manor of Erpingham. From 1379 onwards, he can be seen consciously to be recruiting to his retinue within East Anglian gentry society, and amongst those he recruited was Sir Thomas. Sir Thomas's indenture to serve the duke in peace and war is undated but is to be found in the section of Gaunt's register headed 'retinencia diversorum militum et scutiferorum anno regni regis Ricardi secundo quarto' (retinue of divers knights and esquires in the fourth year of the reign of Richard II, i.e. June 1380-June 1381), following an entry for 23 June 1380 and immediately before one for 25 September of the same year. Elsewhere in the same register there is an order dated 14 June 1380 from Gaunt to his receiver in Norfolk to pay £20 per annum out of the issues of the ducal manor of Gimingham (near Mundesley) to Sir Thomas who is engaged to serve the duke in peace and war. This would imply, therefore, that the indenture was already sealed by mid June 1380. It is also worth noting that Thomas was already a knight at this stage. We do not know when he had been knighted, but it is unlikely that it would have been before he was at least 21 years old. He was soon to receive further largesse from the duke, and by 1396 Gaunt had granted to him the hundred of South Erpingham. In the early 1380s Erpingham was also establishing himself on the local scene, being appointed in March and December 1382 to commissions to preserve local order in the wake of the unrest which had followed the Peasants' Revolt. Three years later he was appointed to the commission of array for Norfolk which was to arrange defensive measures in the face of anticipated French invasion. From 1383 we also see him involved as a witness in local land transactions, and was appointed in June 1384 to enquire into the stealing of 500 sheep from Salthouse.

Simon Walker has shown that Gaunt's main purpose in entering into indentures with men such as Sir Thomas was largely military. By 1380, Gaunt had already led several expeditions to France on behalf of the crown and, as we have seen, Sir Thomas already had much military experience under his belt. His deposition in the dispute in the court of chivalry between Lord Scrope and Sir Robert Grosvenor over a coat of arms implies that he served on Richard II's expedition to Scotland in 1385. His testimony in the Grey/Hastings dispute also mentions his presence in the relief of Brest, which was besieged by the duke of Brittany in 1385-6 and to which we know Gaunt sent men and supplies. Erpingham had sailed from Plymouth on 7 July and later went on to serve in Gaunt's campaign in Spain in 1386, fighting in support of the duke's claim to the throne of Castile and Leon. Gaunt never did succeed in his Spanish ambitions, dropping his claim in 1388. As a truce was agreed between the English and French in the following year, opportunities for military employment, a career to which Erpingham now seems to have firmly committed himself, were diminished. (His personal prowess had been shown in a tournament against a French champion at Montereau in 1387.) Erpingham thus passed by the spring of 1390 into the service of Henry Bolingbroke, earl of Derby, Gaunt's eldest son. It is not exactly clear why or how this happened, but Erpingham's transfer was not unique; by 1399 Bolingbroke had at least 17 knights and esquires who had previously been granted an annuity by Gaunt. It is also interesting to note that on 10 August 1392, Gaunt gave Erpingham 360 florins of Aragon towards his second journey to Prussia with Bolingbroke, implying perhaps that the link with his old master was not completely severed. Indeed the annuity continued till Gaunt's death in 1399. We may speculate that Gaunt had been anxious to place men of experience and proven loyalty into his son's household, most especially because Bolingbroke was about to depart on a fairly hazardous crusade to Prussia.

It was the connection with Bolingbroke, who was of course the future Henry IV, which brought Erpingham his most exotic experiences as well as both his lowest fortunes and his greatest honours. Truce with France enabled and – given all the soldiers likely to be thrown out of employment by the cessation of war – encouraged the resumption of crusading endeavours. Englishmen went to join the Teutonic knights in an attempt to impose Christianity on the Lithuanians. Erpingham thus accompanied Bolingbroke on his crusade to Prussia in 1390-1. He sailed from Boston on 20 July 1390, and is found in receipt of wages in the household of Bolingbroke from 18 August to 30 April in the following year. In these household accounts we also have reference to a Richard Ducheman as a servant of Erpingham, who bought a cap of beaver fur for his master and escorted a horse from Danzig to Konigsburg. It is fairly certain that Erpingham was present at the siege of Vilna, where Bolingbroke and his men distinguished themselves. Erpingham also served on Bolingbroke's second campaign to Lithuania in 1392-3, being paid wages in the household from at least 23 September 1392 to 4 July 1393. We also see him paying out money for two guides and being involved in the purchase of horses, suggesting that he was prominent in his master's commisariat. In late September 1393, Bolingbroke sent most of his followers home but Erpingham was amongst those chosen to remain with him and travel across Europe to the Holy Land. By December he was making offerings on behalf of his master to various shrines in Venice, and he also visited Rhodes and Palestine, although it is not entirely certain whether he accompanied Bolingbroke to Jerusalem. It may have been during this journey that he bought the silk for the chasuble which now bears his name, and which also bears images of camels; another possible reminder of this exciting moment in Erpingham's life.

But things were soon to change. Bolingbroke quarrelled with Thomas Mowbray, earl of Norfolk, and a duel between the two was arranged. However, Richard II intervened, and both men were sent into exile; Bolingbroke for ten years, Mowbray for life. (Bolingbroke had spent some time earlier in opposition to Richard, but the politics of these years are too complex to discuss fully here.) Erpingham had clearly developed a close relationship with Bolingbroke – closer than he had ever enjoyed with Gaunt – and was a most loyal servant, which is why he accompanied Henry into exile in Paris. Before he departed, he conveyed his lands to a body of twelve trustees, who included Sir Simon

Felbrigg. Erpingham stayed with Bolingbroke throughout, witnessing the latter's treaty with Louis, duke of Orléans, on 17 June 1399.

When Bolingbroke undertook his risky return to England in July 1399, Erpingham was in his company – a company which was, not suprisingly, to enjoy its master's largesse following his successful seizure of the throne. Erpingham played a particularly prominent part in the deposition of Richard II. According to a French pro-Ricardian chronicler, the ambush of Richard between Conway and Flint was arranged by the earl of Northumberland and carried out by his men under the command of Erpingham. Another source mentions Sir Thomas as guarding Richard once the latter was imprisoned in the Tower of London. On 29 September 1399, Erpingham and Sir Thomas Gray were sent as proctors of the Commons with a deputation from the lords to receive the abdication of Richard, and three days later Erpingham was amongst those who conveyed to Richard the effective sentence of deposition. The level of the usurper's trust is revealed by the quantity and nature of rewards heaped upon Erpingham. In August, even before Bolingbroke had formally become king, Erpingham was appointed as constable of Dover Castle and warden of the Cinque Ports. These offices were worth over £300 a year to their incumbent and were amongst the most important military appointments in England. It is difficult to know whether Sir Thomas ever spent much time at Dover. As was common with many such offices, day-to-day supervision was commonly exercised by a deputy, and this is precisely what the surviving account rolls of Sir Thomas's period of office reveal. But overall policy and command would have remained with Erpingham, and would have added to his significance as a regular member of Henry IV's council when strategic matters, and most notably the war with France, were being discussed. It is also interesting to note that several of the men in his garrison at Dover were from Norfolk.

Further financial rewards came thick and fast. In November 1399 Erpingham was given custody of the lands of Thomas, duke of Norfolk, and on 11 May 1400 he was granted annuities of £80 from the royal revenues of Norfolk and Suffolk as well as £40 from the fee farm of Norwich, and six months later added a further £66.13.4 from the fee farm of Cambridge. Further custodies of manors, lands and heirs, permission to acquire lands sequestrated from the alien priories, and the grant of 'the Newe Inne' in London followed. He also seems to have become a knight banneret after the usurpation, and is frequently described as king's knight. Such a high level of royal patronage is not surprising given that Erpingham continued in close personal service and proximity to King Henry IV in the first years of the reign. He carried the king's sword before him in the coronation procession from the Tower to Westminster, and antiquarian sources have him appointed as royal chamberlain on the day of the coronation. This office carried with it, as Given-Wilson puts it, 'an immense amount of influence and responsibility', and was almost invariably held by men who were close personal friends of the king.

Erpingham was a dyed-in-the-wool Lancastrian. He was amongst those who petitioned Henry on New Years Day 1400 that Richard should be put to death, and he was involved in the suppression of the revolt of the earls which happened a few days later, being one of the commissioners subsequently appointed to try the rebels. The same French chronicle which credited him with the ambush of Richard in 1399 alleges that he used excessive cruelty in dealing with the revolt, claiming that he attempted to interrogate Sir Thomas Blount whilst the victim's bowels, already removed, were being burned before his gaze. This allows our pro-Ricardian chronicler to put the following words into Blount's mouth: 'art thou the traitor Erpingham? Cursed be the day when thou and he [meaning Henry IV] were born'. Of course, if one is of the opinion that Richard was unjustly deposed then indeed Erpingham was a traitor. Having given his loyalty to the new regime he was obviously anxious to sustain it, particularly in its early years of uncertainty. Significantly, too, it was the stall of one of the rebel earls (Warwick) to which he was elevated in 1401 as a knight of the Garter. He was also applauded in Parliament for his loyalty to the Lancastrian cause.

In the late summer of 1400 he may have seen military service again on Henry's expedition to Scotland: he was certainly involved as chamberlain in organizing men and supplies, and as warden of the Cinque Ports in summoning shipping. The Close rolls give many further references to his activities as warden over the next few years. A regular member of the royal council, he was in 1401 one of the king's delegates to the convocation of the clergy, promising the king's support in the extirpation of heresy and requesting a large clerical subsidy. In October 1401 he was considered as a possible governor of the Prince of Wales, the future Henry V. His candidature was not successful, but the fact that his name stood alongside those of three major peers, Thomas Percy, earl of Worcester (who was given the post), Lord Lovell and Lord Say, shows the status and reputation he enjoyed. He was appointed instead as a keeper of the lands of the king's second son, Thomas, whom he would have known from the days of exile in Paris. It is unlikely, however, that he crossed with Prince Thomas to Ireland, as was once thought. Erpingham was on various commissions in Norfolk and Kent in 1402-3, and active in his Cinque Ports command, but he does not seem to have been present at the battle of Shrewsbury when the king defeated his one-time friends and now rebels, the Percies.

In September 1403 he was appointed steward of the royal household, a post he held until November 1404. He also served as marshal of England in 1404-5, and was on an embassy in 1407 which was charged with negotiating a French marriage for Prince Henry. On this occasion, relations with the French were better than they had been in the more recent past and than they were to be by 1415. Erpingham and his colleagues reported that they had never been so well treated and found no difficulty in negotiating a temporary truce. Indeed the course of our history, and of Erpingham's own life, might have been quite different had not the proposed bride, Princess Marie, refused to contemplate leaving the convent in which she had been placed from birth. If she had married Henry as a result of Erpingham's embassy, there may indeed have been no battle of Agincourt, and no marriage to her younger sister, Catherine. And no Shakespeare's *Henry V*. A frightening thought!

Erpingham's offices kept him largely at court. He therefore did not participate in the Welsh campaigns in which the Prince of Wales, Henry of Monmouth, was making his name and gaining his military experience and members of his own later royal household. Erpingham's developing relationship with the prince is difficult to ascertain. In 1409 he surrendered the wardenship of the Cinque Ports and constableship of Dover Castle to Prince Henry but it is dangerous to interpret this as a sign of either royal or princely disfavour. It is significant that the Prince used the same lieutenant in Dover as Erpingham had done, and it is even more significant that this was Sir Andrew Botiller, the husband of Sir Thomas's niece. What is more, the Prince granted Sir Thomas an annuity of £100 p.a. The fact that the Prince had taken over the offices was more a reflection of his father's need to reward him for his services in Wales and also to provide him with key offices as he began to play more of a role in affairs of state as his father's health declined. The prince was in control of government in 1410-11 when his father was incapacitated. It is possible that Erpingham showed himself too well disposed towards the Prince at this stage and so incurred the disfavour of Henry IV when the latter reasserted his authority in 1411. There is certainly less evidence of Sir Thomas's prominence in central government in the last two years of the reign of Henry IV when the Prince was also in the political wilderness.

Most significantly, the prince appointed Erpingham as steward of the household at his own accession in 1413. Sir Thomas continued to serve in this capacity until 10 May 1417. He was thus a member of the relatively small circle of councillors on whom the new king drew in the early part of his reign. He most certainly participated in meetings which discussed the proposed campaign in France as well as matters such as the keeping of the seas, the defence of Wales, Scotland and Calais, and of course that perennial worry for all governments – especially one that was in the process of pawning its crown jewels in order to invade France – the question of finance. It is likely that he acted as one of the king's leading advisors on the campaign and in the negotiations which preceded it. Present at Southampton with Henry as the troops gathered for embarkation, he witnessed the king's will drawn up on 24 July 1415, and only a week later was entrusted with the rather more invidious task of sitting in judgement on those of the king's friends and relations who had seen fit to plot Henry's death at this very moment. By the end of the next month he set sail, along with the king and his army, for France.

This momentous period in Erpingham's career will be discussed later. But first, the survey of Erpingham's life after Agincourt will be completed. His closeness to the king continued into 1416, when we find him involved in negotiations with the French in Calais and Beauvais in July, and with the subsequent reception of the duke of Burgundy at Calais. As steward of the royal household he accompanied the earl of Warwick to meet Burgundy outside the town and to escort him to his lodgings therein. His office also means that he was likely to have been involved in the Emperor Sigismund's visit to England and in the Garter ceremony of 1416 when the Emperor was admitted to the fraternity. He was also in attendance at the trial of Oldcastle, and legend has it that it was to Sir Thomas that the Lollard spoke his last words that he would rise on the last day. There is no evidence, however, that Erpingham himself inclined towards Lollardy, as Blomefield and others alleged.

As we have noted, he continued as steward of the household until 10 May 1417. This point we must take as marking his effective retirement from court, from the king's personal service and from military activity. He was now in his sixtieth year. Perhaps he had decided he really was too old to accompany the king on his next expedition (due to sail in late July), all the more so when this campaign was intended to last at least a year. Thus he did not benefit from Henry's doling out of lands in Normandy. Ships were requisitioned to take him to the king in France in June 1420 although it is not clear whether he ever crossed. Although he was present at a council meeting in July 1421 (the king having returned to France after a brief few months in England), there is no other reference to his involvement in central government after 1417. He continued to be in contact with the centre and to assist in the levying of troops (in 1419), commissions of array and negotiations of loans in his home county, but it would not be misleading to say that after the death of Henry V Erpingham's interests and activities were exclusively local. His was a life in arms, but it was also a life of service. Even though Erpingham was no longer in arms himself in the early 1420s, when Henry V came the closest of any English king to actually winning the crown of France, his interest in the matter of France continued. It is fitting, therefore, to end with Sir Thomas's own words, written at the end of his letter to the bishop of Durham in July 1420, about six weeks after the sealing of the treaty of Troyes which made Henry heir and regent of France, and about four weeks after the king's marriage to Princess Catherine.

> And worshipful lord also hartily I beseche yow that you likith in recomfort of my symple person to certifie me by the brynger of this lettre of suche goode tydynges as ye have there out of France and of other partyes, the which were to me gret gladnesse joye and ese in hert for to here.

His heart was with King Henry even if the 'agid man' himself could no longer be.

### Sir Thomas and Agincourt

It might be dangerous to say that the battle of Agincourt was the most momentous event for Sir Thomas given that his life was full of interest and action. If anything should be considered as the defining moment, then surely it was the usurpation of Henry Bolingbroke in 1399 which brought Erpingham to the real centre of English politics. But Agincourt must have been for him, as for many others, a tremendous and memorable experience. As far as we know, Erpingham had not been involved in any major pitched battle before, although he had seen plenty of smaller actions. In this context, he was undoubtedly one of the most experienced soldiers present on the campaign of 1415. Given his position as steward of the household and royal councillor, he would certainly have been involved in the discussions that preceded the launching of the campaign. Many members of the royal household, from leading knights to kitchen staff, served on the campaign. Indeed, the household formed a significant part of the king's army (as well as no doubt continuing to serve the king for his comfort), as a quick glance at the lists printed in Nicholas's *History of the Battle of Agincourt* will confirm. This is a point borne out by the manuscripts which still survive in the Public Record Office. There was no separate war office or army department in this period. Armies were raised and administered through the existing offices of state, with the Exchequer playing the major role. Indeed, what we know about the Agincourt army comes largely from pay records. In the case of Sir Thomas's service in 1415, we have virtually a full set of documentary records. Thus his example can be used in helping to explain how the army was organized.

From the last thirty years or so of the fourteenth century, all troops were raised by an indenture (contract) entered into between an individual and the crown. The Agincourt army is distinctive amongst all the armies raised in the later fourteenth and fifteenth centuries in having many contracting to serve with small companies in addition to the customary large retinues offered by the nobility, knights and gentry. To date, at least 250 separate indented companies have been detected. This contrasts with the situation in, say, 1423 when the army of 1,520 men which crossed to France was provided by only four indentees. Only in 1430 when Henry VI himself crossed to France was anything like the Agincourt situation seen, in that 114 men indented with the crown. The dictating factor, therefore, is that a king was present in person. In 1415, too, we can probably suggest that Henry V was trying to raise as large an army as possible – at least 12,000 seem to have crossed – and that he had consciously sought to recruit as widely as he could, bringing in the 'smaller men' as well as the great and good. That is important when appreciating the level of national enthusiasm and pride with which the campaign was undertaken.

Sir Thomas's indenture was entered into on 29 April 1415, as were the vast majority of others. He contracted to serve with a company of eighty men, that is, twenty men-at-arms, including himself and two knights, and sixty archers. All his troops were to be mounted. This was a medium-sized company. The largest retinues were those of the nobility. The king's brother, Thomas, duke of Clarence, for instance, indented to bring 960 men, and the royal uncles, the duke of York and the earl of Dorset, indented for 400 each. Other earls brought 80 to 400 men, barons and knights generally 60 to 120 men, prominent esquires 16 to 40 men, with the remaining indentures being for companies from one to nine men. Companies of archers were also raised from certain areas by virtue of special royal landholding connections. Thus 500 came from Lancashire, and the same number from South Wales. The chamberlain of Chester was ordered to bring 650 archers but pay records reveal that only 294 may have actually served. These companies were accompanied by a handful of men-at-arms but most indentured retinues were in the ratio of three archers to one man-at-arms.

Indentures were so called because they were written out in duplicate and then cut across the middle; one part remaining with the crown and the other with the indentee. In Erpingham's case, the copy kept by the crown survives today in the PRO as E101/69/360 (fig. 16) and that kept by Sir Thomas within E101/47/20 (fig. 17). Whether they would actually fit together is a moot point! After the campaign, Sir Thomas was due to make account with the Exchequer. This will be discussed in more detail later, but it is helpful here to mention that this was how his own copy of the indenture was later returned to the Exchequer, and why it is amongst documents held together in a white leather Exchequer bag marked 'Erpingham'.

*16 and 17. The crown's copy (above) and Sir Thomas Erpingham's copy (below) of his indenture for service in the campaign of 1415.*

The indentures are in French and give the conditions of service. Not only do they tell us the numbers and kinds of troops promised but also the rates and times of pay, rules concerning gains of war, arrangements for mustering, etc. Even though the army was being provided by individuals, it was most certainly a royal army as there was central control of wages and conditions. Sir Thomas was to be paid 4 shillings a day, and his knights shillings per day wherever the army fought. The ordinary men-at-arms would each be paid forty marks (£26.13.4) and the archers twenty marks (£13.6.8) for the whole year if the campaign went to Gascony, but if it went to France the rates would be one shilling per day (£18.5.0 p.a.) for the men-at-arms, plus a special regard calculated at one hundred marks for every thirty men-at-arms each quarter, and 6d per day (£9.2.6 p.a.) for the archers. Service was to be for the whole year following the date of the muster at the sea-coast, which was set for 1 July. The indenture also mentioned that Erpingham would be informed by the end of May about the location of the muster.

Two interesting issues arise. The first concerns the arrangements for giving out pay. The indentee received pay for the whole of his company, and would normally expect to be paid for a substantial part of the campaign before the army set out. But Henry did not have enough money in hand. So half of the wages for the first quarter were paid at the time of indenting, no doubt as an aid to recruitment, with the other half paid at muster. For the second quarter, no wages were paid, but indentees received royal jewels and plate as guarantee of payment in the future. Redemption was planned for nineteen months later. Thus indentees would have begun the campaign knowing that if it lasted for more than three months, they would essentially be paying troops out of their own pockets, but would have some prospect of repayment. If it continued into the third and fourth quarters of the year, the crown would try to pay wages, but if it could not, then the indentees were at liberty to withdraw their services. A good quantity of documents survive concerning the payment of wages for the first quarter and the issue of jewels. For Sir Thomas we have an Exchequer warrant for payment for the first instalment of wages following the indenture (PRO E404/31/156). This payment, totalling £173 18s 4d, is also recorded on an Exchequer issue roll, E101/45/5, and was made at the Gascon rates. There also survives a receipt for the second instalment of £119 15s $6\frac{1}{2}$d dated 1 July within his post campaign account bag (E101/47/20). This payment was made adjusting the pay for the first quarter for France, not Gascony. We also have a receipt for the jewels he was given as security for the second quarter, made in the form of an indenture and dated 18 June. All of these receipts also feature in the accounts drawn up after the campaign.

The second interesting issue brings us closer to the battle itself. This concerns the intended location of the campaign. The indenture leaves the destination vague, mentioning 'the expedition which it had pleased the king to undertake into the duchy of Guienne [Gascony] or the kingdom of France', and allowing for two different wage rates depending upon location. What Henry intended to do in France remains unclear. He may have first thought of going to Gascony, hence the level of pay issued for the first half of the first quarter, and then changed his mind. The pay for the rest of the first quarter was adjusted for the French theatre, as was the value of the jewels issued as security for the second quarter. The indentures were for a year's service. Henry may have hoped to capture more places than merely Harfleur, and perhaps even to conduct a *chevauchée* from the Seine down to Bordeaux. Erpingham's proximity to the king makes it likely that he was better informed of Henry's plans than we are now.

Erpingham mustered his men on Southampton Heath along with other companies in the royal household on 13 July. This muster is still extant and is in the form of an indenture so that Sir Thomas and the crown could both have a copy. (It is interesting how much effort was put into avoiding any opportunity for fraud.) This gives the names of Erpingham and nineteen other men-at-arms and of sixty archers. We should note that he had not been able to find two knights, as his indenture had required. Only one, Sir Walter Goldingham, is named in the muster. But four extra (named) men-at-arms and thirteen extra (unnamed) archers had been recruited beyond the indenture terms. This may be a reflection of Erpingham's reputation which made it possible for him to recruit more troops than he had promised, or it may be indicative of the fact that he was someone to whom men indenting as individuals or in small groups could be attached. He may also have deliberately chosen to take extra troops to

*18. Quittance (receipt) by Sir Thomas Erpingham for the payment of the first instalment of wages for the campaign of 1415.*

*19. Indenture recording delivery to Sir Thomas of royal jewels as security for payment of the second quarter's wages.*

fill any vacancies which might arise, although this would have been at his own expense.

The army did not cross until 11 August, departure being delayed by the detection of a plot by the earl of Cambridge, Lord Scrope and Sir Thomas Gray against the king. But neither Erpingham nor anyone else could have known as they sailed from England that they were going to fight a major battle against the French. They soon discovered that they were going to besiege Harfleur. The chronicler, Thomas Walsingham, asserts that Erpingham was appointed along with the earl of Dorset and Lord Fitzhugh to treat with the burgesses for surrender, an observation also found in versions of the vernacular chronicles, the *Brut* and the *London Chronicle*. This suggests that he was a senior member of Henry's command staff. But he is not noted in connection with the campaign in the best contemporary account, the *Gesta Henrici Quinti*. That chronicle only mentions him in relation to the negotiations at Calais with the duke of Burgundy in 1416. In fact he is not featured in any account of the battle written in England. He does get a passing mention in two Middle English poems on the battle, written in the 1440s, one of which is inserted in a version of the *London Chronicle*, but these note only his presence at the battle and his valour in general terms, as they do for many other English nobles and knights. They do not assign to him any special command role.

*20. Muster in indented form recording the troops brought by Sir Thomas Erpingham to the muster point in July 1415.*

*21. Account (left) and particulars of the account (right) drawn up concerning Sir Thomas's service in 1415. These documents were drawn up after his death.*

It is in three works written in France, the chronicles of Enguerrand de Monstrelet, Jean de Waurin, and Jean Le Fèvre, sire de Saint Rémy, that we have the famous passage referring to his command, already mentioned in Chapter Two, and where reference to his greyness of age is made. Firstly, the account in Monstrelet:

> Elsewhere the king of England sent about 200 archers behind his army so that they would not be spotted by the French. They secretly entered a meadow near Tramecourt, quite close to the rearguard of the French, and held themselves there secretly until it was time to shoot. All the other English stayed with their king. He had his battle drawn up by a knight grey with age called Thomas Erpingham, putting the archers in the front and then the men-at-arms. He made two wings of

men-at-arms and archers, and the horses and baggage were placed behind the army. The archers each fixed in front of them a stake sharpened at both ends. Thomas exhorted them all on behalf of the king of England to fight bravely against the French in order to guarantee their own survival. Then riding with an escort in front of the army after he had set up its formation, he threw high into the air a baton which he had held in his hand, shouting 'nescieque'. Then he dismounted to join the king and the others on foot. At the throwing of the baton, all the English suddenly made a great cry which was a cause of great amazement to the French.

Waurin and Le Fèvre connect Erpingham more explicitly with the deployment of the archers. Their accounts are identical, save for Waurin's inclusion of Erpingham's word of command.

Some on the French side say that the King of England sent 200 archers towards the French and behind their army, secretly, so that they could not be seen, towards Tramecourt to a meadow close to where the vanguard of the French were positioned. The purpose of this was that when the French marched forward, the 200 archers could fire on them from the side. But I have heard said and certified as true by a man of honour who was there on that day in the company of the king of England that nothing like this happened… The king of England ordered a veteran knight, called Sir Thomas Erpingham, to draw up his archers and to put them in the front in two wings. Sir Thomas exhorted everyone on behalf of the king of England to fight with vigour against the French. He rode with an escort in front of the battle of archers after he had carried out the deployment, and threw in the air a baton which he had been holding in his hand. [Waurin adds that 'he cried 'Nestroque' which was the signal for attack'.] Then he dismounted and put himself in the battle of the king of England, which was also on foot, between his men and with his banner in front of him. Then the English began suddenly to advance uttering a great cry which much amazed the French.

At this point, the accounts of Monstrelet, Waurin and Le Fèvre become identical.

When the English saw that the French were not advancing on them, they moved forward in good order and again made another great cry before taking a rest and catching their breath. Then the archers who were in the meadow also raised a great shout and fired with great vigour on the French. Straightaway the English approached the French; first the archers, of whom there were a good 13,000 [Le Fèvre says 10,000, Waurin does not give a number] began with all their might to shoot volleys of arrows against the French for as long as they could pull the bow.

As can be seen, Sir Thomas is associated with men-at-arms as much as archers, and of exhorting *all* to fight hard against the French in order to guarantee their own survival.

At his command, the English move forward and form up again with another shout. The firing of the arrows which then follows in the accounts is not necessarily directly linked to Erpingham's actions of deployment. He is never explicitly recorded as ordering the archers to shoot. Moreover, we must remember that these French accounts were written relatively late in the day: Monstrelet in the mid 1440s; Waurin in the 1450s or 60s; and Le Fèvre in the early 1460s. Monstrelet's account was drawn on by Edward Hall in his *Union of the Two Illustre families of Lancaster and York* (1542). There, Erpingham's throwing up of the baton was followed by a great shout, which was the sign for the archers in the meadow to shoot. Holinshed copied this into his own account of the battle in his chronicle of 1586-7. By such means it entered the English historical tradition and was later elaborated well beyond what the contemporary and even the sixteenth-century sources said.

It is perhaps surprising – if Erpingham was so important to the battle – that he is not mentioned in the *Gesta*. There, command of the centre battle lies with the king, of the right with the duke of York and the left with Lord Camoys, although it is interesting that it is only in the *Gesta* that the latter is named in this context. Other later fifteenth-century chronicles written in England mention York in connection with the command of the archers. Now, it may stand to reason that someone did issue the command to shoot, and also to advance. But if one supposes that the archers were on the flanks, or even if one accepts that they are interspersed in groups amongst the men-at-arms, there would need to be a way of transmitting that order. It is unlikely that all could have been in view of one signal. It is more likely, surely, that a central signal was given, possibly by Erpingham, and echoed down the line.

In this context it would be helpful to know more about the deployment of the army. All chronicles are unhelpful on the positioning of the archers. We know, however, that there were more than three times as many archers at the outset of the campaign than there were men-at-arms. Both categories of troops had suffered from sickness at Harfleur and had seen some of their number invalided home. Men-at-arms and archers had been left in garrison in the conquered town. Although we have some figures for these losses in the account material, survival of records is not quite enough to be sure exactly how many of the army went on to participate in the battle, nor what the ratio of men-at-arms to archers there was. The 'Agincourt roll' – a sixteenth-century partial transcript of a now lost fifteenth-century list of those at the battle – names 770 men-at-arms and 2,496 archers, still, roughly speaking, a ratio of one to three. It lists these men in companies under their leaders (the indentees), just as the musters taken at embarkation do. Erpingham is in this roll, with two knights (Sir Walter Goldingham, and Sir Hamo Strange) and twelve other men-at-arms whose names are given. A total of forty-seven archers is given, but the sixteenth-century transcribers did not give the names of the archers.

As it happened, the campaign did not last for the whole year. The army moved on to Calais and thence to Dover, where Erpingham landed around 16 November. That was not the end of the financial business, however, for Erpingham and his fellow indentees had still to account for their receipts and expenditures on the campaign. All of this was most complex. The indentees had received pay for a certain number of troops but some

*22. Brass of Thomas, Lord Camoys, leader of the left battle at Agincourt according to the* Gesta Henrici Quinti.

had died at Harfleur and thus not served for the whole period. Their pay was due to be refunded to the crown. In addition there were gains of war for which the crown was entitled a share. And there were the jewels issued as security for the second quarter's pay to redeem. Erpingham's account was not submitted for settlement until after his death. It was by no means uncommon for Agincourt accounts still to be outstanding in the late 1420s, but the crown continued to be anxious that it should not be defrauded by captains. Thus Erpingham's executors were obliged to present all the evidence: Sir Thomas's copy of the indenture; an account of the pay he had received for himself and his men; details of what had happened to each and every man of his retinue. These materials were checked against the royal Exchequer records. After the account was settled, the documents were filed in a white leather bag, where they still are today.

Within this bag is a list of all Erpingham's men. Sir Thomas heads the list, followed by two knights, Sir Walter Goldingham, who had been on the embarkation muster list as a knight, and Hamo Strange, who had not been noted as a knight on that list but who had obviously been knighted during the campaign. A note in the margin explained that both had been at the battle of Agincourt. Seventeen men-at-arms are listed. The

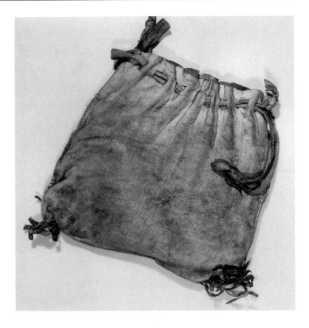

*23. Exchequer account bag containing materials relating to Sir Thomas's service in 1415.*

marginal note tells us that two of them, Thomas Geney and John Calthorpe, had been knighted at the landing at the Chef de Caux. Both had then become ill at Harfleur, and had died shortly after being sent home. Another man-at-arms, John Rous, had also been invalided home. Sixty archers are listed. Two of them, Henry Prom and Robert Beccles, are also noted as dying at Harfleur, another, John de Boterie, had been invalided home. Perhaps Erpingham and his men, or at least some of them, were in the part of the army where dysentery was most virulent, with the duke of Clarence, who was himself invalided home. Remember that Erpingham had earlier links with the duke in 1401, and was one of his executors following his death at the battle of Baugé in 1421. Another archer, Richard Charman, was killed on the march from Harfleur and Agincourt.

All of the others, Sir Thomas included, served in the battle. Only one fatality was noted as occurring at the battle: an archer, Stephen Gerneyng. A man-at-arms, John Aungers, died at Calais on the way back to England. This list raises several interesting points. The first is that none of Sir Thomas's men were put into garrison at Harfleur. Was he seen as someone the king wanted with him on the inevitably dangerous march? Were his men equally vital? The second is that, fascinating as the list is, it cannot help us much with the deployment of troops at Agincourt. We have seen that the army was recruited, organized and paid in units of mixed troops, men-at-arms and archers, under an indentee. But that does not mean that in a military action all these troops would necessarily have served together. Indeed, wherever one puts the archers at Agincourt, it is assumed that there were groups of archers together, presumably drawn from several retinues, and separated from 'their' men-at-arms. Did they then train together as archers? Was their command and grouping reorganized on the battlefield only? Had they served in their mixed companies at Harfleur? Unless we are getting the whole thing wrong, and mixed retinues of men-at-arms and archers *were* kept together in

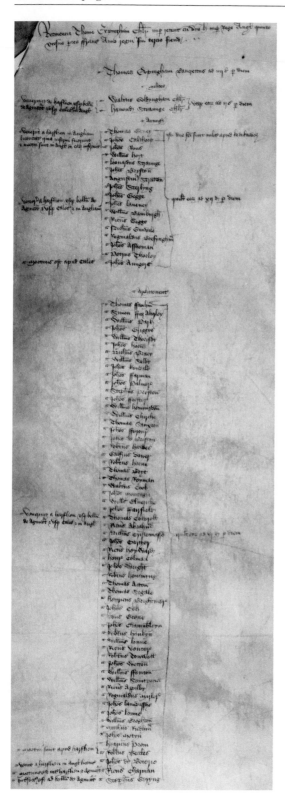

*24. Retinue list presented with Sir Thomas's account after his death. It notes what happened to each of the men in his company on the campaign of 1415.*

battles. Perhaps only the companies of archers alone, drawn from Cheshire and Lancashire, were kept separate.

The third point concerns the specific names in the list. It would be possible to investigate this more thoroughly, but here are a few examples. John Leveriche, an archer, was a member of a family based in Susted with which Sir Thomas had been involved as a feoffee as early as 1383. Connections between the Erpingham and Geney families are also known, and two of the men-at-arms, William Bamburgh and Richard Gegge, were among Erpingham's executors in 1428. Robert Bresingham, a kinsman of the William Bresingham who had been Erpingham's marshal at Dover castle, was in Erpingham's retinue at Agincourt as a man-at-arms. Thus we can see that Erpingham recruited amongst friends and neighbours in Norfolk at least for some of his company in 1415. Some of his men may have been drawn from his own household servants: the name, John de Boterie (Buttery), is indicative here. We can also see that for the men-at-arms there is consistency between the muster list of 13 July 1415 and the retinue list presented against the final account (and with the 'Agincourt roll'). But this is not the case for the archers. Many names appear only in one of the lists, not both. Perhaps by 1428 no one knew exactly which archers had been with Sir Thomas? Could it be that after the siege of Harfleur, in the light of deaths and invalidings home, there had been some reorganization of companies? Or is it merely a problem of surnames? There was inevitably much inconsistency of spellings for men of all ranks, but it would seem that there was a greater stability in the surnames of those of higher rank – the men-at-arms – than in the names of the archers.

This is only one of many puzzles which continue to perplex us when looking at Sir Thomas Erpingham and the triumph of the English archers at Agincourt. Yet we can find out a surprisingly large amount about him and his men, and further research in documentary sources would no doubt reveal more. What can also be suggested is that however the archers were commanded and positioned, both they and the men-at-arms reaped the benefit of having been together for four months or so already, over half of which had been spent on enemy soil. Surely it would not be incorrect to assign to them a considerable degree of mutual trust, both one to another, and between the rank and file and commanders. In such a scenario, it is not surprising that they had the edge over French troops hastily thrown together and unpractised in concerted deployment. Nor would it be surprising if a veteran warrior such as Sir Thomas Erpingham, distinguished by the badge of age, should be seen as a reliable and inspiring leader. Many men in the army would have known him personally or by reputation. His contemporary prominence cannot be doubted. An account roll for the gild of St George in Norwich notes the purchase of hoods of St George and also of Erpingham for use in processions. Such a tangible expression of Sir Thomas's fame and importance, juxtaposed with that of the saint whose invocation at Agincourt is well documented, provides a fitting conclusion to this study of 'a life in arms'.

# Norwich, Norfolk and Sir Thomas Erpingham
## Ken Mourin

Although Sir Thomas became a national figure, influential and esteemed at court, and widely travelled for his times, he had his roots in the Norfolk countryside and the city of Norwich. His father, Sir John Erpingham, who was bailiff of Norwich in 1352 and 1360, spent most of his life there, owning a house there in 1370 (possibly earlier). Blomefield's map shows it located on the corner of Cattlemarket Street and Conisford (Konigsford) Lane, which is now called King Street (Site A). Presumably his son Thomas was brought up in part here, and possibly was even born here. Sir John died on 1 August 1370, and was buried in Erpingham church, where his tomb with its brass effigy of a knight in full armour survives. The Erpinghams had held the manor of Erpingham since about 1234 but there is no documentary information about a manor house or residence at Erpingham, though the site of a manor house has been identified there.

Sir Thomas was married sometime before 1389 to Joan, daughter of Sir William Clopton, of Clopton Green in Suffolk. It is likely that they lived at the family home off Conisford Lane. She died in 1404, and Clopton manor descended through her to him. In 1409-10 he married his second wife – Joan Howard, widow of Sir John Howard of Fersfield, and daughter and heiress of Sir Richard Walton – acquiring a house called Berney's Inn in Norwich built by the Berney's in the early fourteenth century, on World's End Lane (site B). The site is now occupied by the car parks of the Magistrate's Courts; archaeological evidence locates it west of the Calthorpe's house shown on the map.

A bay window ascribed to his house and re-erected at No. 10, St. Martin-at-Palace, came from Hall House (now lying under the Magistrate's Courts themselves), rather than Berney's Inn. Erpingham's house was even further east over towards the river, mostly under the site of the westernmost of the two gas-holders built there in the nineteenth century, in front of the bishop's palace. It was very substantial, with a small central courtyard surrounded by the main blocks and by two wings running north to south; the site was large, and the house set well back from the road. It must have housed and supported a number of people, since one of Erpingham's servants, John Middleton, left legacies to seventeen people, including his lord's butler, his personal servant, cook, barber, five stable hands, a skinner and five poor people living there.

After Erpingham's death, the house went to his nephew and heir, Sir William Phelip, whose widow Joan left instructions that it should be sold on her death, which occurred in 1446. It was bought by Sir William Calthorpe together with much of the furniture and equipment, for 350 marks (one mark was worth 13s 4d, or 66p in today's coinage). The widow of his son, Sir Philip Calthorpe, listed a great chamber, a gallery, and a wardrobe, as well as other rooms, some hung with tapestries. In 1858 it was said that the banqueting room, with carved chestnut panelling, was 35ft by 17ft in dimension, with a 10ft window on the south side, and it could still be discerned, with an external stairway faced with stone, probably roofed, leading to it. Set in spacious gardens, on the banks of the Wensum, it must, as Druery says, 'have been an ornamental and handsome residence'.

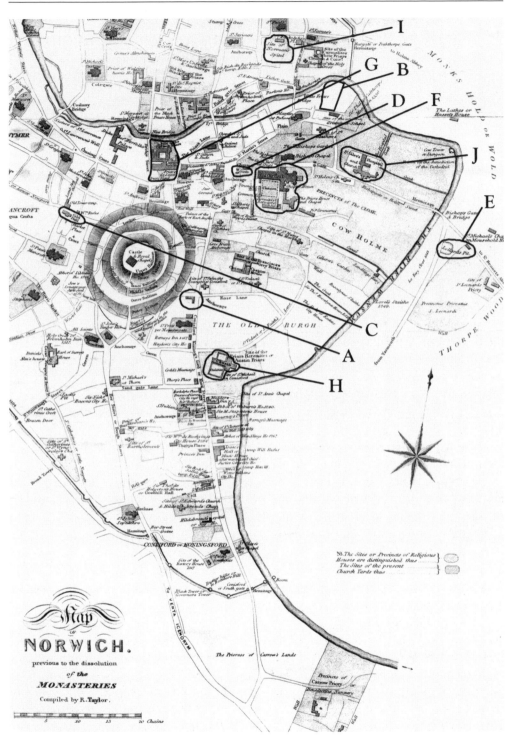

*25. Sites in Norwich associated with Sir Thomas Erpingham, based on Taylor's map of the city, 1821.*

*26. The window from St Martin's at Palace Plain.*

A tenement in London called 'The Newe Inne', near Paul's Wharf, was granted to Erpingham for life, shortly after Henry IV's accession. Erpingham had been made chamberlain, and this was possibly so that Erpingham had a town house in London readily accessible to court. The house went to his heir, Sir William Phelip, on his death.

However, despite his increasing prominence on the national scene, Sir Thomas's connections with his home county remained strong. Lancastrian supporters in East Anglia looked to him for leadership, especially after the accession of Henry IV. As Trevor John and Helen Castor have shown, Henry IV was keen to build up a royal affinity in Norfolk based upon his duchy of Lancaster holdings which lay principally in the north of the county. Erpingham was central to the development of royal interest in the shire in the early fifteenth century. As John affirms, Sir Thomas was 'the centre of a web of influence and connection stretching from the central government to local society, and binding them together'. Castor also shows how, as prince of Wales, Henry V developed a strong interest in the county. This developed especially after 1409 when the prince gained the keeping of the Mortimer lands previously in the custody of Erpingham. But this was not symbolic of a fall from grace of Erpingham, as the latter retained control of three of the manors and was given an annuity by the prince. It is interesting to note that John Phelip, the younger brother of William, was in Prince Henry's household, and also served on the Agincourt

*27. Sir Thomas Erpingham's house (Berney's Inn) on World Lane End in 1851, from Winter's Norfolk Antiquities (1885-8).*

campaign, dying at the siege of Harfleur. The Phelip brothers were, of course, Sir Thomas's nephews. They, along with others such as John Winter, formed a group of Norfolk men in Henry V's service as prince and king. Indeed, Castor concludes that Prince Henry 'developed a much closer association with the Lancastrian network in East Anglia than in many other areas of the duchy [of Lancaster], and also that his association was stronger than his father's links with the region'. In this context, Erpingham served as a crucial link between the court and the locality.

Erpingham had already served as a justice of the peace under Richard II, and was to do so on many occasions in the reigns of Henry IV, V and VI. Indeed, under Henry IV he was named on every commission of the peace in Norfolk, and served on other commissions with local and national connotations. His reputation was high. Although the parliaments of Henry IV frequently complained of royal extravagance, Erpingham was specifically exempted from criticism and his services to the king and the country commended. Likewise his importance as a patron of the city of Norwich should not be underestimated. At Erpingham's instigation, Henry IV gave Norwich its new charter in 1404. This made the city and suburbs into 'the county and city of Norwich', extinguished the office of the bailiffs, and enabled the citizens to elect a mayor and sheriffs. Erpingham attended the great assembly held in Norwich Guildhall (site C) on 5 February 1414 and the first assembly of 24 July 1422. He also left money in his will for the benefit of prisoners at the Guildhall, and those at the Castle. He was also important in the rehabilitation of Bishop Henry Despenser of Norwich who had sent four or five knights to join the rebellion of the 'duketti' against Henry IV at Epiphany 1400. The bishop claimed later that his action had been intended merely to exhort them to be loyal to Henry but with his past loyalty to Richard II, that was a bit too much to swallow. Erpingham laid the facts before parliament in 1401, supported by the city of Norwich and many of its important citizens. The bishop backed down and declared his acceptance of God's will in the new rule. Erpingham is said to have procured the bishop's release from prison. The king commended Erpingham before parliament for his actions, rebuked the bishop, and then made them shake hands in friendship. Indeed, it seems as though true friendship did develop. He also acted alongside the earls of Northumberland and Worcester in mediating a long-standing dispute between the bishop and the prior of King's Lynn in 1403.

His relations with the cathedral are also worthy of attention. There will be a fuller discussion of the Erpingham gate (site D) in due course, but Sir Thomas was a benefactor of Norwich Cathedral (site F) in other ways. There are carved shields on elbows and misericords of a choir stall on the dean's side. Portraits of him and his wives were also in the window adjacent to the tombs, now lost, and the pillars on either side were decorated with figures and inscriptions; both were recorded by Sir Thomas Browne. A fragment of glass (possibly from these portraits) now in the north ambulatory aisle window, reconstructed by Mr. King, has Erpingham's motto 'yenk' (thought to mean 'think' or 'remember') on four of the petals of a forget-me-not, the type of flower being significant – 'remember', 'forget me not'. His tomb, and that of his two wives, was probably on the north side of the presbytery, in the first bay, where a banner bearing his arms was raised in 1996 to commemorate this great knight. Bishop Goldwell (1472-99) encased the original arcade and reformed the arcades, but the bay where Erpingham was buried was known to have been decorated at the time. The cloisters were finished by 1430, financed by several families whose arms were placed in the windows: Morley, Shelton, Scales, Erpingham, Gournay, Mowbray, Thorp, Savage and others. Bishop Goldwell placed on the walls and in the windows of the cathedral the many arms of worthy benefactors that contributed to the work, though 'none so often occur as the arms of Sir Thomas Erpingham and his two wives and Sir William Boleyn and his wife'.

A fire destroyed much of the city of Norwich in *c*.1414, including the convent of the Friars Preachers (where, it has been suggested, Erpingham's putative brother, Robert, may have been a friar). Erpingham rebuilt the Blackfriars church, now called St Andrew's Hall (site G). Outside on the south there is a row of Erpingham's arms in stone between every

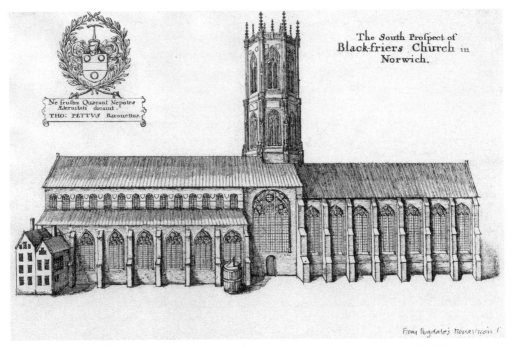

*28. Blackfriars Church, now St Andrew's Hall, from Dugdale's Monasticon (1718-23).*

window of the clerestory of the nave. The chancel is now called Blackfriars' Hall. There was a hexagonal tower between the two, but that fell in 1712. St. Andrew's Hall was acquired by the city corporation and has been used for many purposes before becoming the present concert hall; the chancel became for some years the 'Dutch Church' for the use of Dutch people who settled in the city and developed the cloth trade.

In 1419, the great East chancel window of the church of the Austin Friary in St Michael Conisford parish (site H, demolished in the sixteenth century), was glazed by Sir Thomas Erpingham, with eight panes containing eighty-two coats-of-arms, with an inscription in Latin, translated:

> Sir Thomas Erpingham, Knt., made this window in honour of God and all
> the saints, in remembrance of all the lords, barons, bannerets, and knights,
> that have died without male issue in the counties of Norfolk and Suffolk,
> since the coronation of the noble King Edward the III, which window was
> made in the year of our Lord 1419.

A note in Blomefield's *History* says that after this time, twenty-five more knights and esquires with more than £100 per annum, dying without male heirs, had their arms put up in the church. Perhaps Sir Thomas's own lack of children prompted this sad remembrance of mortality without continuance, or perhaps he was keen to remember dead companions in arms and in royal service. One fragment of this building survives: an arch built into a brick wall in King Street.

Along with other members of the Norfolk gentry, Erpingham was a member of the gild or confraternity of St George in Norwich, which had been founded around 1385. In 1420-21, the city of Norwich gave Erpingham a pipe of 'white wine of Gascoigne for his good counsel against the king's coming', though it seems the king never came to the city during his progress round England in the spring of 1421. Prior to his death, Sir Thomas Erpingham gave 300 marks to the prior and convent of Norwich to found a chantry for a monk to sing daily mass for him and his family for ever, at the altar of the Holy Cross in the cathedral, and to keep his anniversary before the whole chapter. This chantry was later combined with that of Bishop John Wakering. Erpingham also left ten marks to St. Paul's Hospital, known as 'Norman's Spital' after the first warden (site I), which cared for poor and sick people; this was located just over the river to the north-west of Erpingham's house, though nothing remains. A further 10 marks was left to the Great Hospital (site J), which had been founded in 1248 by Bishop Walter Suffield for the sick poor, especially the poor chaplains of Norwich; seven poor scholars of the Cathedral School were fed there daily. Its church of St. Helen, with a late fourteenth-century roof decorated with 252 painted eagles, still stands, to the south of the site of Erpingham's house.

Rye says that Erpingham, together with his heir, William Phelip, and Bartholomew Appleyard were benefactors of Carrow Abbey, a Benedictine nunnery lying to south of the city walls; and their arms were to be found there. He left money in his will to the recluses of Norwich, the nuns at 'Carhowe' (Carrow), Bungay, Thetford and Crabhouse (?), and the canonesses of Flixton and the minoresses of Bruisyard, both in Suffolk. From the Patent rolls we know that the 'king's knight Thomas Erpingham' was given in 1421 a licence 'to build a bridge across the water between the counties of Norfolk and Suffolk where the king has a passage, a ferry called 'Saint Tholaves ferry alias Seynt Olcoff ferry' (St Olaves) or elsewhere'. Erpingham had the manor and advowson of Haddiscoe, the adjacent parish to the west in Norfolk, but he had no manors or possessions in Suffolk near the crossing. Even Framlingham Castle had been relinquished long before, and it was hardly the most direct route thence from Norwich. There is no evidence that this bridge was ever built; the first at that site appears to have been the bridge constructed at the sole expense of Dame Margaret Hobart during Henry VII's reign (1485-1509). But what is significant is that Erpingham proposed to build the bridge for the relief of the area, and for the good of his soul, that of his wife and of their ancestors, as well as of the souls of his Lancastrian masters, Henry IV and John of Gaunt – an interesting reflection of Erpingham's concern for both local and national contexts.

## Erpingham's Manors and Possessions

John of Gaunt, duke of Lancaster, had granted Sir Thomas the hundred of South Erpingham in 1386, confirming this for life in 1396. Sir Thomas already held the manor in Erpingham (1) from his father. (The numbers in brackets identify the locations in Norfolk on the map opposite.) Gaunt had acquired the manor of Aylsham (2) from the king in 1372, when it became the principal town of the duchy of Lancaster in Norfolk.

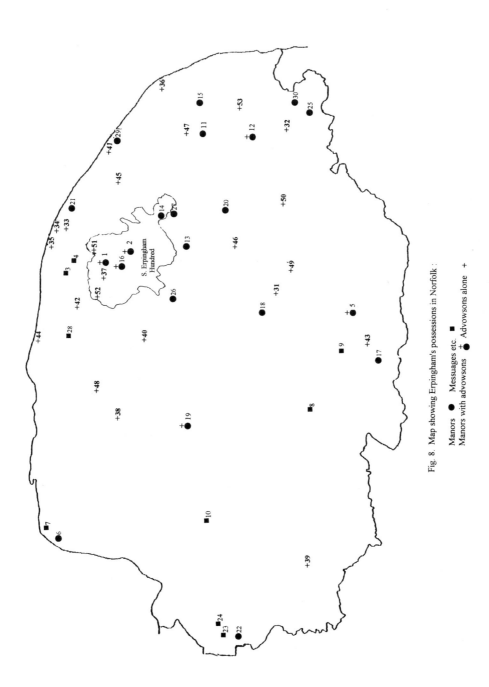

Fig. 8. Map showing Erpingham's possessions in Norfolk :

Manors ●   Messuages etc. ■
Manors with advowsons ●   Advowsons alone +

*29. Map of Sir Thomas Erpingham's possessions in Norfolk.*

Gaunt helped to build the church there; his arms are in the porch and on the east side of the font pedestal. After reverting to the crown on the death of Gaunt's widow, Aylsham was granted to Sir Thomas Erpingham until 1414.

Sir Thomas acquired 'a messuage in Gresham (3) called Manclerks, and two inclosures in Susted' (4), with others, from one John Leverich of Susted in *c*.1383. In 1384 he granted the manors at Banham (5) to the widow of Sir Thomas de Felton. Earlier that year he had, with thirteen others, agreed by charter to hold the lady's manor of Fordham, Cambridgeshire, during the lives of herself and her daughter, a minoress of the Abbey of St Clare without Aldgate. In 1391, with others, Sir Thomas received a charter of the manor of Hunstanton (6) and all its lands in Holm (7), Tottington (8), Snetterton (9), and East Winch (10), all rents, marshes etc, from Sir John le Straunge (Lestrange) of Hunstanton.

Not all his lands remained his. The tenure of manors seems frequently to have been given 'for life', and as frequently removed and given to others well within that lifetime. In 1398, the king ordered 'the escheator in Sussex… to give Katherine wife of John lately duke of Aquitaine [John of Gaunt] livery of the castle and lowry of Pevensey, the manors of… the hundreds of North Erpingham, South Erpingham granted to John and his wife and his heirs… and of the said hundred of South Erpingham which was held for life by Thomas de Erpingham knight and his heirs'.

In passing, South Erpingham was given to the archbishop of Canterbury, the bishops of Norwich, Winchester and Durham, the duke of York, and a number of other peers and knights, in July 1415, as part of a massive grant from the king. Included were seven castles and the associated manors and lands, ninety-five other manors, twenty-seven towns or hamlets, six hundreds (including South Erpingham), five wapentakes, ten other areas of land, with mills, marshes, parks, chases, feefarms and bailliwicks, *plus* all the castles, manors, etc. of the king's late grandfather, the earl of Hereford. As all the bishops and peers were at the war council held at Westminster on 16 April it might be that the land was given as a reward for their support or offers of financial or military help, or even as a mortgage. Bishop Courtenay died in France of dysentery. The duke of York led the right wing, and died at Agincourt. Thomas, Lord Camoys, had had a small grant of manors in April, possibly to induce his support; no such information can be found about Sir John Cornwall, who commanded the vanguard, or Erpingham, commanding the archers. Nor were any of them rewarded by the king after the battle, though of course they may have had their share of the spoils and ransoms.

Lands, rents and services in Little Glenham came to Erpingham, Simon Felbrigg, knights, William Phelip and Julian his wife (Erpingham's sister), and to their heirs and assigns from John Glenham in 1399. Thomas Erpingham, Edmund Oldhalle, Nicholas de Wychyngham, Ralph Bateman and Stephen Bastwyke jointly possessed the manors of Upton (11) and Cantley (12) with wards, marriages, escheats, etc, purchased from Hugh, Lord Burnell. Similarly, Erpingham – jointly with William Phelip the younger, John Wynter and Nicholas Wychyngham, and others – had part of the manors of Horsford (13), Great Hautbois (14), and Burgh (15) in Flegg (and parts of others in Suffolk) from Hamon Lestraunge, with the associated advowsons. Thomas Erpingham and Robert Berney bought Blickling (16) manor from Eleanor, widow of Sir Nicholas Dagworth, for a rent of 25 marks to her for life. This was, of course, long before the present magnificent Blickling Hall was built, in the care of the National Trust. Dagworth's brass remains in Blickling church; he too had been in King Richard's party, and was imprisoned in 1388. Erpingham had £100 for life from the estates.

Elizabeth Furneaux settled Middle Harling (17) manor and advowson, with the reversion of Kimberley (18) manor, on Sir Thomas and others in 1401. In 1408, Sir Thomas Erpingham bought from Sir Hamo de Felton's granddaughter the manor of Netherhall in Litcham (19) together with the advowson of the church, and six years later disputed with Thomas, earl of Arundel, the ownership of two crosses found on Litcham common. He purchased a manor in Norwich with Simon Felbrigg and Robert Berney, called 'Tolthorphalle' (apparently at Thorpe) (20), in 1410.

There can be no doubt that Erpingham's closeness to the Lancastrian dynasty led to many gains. He convinced the king that he had held Weybread manor in Suffolk all his life, though there is no evidence as to how he came by it. He had 100 marks annually from the manor of Saham, Cambridgeshire, another 100 marks from Cambridge for life from the death of Sir Nicholas Dagworth who had previously had that fee, £80 a year from Norfolk and Suffolk, and £40 from the fee-farm of Norwich, all given by the king. Another £20 came from the manor of Gimingham (21) in about 1422. The king gave him 50 marks from the manor of Newton Longville in 1400.

Soon after returning to England in 1399, Henry Bolingbroke (Henry IV) gave Erpingham the position of constable of Framlingham castle, with the manors of Framlingham, Earl Soham and Kelsale in Suffolk, and Southfield, Framingham and Hanworth in Norfolk. These were part of the Mowbray estates which had reverted to the king during the minority of the heir of Thomas Mowbray, the first duke of Norfolk, who died in exile in 1400. The king received £321 8s 10d a year from Little Framlingham manor, and £350 from Southfield; Erpingham probably received twice that amount. Three more manors were given him next year, with £40 to cover the costs of the constableship. Norfolk's son, Thomas, objected to losing the title – which was withheld on the grounds that Richard's parliament had no right to confer it – and he joined the rebellion of Scrope, archbishop of York, but was arrested and beheaded without trial at York in 1405. His brother John succeeded on his majority, and obtained livery of the estates, which Erpingham surrendered in 1406, except the manors of Little Framingham and Southfield, which he held till 1410. The constable of Cardigan Castle was ordered in 1403 to deliver to Sir Thomas Erpingham the king's gift of a barge which had belonged to Thomas Percy, earl of Worcester, who had been killed at the battle of Shrewsbury after rebelling with his kinsmen. There is no evidence of his having used it, but this appears to have been another significant mark of esteem. With five others, Erpingham held most of the estates in Norfolk, Suffolk and Essex of Roger Mortimer, the late earl of March, from 1399 until 1401. The king received £200 from the estates, which was probably about one third of their value. Two years later, Erpingham was appointed keeper of some parks on the Mortimer estates in Suffolk, together with the castle, manor and town of Clare and almost all of the remaining estates in Norfolk, Suffolk and Essex, until 1409, when he gave them up. He held the estates of Alexander, the bishop of Norwich, on his death in 1413, paying rents of 200 marks to the Exchequer, and, in 1417, all lands late of Thomas Bardolf, until his son and heir came of age, and the estates of Michael de la Pole, earl of Suffolk, who had died at Harfleur, on behalf of his wife and son.

Erpingham also benefited from the royal policy to prevent alien (i.e. French) abbeys enjoying their possessions in England. Erpingham was given the king's permission in 1421 to purchase 'the priories of Toftes and the manors of Tofts (Toft Monks) (25), Norfolk, Wermyngton, co. Warwick, Spectebury, Dorset, and Aston, Berks, the manor of Wychyngham [26] called "Longevyles", part of the possessions of the priory of St Faith de Longueville [Normandy], and the manor of Horstede [27], Norfolk', which had belonged to the priory of Caen. The manor of Walsoken (22) with appurtenances in Walsoken, Walton (23) and Wallope (probably Walpole) (24), came to him in 1420. He had to pay to Henry, archbishop of Canterbury, and other feoffees £100 a year from the manor and soke of Kirton in Lyndesey. He held lands and tenements in Saxlingham (28) from the prior of Walsingham. He had the farm of Lessingham Manor (29) from the duke of Bedford, and farmed the manor of Haddiscoe (30), in 1402 when he presented to the living there.

Thus he held at least forty-three manors, thirty in Norfolk during his life, though not all permanently. He had inherited three manors or properties from his father, and during the next twenty years acquired another seven. The biggest group of thirteen manors came to him in 1399 – eight of them being given by the king, Henry IV. He acquired another seven in the next ten years (five in 1401), but the giving of individual manors had stopped, though he had the Clare manors in his charge from 1403. Interestingly, it seems as though he bought every one of the twelve manors that he acquired between 1410 and 1421, the date of his last acquisition. It might have been expected that his leadership at Harfleur and Agincourt would have been rewarded by Henry V; but as has been said, this does not appear to have been so. The Garter had been given by Henry IV in 1401 – a reward for his support in seizing the throne. Henry V ascended to the throne in 1413, but even the care of the bishop's and the de la Pole estates predate Sir Thomas's military service at Agincourt.

## Churches

Erpingham's influence in the county and patronage of the church is also revealed. The base of the tower of St Mary's Church, Erpingham (1), has the arms of Sir Thomas Erpingham on one face as patron, plus a number of other arms. The tower and south aisle were begun in his time and at his expense, and were roofed by his heir, Sir William Phelip, Lord Bardolph and his lady, who have their arms on the roof. (Phelip's arms are also found above the doorway at Cantley (12), quartering Erpingham and Bardolf). Another church that appears to have been given his patronage is Wymondham Abbey (31), where his arms are still to be found in the roof of the nave. The sheriff of Norfolk and six others including Erpingham were appointed in 1410 to hear the grievances of the prior of Wymondham against 'evildoers', and he may have been persuaded then to help the church financially. Erpingham's arms are also to be found in Heckingham (32) church in glorious coloured glass, with another shield of Wilton impaling Erpingham.

At Banham (5), Erpingham's arms are in a window of the chapel; he held the manor there in 1384. Rye records that there were further traces at Gunton (33), which came to Sir

*30 and 31. Cley Church (Norfolk) (above and detailed below), one of many in the county bearing Erpingham's arms, on this occasion on the porch.*

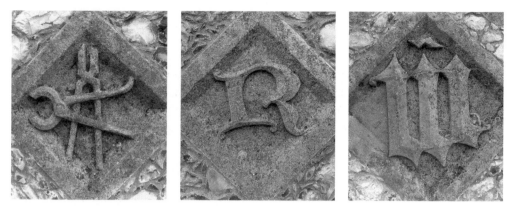

*32, 33, 34. Decoration from the tower of Erpingham church, believed to be work commissioned by Sir Thomas. In addition to the instruments of the passion (left), there are individual letters which together spell out 'Erpingham' ('r' and 'm' shown).*

Robert Berney in 1398, in the chancel window (Erpingham also presented to the living in 1396): '*Vert a scochion and an vrle of m'les argent*'; and at Overstrand (34): Erpingham impaling Clopton: '*Arpingham in his coate armore on the southe syde of the churche his timber and creste a plume of fethers argent oute of a crowne goulis*'. His arms were also in the window of Cromer (35) church, and in the chapter house at Canterbury, presumably in further gratitude for donations. Blomefield also records that his arms were in Blickling church (16), Somerton (36), Calthorpe (37) (*Erpingham* impaling *Calthorp,* and *Erpingham* impaled by *Felbrigg,* which may indicate other branches of the family), Sculthorpe (38) (with Gaunt), Hilgay (39), Foulsham (40), Happisburgh (41), Hempstead (42), East Harling (43), Cley (44), Honing (45) and St. Gregory's, Norwich, (quartering Boleyn) (46) churches, and his arms were on the gateway of St. Benet's Abbey, Horning (47), along with other benefactors such as Arundel, Hastings, de la Pole, Beauchamp, Clare, and Valence, earl of Pembroke. At Great Snoring (48) Sir Thomas's effigy, arms and crest were in the window, with a motto 'Pinche' or 'Pinke'. This word, possibly 'Yenk' but misread, was also said to be recorded at Great Snoring, on the tomb of Thomas Antingham who was Sir Robert and Beatrix Erpingham's trustee and on whom they settled lands in 1312. Erpingham presented to the livings of Wreningham Parva (49), Little Poringland (50), Aldby (51), Haddiscoe (30), Toft (25), Berningham Winter (52), Gunton (33), Oxstrand (this appears to be the old church of Overstrand, now ruinous) (34), Lessingham (29) and Wickhampton (53), among others.

In later years, he was fair, just, and trustworthy, a good counsellor, a reliable and honest feoffee and trustee, dealing fairly with the lands and wards in his care, and in his work for the city of Norwich. He was pious and a great benefactor of churches, friaries, and hospitals, and did not forget the imprisoned, nor the care of his own soul after death. Perhaps because he was himself childless, he commemorated those knights dying without sons, over nearly a hundred years. For himself and his wives, he left a magnificent memorial in the gate, and he supported the artistic renewal and decoration of the Cathedral church to the glory of God. All around Norfolk, if only we look, there are memories of one of our most worthy Norfolk knights.

# The Erpingham Gate
Tony Sims

What is now known as the Erpingham Gate provides an entrance into the close of Norwich cathedral from the area of the city known as Tombland. Before the eighteenth century, as the sacristy rolls of the Dean and Chapter now in the Norfolk Record Office reveal, it was known as the Church or Lower Gate, being located almost directly opposite the west front of the cathedral. Pevsner describes it as 'one of the proudest of cathedral gateways'. Although no documentary evidence of its construction has so far come to light, its connection with Sir Thomas is confirmed by heraldic evidence, as we shall see in due course. More obvious to the casual observer, it houses in a niche on its west side a kneeling effigy of the knight. This was not the case in 1712, however, according to an engraving in Sir Thomas Browne's *Repertorium*. It is suggested, therefore, that the kneeling figure was originally made not for the gateway but for Sir Thomas's tomb in the cathedral. A depiction of the Trinity, now lost, may once have filled the niche. As we shall see, that would certainly make sense iconographically. Other changes have also occurred over the years. A comparison of the gate today with the etching of 1712 and a watercolour of 1786 suggests that a cross once found at its apex has been lost. But there remains much of interest in this splendid example of fifteenth-century architecture. Much of the sculpture reminds us of Sir Thomas's devotion to the church. The remainder, being largely heraldic, reminds us of his pride in family and service.

First let us describe the gate as it survives today. To the gable apex the building is 14m, the equivalent of five perches in medieval measurements. The height of the arch is 8.5m, the figures atop the turrets are 1.5m. The building width is 7.54m and the depth from the eastern to western arches 7.75m. It is hardly a large structure, but it possesses a sense of loftiness generated by the upward thrust of its pillars from a deep plinth at the base and the tallness of its arch. Above the arch is a horizontal string course which also serves to integrate the two semi-hexagonal turrets on either side of the arch. Above the string course, the gable is built of faced flints and in the centre is a tabernacle with a rich canopy reaching almost to the gable apex. It is in this tabernacle, or niche, that we now find the figure of Sir Thomas. There are two square panels of stone either side of the tabernacle containing shields within the cusped edging, that on the north bearing the arms of the bishop of Norwich (azure three mitres or), and on the south, the arms of the Norwich Cathedral Priory (argent a cross sable). The turrets are topped by figures: on the north side a secular priest with a book apparently instructing a boy standing next to him, and on the south side a monk also with a book in his hand. The faces of the two turrets are in four tiers, separated by string courses. The top two tiers of both turrets are tabernacles enclosed by arches of two-centred heads, the bottom two tiers contain Erpingham devices, surrounded by chain at the third tier and by oak foliage on the bottom tier.

The gable is built of faced flints, which are found also in the passage of the gateway itself, but the stone which forms the pillars, vault and other decorative features is probably Ancaster stone, an oolite limestone from mid-Lincolnshire. The effigy is likely to be of the same stone. The gate had a proper usable upper chamber reached by a vice which can be seen outside the north west corner, and this can be seen as an integral part of the north side wall as was the rest of the porter's tenement . From 1539 onwards in the Dean and Chapter lease books there are

records of the upper room lettings which were, apparently, the porter's perks. It is not clear whether the upper rooms referred to include the gate room as well as the tenement upper room. The side of the gate facing the cathedral was meant to be of stone, but plainer and less decorated than the west face. Either this was never finished or it may have collapsed. There is reference to one of the cathedral gates being mined during Gladman's Riding in 1443. It was finished or rebuilt with rubble side walls and a substantial timber-framed west end wall, arch and capitals in wood, with a roof of the type with side purlins and wind braces. The roof would be typical of the sixteenth century but could be as early as 1470. Some trouble was obviously taken over this phase to make it a worthy completion of the original design.

The two angle buttresses that support the east end are of flush tracery filled with squared flint and do not appear to be adequate for the height of the building. The vault between the arches is now of plaster, but was once of groined stone, one of the springers at the south-west angle is still visible with what looks like the broken off boss head at the inner arch apex. The building has over the years been seriously altered, the stone vaulting has been removed or it has collapsed. There is a definite dislocation in the great arch and a wooden room was removed sometime in the eighteenth or early nineteenth century. Another, perhaps relevant, event is the city fire of 1508. Cathedral records show that the *Trasour* near the inside of the gate, was burnt down. On close inspection of some of the lower stonework on the western side, fire damage can be seen. Perhaps the great wooden gates burnt, causing considerable heat and affecting of the remainder of the structure.

## The decoration scheme

Within the two principal orders of concave moulding on the great, or western, arch are two programmes of twelve sculptured figures. The inner is of female figures with, at the arch head, a shield of the Five Wounds of Christ, supported by an angel at each side. The angel on the north side has a shield hanging from the neck bearing a cross. Judging by the black traces on the cross edges this would seem to be the arms of the priory. In all probability the whole scheme was originally painted. All figures stand on pedestals with carved foliate vaulted canopies above them. Those of the female programme have what seems to be mulberry foliage with the fruit in abundance and the male canopies are of hawthorn with its pendant berries or haws. Mulberry was a symbol of virginity in the fifteenth century and perhaps the thorn is symbolic of the male. All identifications have been taken from photographic surveys and close inspection of the arch itself when scaffolded, and also from reference to older works. All the male figures have long hair and all except two have beards. Unfortunately only a few of the male figures can be identified.

North five, with a scimitar, is probably St Matthias. North two wears a mitre of low design. This may be St Theobald of Provins or Theobald, Archbishop of Canterbury. A panel at Hempstead (Norfolk) depicts a St Theobald presented as a bishop. South two is probably St John, as the image is clean-shaven and bears a traditional resemblance to the saint. However, it must not be forgotten that originally on the gable were the four Evangelist symbols amongst whom would be John. South four, bearing in his right hand a broken rod or staff, is St James. South five, with a boat in the left hand, is St Jude. The rest of the male

35. *The Erpingham gate as portrayed in Thomas Browne's* Repertorium *of 1712, when the effigy does not appear to have been housed in the niche.*

36. *The north side of the gate. The outer carvings are likely to be of, in ascending order, St Mary Magdalene, St Agnes, St Petronilla or St Sitha, St Margaret, a shield bearing the five wounds of Christ. Only the third male saint from the bottom has been definitely identified, as St Matthias.*

figures have either lost hands and emblems, and some have scrolls which are now plain and some are broken. There are seven which are unidentified at present.

In describing the female figures there is more extant detail and there are Tristram's photographs of the 1930s which show detail now eroded away. Of great interest are the five crowned queens. North one is cautiously attributed to St Catherine; to the left side of the garment below the waist are remains of a wheel rim. North two is the sainted Abbess Queen Etheldreda with long loose garment and very wide sleeves, a wimple and crown, and a gorget which covers throat and shoulders. The right hand is gone but there are indications on the body of its having held a long staff or crozier. The left hand holds a hillock on which stands a church or monastery. In north three, the right hand appears to be holding a pot with a tall spire-like cover, which held the aromatic ointment spikenard; the emblem of St Mary Magdalene. North four, a circlet of flowers around the head and a lamb in her right hand, is the emblem of St Agnes. North five, a circlet of flowers around the head and a book with clasps in the left hand, could be St Sitha or St Petronilla. North six stands on a very strange animal which most authorities have as a dragon with, on the garment's left side, attachments for the spear which was thrust into its head by St Margaret.

The south order again commences with two queens. South one wears a long loose flowing garment and over it a mantle, a wimple and crown on her head; there is no emblem for identification. South two, similarly dressed to north two, is perhaps Etheldreda's sister, Withburga. South three, hair bound with a circlet of flowers, holding in her right hand a

*37. The south side of the gate. The outer carvings are likely to be of, in ascending order, Queen Withburga, St Barbara, St Helen, unknown, St Mary of Egypt. The male saints, from the bottom, are probably St John, unknown, St James, St Jude, unknown.*

building with four circular towers at the corners, battlemented, and a tower rising from the centre, represents St. Barbara. South four holds what could be the upright of a cross shaft in the right hand and a partly open book, leaves to the front, in the left hand. This may be St Helen, the mother of Constantine, who was the discoverer of the True Cross. South five cannot be identified, but south six, who wears a jewelled diadem on her head, an undergarment of skin with tails as the skirt hem, and has long flowing hair and bare feet, is probably St Margaret of Egypt.

At the base of each order of figures on both north and south there is a horizontal scroll with a single vertical oak branch (or trunk) and foliage reaching to the first pedestal. The scroll contains the Erpingham motto, 'yenk' ('think' or 'remember'). Each side of the trunk is a crowned falcon, rising. This is an Erpingham device used on contemporary seals, one of which was used as a pattern for the design of the wooden achievement of arms on the eastern gable of the gate. The motto and falcons also appear on the Erpingham chasuble. A very small quarry of glass in what is now known as the 'Erpingham window' in the north ambulatory aisle of the Cathedral, which contains the falcon rising with a rose thereupon which bears the letters of the motto on each petal. This last device is also present on the Erpingham chasuble and on the gate.

The spandrels of the great arch are filled with three cusped circles of tracery containing shields. Small daggers of tracery fill up the remaining space of the acute angles. The north side contains ecclesiastical heraldry with the large central shield being emblemmatical of the Trinity, the Shield of Faith. In 1246 Pope Innocent IV instigated, as part of the devotion of the Passion of the cult of *Arma Christi*, the Instruments of the Passion on heraldic devices, which were seen as Christ's mystical weapons against Satan. The smaller upper shield is of the three chalices with wafers above and the lower shield of a particularly youthful crucifixion. The south side is personal heraldry with Erpingham in the large central shield, (vert, an inescutcheon within an orle of eight martlets, argent.) The smaller upper shield is Walton for Sir Thomas's second wife (argent, on a chief indented sable, three bezants). The lower shield is Clopton for his first wife (sable, a bend argent, between two cotises dancettee, or).

The semi-hexagonal turrets also bear carvings. The faces are in four tiers separated by string courses. The top two tiers of both turrets are tabernacles enclosed by arches of two-centred heads, beneath which is similar foliate decoration to the arch figures, but in this case oak, which spreads to fill the space between the arch heads. The top series of tabernacles contain figures bearing shields of the instruments of the Passion, but some of these, due to weathering, are not now identifiable. The only shield on the north side, on the north face, was identified as a cross. A present day photograph shows a cross on the south face also. The second series of tabernacles contains figures with shields of Erpingham and his wives. The south turret has on the north face the suggestion only of the indented chief of Walton and then following round, Erpingham and Erpingham impaling Clopton. The third tier is especially interesting in that the faces are recessed and arched panels, with Erpingham devices all surrounded by an endless chain. This is also used to subdivide it into six panels, within which are these devices and upon which the shields are hung by straps. The use of chains demands the question, why? There is reference to being 'bound by one's sins' during the feast of St. Peter ad Vincula (1 August), which is interestingly the date on which Henry V began his conquest of Normandy in 1417. The device of a prisoner's chain, borne as the outward and visible sign of a binding vow, is one that is encountered often. Was it perhaps a symbol of loyalty to the house of Lancaster? The Le Gros tomb at Sloley, Norfolk also bears a chain surrounding the shield; he was also a Lancastrian supporter.

The subdivision of the six panels is uniform across both turrets, as can be seen from the plan, with matching devices: forget-me-not, shield, crowned falcon rising, rose, falcon and shield. The top shield in each panel on both turrets are single family shields reading Walton, Erpingham, Clopton, on each turret. The lower shields are, in the majority, impalements. The bottom tier has panels of the same shape with a vertical oak branch or trunk with the crowned falcon rising, at either side. Hung at the top of the foliage, an Erpingham shield faces west on both turrets. The other shields across this level are impalements of his two wives in the same pattern as above. The overall scheme becomes clear on studying the plan: the north faces are all Walton; the west faces, Erpingham (except one); and the south faces, Clopton.

## The effigy of Sir Thomas Erpingham

The overall height of the kneeling effigy is 1.2m. Much detail of the armour and jupon, or surcoat, is now lost. What can be seen is that the arms and legs are fully encased in armour. A short sleeveless coat reaches to mid thigh, opening at the front below the waist. On the chest are the Erpingham arms, an inescutcheon within an orle of eight martlets. The

*1. Henry V at the battle of Agincourt, armoured and with his coronet displaying the supposed damage from his fight with the duke of Alençon.*

*2. Sir Thomas Erpingham.*

*3. Mounted archer, in marching order on the march from Harfleur, horse with baggage and cased bow slung across the bowman's back.*

*4. Bowman preparing the defensive stakes planted before the battle. Bow slung, but equipped for battle with bascinet helmet and padded jack below English livery.*

*5. Well-equipped bowman, dismounted archer, but wearing riding boots, drawing back his bow with a bodkin headed arrow. He is rather well-to-do, with mail shirt beneath jack, bascinet and long misericorde dagger, sword and buckler.*

6. *Two archers at full draw, protected by their stakes, showing different features of dress and equipment. The figure on the left wears a kettle hat and padded jack, and is armed with falchion and buckler. His hose are rolled down for the possible easement of troubled bowels. The figure on the right wears a bascinet with a hood worn beneath for extra padding, a jack featuring riveted plates, and riding boots, and is armed with a normal cut and thrust sword.*

*7. Jean, sire d'Aumont, nicknamed 'the brawler', a French knight, who was killed in the first cavalry charge of the battle. This picture gives some impression of the volume of arrows.*

*8. Guillaume Martel, sire de Bacqueville, bearer of the oriflamme at Agincourt. He was also killed on the field and the standard lost.*

9. Paul Hitchin prepares to draw.

10. A close up of a modern reproduction of a bascinet.

11. Modern reproductions of the equipment of the medieval archer.

*12. Erpingham Church.*

*13. The Erpingham gate.*

*14. Fragment of glass bearing the arms of Sir Thomas Erpingham (Burrell Collection, Glasgow).*

*15. The Erpingham Chasuble (back) (Victoria and Albert Museum).*

*16. William Bruges, first Garter king of arms, kneeling before St George, patron of the order of the Garter, c.1430. (British Library, Stowe MS 594 folio 5b).*

*17. The Garter stall plate of Sir Thomas Erpingham.*

*18. French battle banners. Left to right: St Denis; St Martin; Brittany; the Constable of France (x2).*

*19. English battle banners. Left: St George; right: the Trinity.*

20. *French royal banners. Left to right, top row: Charles VI; John, Duke of Alençon; John, Duke of Bourbon; Anthony, Duke of Brabant; John, Duke of Burgundy. Bottom row: Louis the Dauphin; Charles of Artois, Count of Eu; Philip of Burgundy, Count of Nevers; Charles, Duke of Orléans.*

21. *English knights. Left to right: Sir Thomas Erpingham; Sir John Fastolf; Henry Lord Scrope.*

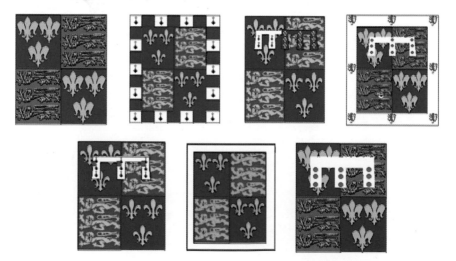

22. *English royal banners. Left to right, top row: Henry V; Thomas Beaufort, Earl of Dorset; John, Duke of Bedford; Richard, Earl of Cambridge. Bottom row: Thomas, Duke of Clarence; Humphrey, Duke of Gloucester; Edward, Duke of York.*

23. *Henry Paston-Bedingfeld,*
*York Herald of Arms.*

24. 'Lend me thy cloak, Sir Thomas': portrait of Robert Hardy as Sir Thomas Erpingham, by Howard Morgan.

25. The Erpingham banner embroidered by Penelope Knee, presented to the Cathedral by the Norfolk Heraldry Society on the occasion of the Erpingham symposium, October 1996, and placed above the supposed location of his tomb.

*38 and 39. The effigy of Sir Thomas as it is in the niche on the gate today.*

martlets are original but the shield or inescutcheon and the praying hands have been incorrectly replaced as can be seen when compared with a photograph taken in 1879 when the effigy was on the ground. What is seen now, therefore, is a larger shield with, for some reason, a saltire thereon, for which there is no precedent. Above the surcoat is worn a gorget and around the neck is a collar or strap with the buckle easily recognizable, the whole seemingly holding a shield against the chest, which is an incorrect interpretation as this should be the inescutcheon and not a separate shield. An 'S' is still discernible just above the buckle and is in an unusually vertical position, which suggests this is an early representation of a Lancastrian collar of SS. The face is bearded, the hair shoulder length and shown in such a way as to have the appearance of wearing an arming cap, i.e. to support a heavy helmet. However, on close inspection there is a peculiar curling of the hair around the crown of the head, leaving the latter with a distinctly bald appearance and absolutely smooth.

The visible side of the base shows well-worn carved drapery and at the very rear there are traces of red paint. A lead plug in front of the knees was perhaps where a helmet rested. A small cushion the same width as the base sits to the front, on which the knight kneels with the left foot encased in a sabaton resting over the rear edge of the base. A rusted iron stirrup still remains but the rowel attachment is missing. Just below the knee the strap of the order of the Garter is clearly visible. The right leg was never modelled below the ankle; in fact the stonework is cut at a right angle towards the left foot, and there is no material detail below the knee. A modern scabbard in copper rests against the left hip but the original, rather narrow, carrying straps are still clearly visible right around the waist. These do not look strong enough for the purpose of carrying a sword, but perhaps carried a small dagger. The right base up to the shoulder is uncarved and appears as a flat slab which could suggest the effigy was originally positioned elsewhere. Unfortunately, even on close inspection from scaffolding, the effigy is now so closely fitted against the niche on that particular side that it is impossible to ascertain whether there are old fixing points from a different structure. The existence of the spur stirrup and the carving of the Garter were surely meant to be seen at close quarters and not to be invisible in the present position.

Looking at the rear of the niche from within the upper room of the gate, it can be seen that the niche has been broken away to take the rear base section of the effigy enabling it to fit wholly on the ledge. A probable solution is that the effigy stood atop Erpingham's tomb on the north side of the cathedral presbytery, or perhaps against the western Norman pier of his tomb praying towards the high altar.

Sir Thomas's testament expressed his wish for 'my body for to be beried withynne the cathedrall chirche of the Holy Trinity in the cite of Norwich beforn the croos cleped the browne rode wher as my sepulture ys made and ordeyned'. Sir Thomas's tomb was at least in part made before his death. But what of its location? A cross or rood was renewed in Norwich in 1297 and 'according to Beeching, probably occupied much the same position as the cross at Westminster Abbey, figured in the Islip roll', i.e. over and above the high altar. There are references at Norwich in 1304 to 'the old cross in the presbytery'. This seems to have generally been called the 'black cross' after 1400, but is likely that it was named by Sir Thomas as the brown rood. We thus can suggest the site of the tomb as lying immediately to the west of the reliquary chapel. Sir Thomas Browne noted in his *Repertorium* that 'on the north side of the choir, between two arches, next to Queen Elizabeth's seat, were buried Sir Thomas Erpingham and his wives, the Lady Joan etc, whose picture were in the painted glass window next to this place with the arms of the Erpinghams'. Queen Elizabeth's seat was so named because that was where the Queen sat when she attended services at Norwich; it was, according to Harrod, in a quatrefoil opening between the pillars below the reliquary chapel. Browne thus provides us with the earliest definite fixing of the site, written in the 1680s, although there is a reference in John Weever's *Funeral Monuments* (1631) to an inscription (now lost): 'here lieth the body of Jone the wife of Sir Thomas Erpingham K.g. as appeareth by her will made by licence of her husband the last of May 1410 and proved 14 of July next following'. There certainly was a chantry associated with his tomb which by at least 1457 had been combined with that of Bishop John Wakeryng (d.1425), a man whom Erpingham would have known well.

Erpingham's tomb may have been altered when the presbytery piers were encased in 1472 by Bishop Goldwell or, alternatively, destroyed at the Reformation or a century later in the Civil War. It is not clear today whether anything of its fabric survives. It is a great pity that no documentary material has emerged to shed further light on this issue. We can be sure, however, that there are other examples of this type of kneeling tomb effigy which can reinforce the idea already stated. There is, for instance, the figure of Edward, 5th Lord Despenser in Tewkesbury Abbey, kneeling on a cushion with hands upraised in prayer. He died in 1375. His widow, Elizabeth, daughter of Sir Bartholomew Burghersh, put up the effigy before her own death in 1409. As Erpingham knew the Despenser family it is interesting to wonder whether he saw the effigy at any time and thought he would do something similar. There are continental examples too of the late fourteenth and early fifteenth centuries: Marshall Huglin von Schonek, leader of the papal knights and builder of the chapel to St. Theobald 1362-69, in

*40. A detail of St Petronilla or St Sitha.*

*41. Erpingham's motto 'yenk' as carved on the gateway.*

*42 and 43. The Erpingham window, once in the north choir isle of Norwich Cathedral, now lost.*

the church of St. Leonard at Basle; Antoine des Essarts in Notre Dame in Paris; Duke Philip of Burgundy at Dijon; the duke and duchess of Bourbon at Bourges.

## Dating of the gate

On the heraldic evidence of the Walton shield on the south spandrel, the gate was not built until after 1409-10 when Joan Walton's first husband, Sir John Howard, died. However it had been built by 1470 when the Sacrist rolls mention that the Chaplain refectory hall had been 'turned round' because the gate was taking the light. John Harvey claims that James Woderofe (fl. 1415-1451) was almost certainly the designer of the Erpingham gate, and suggests that it was constructed between 1416 and 1425. Woderofe was also the architect of the remodelled west front of the cathedral, constructed between 1426 and 1450. Woodman has suggested the existence of a Mancroft workshop in early fifteenth-century Norwich as probably responsible in its early days for the Erpingham gate. He cites the similarities of the moulding profiles between the west and north door of St. Peter Mancroft in the city with those of the gate, dating it to around 1430. Both the west door of St. Peters and the Erpingham gate display a total disregard for the niceties of providing shafts with capitals and bases. The theme, then, of a Norwich workshop emerges with co-operation perhaps between different groups, including the Woderofe brothers and Reginald Ely among others, as leaders of their craft.

When looking at the structure's style, the important factor is not necessarily to search for the building date, but when the patron – whoever he was – commissioned a designer at the outset and when the finished plans were completed. Any number of factors may delay building commencement and indeed the duration of the building programme – lack of money, death of patron and designers and failure of the structure in building being not the least among these – but the early plan, in most cases, still remains. The same design from the same pattern book or templates could be ordered by different patrons at the same time, but some of the above factors coming into play could mean a gap of many years in the construction and completion of the respective structures. Attempts have been made by Fawcett to give a later date for the gate, citing for comparison the similarity in style of the Morley tomb at Hingham, Norfolk. However one has also to consider the Bovile and Wingfield tombs at Letheringham, Suffolk which also seem to be of a remarkably similar construction. The Morley similarity is not denied but its date of building must have been sometime after 1442 when Morley's son Robert married, as their arms are displayed there.

The 1420s marked a period when Erpingham was particularly active with other building projects in Norwich, and more important still is the obvious link between the cathedral west porch and the Erpingham gate. Erpingham and Bishop Alnwyk (who paid for the porch ) were known to be associates, and it would seem natural to have been in consultation on design matters in this instance. There is no doubt that one structure complements the other; in fact the gate provides the picture frame for the west end of the cathedral in general and the Alnwyk porch in particular, thus completing the whole picture. Hence the huge size of the great arch of the Erpingham gate in comparison with the much smaller arch of the Ethelbert gate which forms the south western extremity of the cathedral precinct and which was built by the citizens of Norwich in 1316.

Erpingham may have helped to fund the choir stalls of early 1420s type. On other stalls of the same group are found the arms and devices of his warrior society and colleagues, Morley, Woodhouse, Wingfield and de la Pole, and Bishop Courtney, who died at the siege of Harfleur. All these projects should perhaps be taken together with the granting to John Woodhouse of his chantry in the chapel crypt just inside the gate, traditionally known as the Agincourt chantry. In the crypt of the chapel of St. John the Evangelist, Sir John Woodhouse was granted a charter on 8 June 1421 to found a chantry dedicated to the Five Wounds of Christ and the Holy and Undivided Trinity, for the good estate of the king, Henry V, of his consort, Katherine, and of himself. On each Friday, five poor people were to receive a dole of one penny each in commemoration of the Five Wounds of Christ, and every other day three poor people were to receive a similar sum in honour of the Holy and Undivided Trinity; all of these persons were to attend the said masses with the chaplains. On the feast of St. Blaise after Vespers and Compline, the priest was to celebrate Placebo and Dirige (i.e. service for the dead) with nine lessons and Lauds, calling in the principal of the upper chantry with his five fellows for the soul of the king's grandfather John (of Gaunt), duke of Lancaster and, on the morrow, for the soul of Henry IV. (The crypt is underneath the chapel of St. John the Evangelist built in 1316 by Bishop Salmon as a charity for his soul and his parents, as well as for those of his predecessors and successors as bishops of Norwich.) The original purpose of the vault or crypt is clearly defined as a repository for human bones buried in the city of Norwich and clean of flesh, to await the general resurrection. School house, to the west of the chapel was formerly the college where the chantry priests lived. The west end of this building and the porter's tenement of the Erpingham gate form the north west corner of the upper cathedral close. In the Sacrist rolls of the Norwich Dean and

*44. A carving of Sir Thomas's arms on the choir stalls of Norwich Cathedral.*

Chapter records for the years 1439-40, payment is noted for a new door and gates in the wall of the preaching yard reaching from the chapel to the north western corner of the cathedral. This formed the rest of the north side of the upper cathedral close.

It is thus suggested that Erpingham commissioned the gate in the early 1420s as a conscious personal monument to himself, Agincourt and the Lancastrian house to which he had devoted his life. This is borne out in the conception and design of the gate incorporating the shield of the Five Wounds of Christ at the apex of the arch, the Trinity shield on the north spandrel and together with the crowned figure of St. Catherine who commences the scheme of female saints on the north side. All tie in with the extant 'Agincourt' chantry foundation charter dedication. In 1440 James Woderofe was paid for building a wall and gates from the main chapel of St. John to the cathedral west end, which suggests the Lower (or Erpingham) gate was open by now, and that the area of the precinct was a lot busier than it had been previously. It would make sense if there was a Trinity group in the niche, similar perhaps to that seen on the Cathedral cloister boss of Robert Knollys and his wife Constance Beverley, dated about 1421. There were the four Evangelist symbols above on the gable as the spreaders of the Word, so that therefore, the Word Himself might have been expected below in the centre. The now broken pendant drop-head canopy would have meant a smaller sculpture and, if complete now, would certainly serve to emphasize the incompatibility of Sir Thomas's position there; his head would be completely obscured and heavily shaded, even from below. The Trinity is also depicted on the cross orphrey of the Erpingham chasuble, and was a popular image of the late fourteenth and fifteenth centuries. The Black Prince was known to have been a keen devotee of the cult of the Trinity (he was born on Trinity Sunday). He lies on his tomb in Canterbury cathedral looking up at an illustration of the Trinity on the underside of the tester above. Edward, Lord Despenser – who was also a knight of the Garter and known to Erpingham – likewise had a Trinity in his chantry chapel below his kneeling effigy in Tewkesbury Abbey. Erpingham may also have

*45. The boss of Robert Knollys and his wife Constance Beverley from the cloisters of Norwich Cathedral. It is suggested that the niche on the Erpingham gate may once have held a portrayal of the Trinity similar to that in the centre of the boss.*

followed such examples on his gate before the cathedral dedicated to Christ's church and the Holy and Undivided Trinity.

As noted earlier, the engraving of the Erpingham gate in 1712 shows no effigy in the niche. Blomefield comments thus in the 1740s: 'but the effigy of Sir Thomas on his knees which is now in the niche, was not then found and placed there, as it hath been since, so that it doth not appear in the plate'. So far there is no answer as to where it was found and when it was placed in the niche. Bishop Goldwell encased the presbytery piers in 1472; during this operation he may have had to dismantle Erpingham's tomb. The effigy could then have been moved to, for instance, the 'Agincourt' chantry under the chapel of St. John the Evangelist commissioned by Woodhouse. The chapel was suppressed very early in 1476 and possibly fell into disrepair. The great city fire of 1508 might have caused the dislocation or partial collapse of the great arch of the gate; any such movement could have dislodged the proposed 'Trinity' sculpture in the niche causing it to fall, never to be replaced. In 1724 much debris was removed from underneath the Woodhouse chantry, at that date known as the Free School. Was Sir Thomas then uncovered and hauled aloft to his present position? When writing about the effigy Blomefield says it had recently been found, but unfortunately he does not say where, and only from that time did the gate become known as the Erpingham gate.

With the existence of a European fashion for kneeling, praying tomb figures as discussed earlier, it prompts the reiteration that this figure was probably situated on, or in the vicinity of, the tomb of himself and his two wives. Thus it may be that, as Sir Thomas Erpingham had fully intended, crowds would have witnessed his funeral cortege in 1429 moving through the great arch of which he was patron, past the chantry of his friend and companion in arms, and on into the cathedral, with his military accoutrements being hung over his armoured, spurred and gartered effigy kneeling in prayer over his tomb.

# The Erpingham Chasuble
Gilly Wraight

Trapped in a glass display cabinet in the medieval treasury hall of the Victoria and Albert Museum, South Kensington, London, is an embroidery silk vestment, a chasuble that deserves more than a fleeting glance. Despite its age, it has a strength of colour and of design that is arresting to the eye. The embroidery is thought to have been worked in England between 1380 and 1400, and the silk fabric to have been woven in Tuscany or Northern Italy between 1400 and 1415. (This difference in dating may at first seem strange, but is explained by the fact that fine embroidery would be taken from older silk and reset on new.) The two heraldic shields stitched onto the back of the chasuble tell us that it was owned by Sir Thomas Erpingham and it would seem a reasonable supposition that he also commissioned the making of the chasuble.

This chasuble may have been part of the fabric of the church that Sir Thomas had partly rebuilt at Erpingham, although there is no firm evidence for this. Inventories of church goods for the archdeaconry of Norwich sadly do not give sufficient detail for it to be possible to match the chasuble in the Victoria and Albert Museum with their entries. However, inventories do list chasubles, of red and gold, to be of Erpingham's patronage. Furthermore, in different parts of England certain colours were favoured for ecclesiastical vestments, and inventories dated to 1368 indicate that the most commonly favoured colour in Norfolk was red. That the background of this chasuble is red may be coincidence and not of help in regional appropriation, but the colour does strengthen the association with Sir Thomas Erpingham himself. The falcon depicted on Sir Thomas's device bears a red rose on his chest, which is inscribed with his motto 'yenk' ('think', or 'remember'). Probably the most distinctive element of the whole piece is the repeated camel motif on the silk fabric. The design is bold and clear. Is the observer to bring to mind Matthew 19:24 , 'And again I say unto you, it is easier for a camel to go through the eye of a needle than it is for a rich man to enter the Kingdom of God'? Certainly Sir Thomas was a rich man, as illuminated in this chapter's study of his landed possessions.

Other animals and birds are depicted on expensive brocades of a similar date but this may be the only extant example of the depiction of camels. It may also reflect the choice of a man such as Sir Thomas, who had travelled widely and to whom camels would not necessarily be alien for he might have seen them on his journeys to Jerusalem, Cyprus and Rhodes. It might be speculated that he commissioned the weaving of the fabric by Venetian silk weavers. It is certainly of the finest quality possible. Therefore that the patron specified the design becomes quite plausible. The chasuble was acquired by the Museum in 1968 and it is believed to have been owned by a Catholic family in Monmouthshire. The chasuble was altered to the present shield shape, at an unknown date. It was reduced from its original size and the off-cuts were made into a stole (a narrow band worn round the neck) and maniple (worn over the forearm), which are also at the Victoria and Albert Museum.

It is remarkable that this chasuble has most clearly been carefully stitched throughout its history. First, the embroidered panels are very fine examples of the best of English work, and secondly, great care and consideration was taken when the embroidered panels were stitched

on to the new background silk. It is difficult to imagine that this was chance positioning. Whilst the later alterations that reduced the size of the garment have inevitably disfigured the camel motifs at the side seams, originally these motifs would have been clearly visible. The back of the chasuble carries the most significant embroidery in theological terms: the Crucifixion. There, the camel motifs are fully visible to the left and right of the embroidered panel. There is only one exception. This is around the panel depicting two female saints, which is immediately below that large panel that depicts the Crucifixion. Here the embroidered panel has been most carefully placed on the background fabric, such that there appears to be a rather long-bodied camel visible to either side, as if it were 'walking' behind the embroidery.

However on the front of the chasuble the arrangement is different. This perhaps demonstrates that this 'camel fabric' was of great value and that the original chasuble was thoughtfully cut from a rather small length of fabric. Again the embroidered panels have been carefully placed so as to respect the integrity of the camel design of the background silk, but on this aspect the camel design is placed vertically. The arrangement is such that it must be that the front of the garment has been formed by joining two pieces of fabric together. Once more, care has been taken when joining the fabric pieces so as to align the level of the camel designs, horizontally, across the garment. The flowers and leaves of the motif are covered, as the heads of the camels just touch the sides of the panels.

As mentioned earlier, there exist also a maniple and stole made of the same camel decorated silk fabric. However these are 'assemblages' perhaps best described as a laborious patchwork of the most tiny fragments of material. Triangles barely a quarter of an inch wide at their widest and perhaps an inch and a half long taper away to nothing. Certainly this was a labour of love and devotion to have assembled maniple and a stole some yard in length from so very many minute scraps of fabric. Both the maniple and stole are edged with the same braid as that which edges the orphrey on both front and back of the chasuble.

English embroidery, *Opus Anglicanum*, was characterized by a very high technical standard and an expressive artistic designs. This was achieved in a style of embroidery in which the entire surface of the fabric was covered with stitches. Such a density of stitches tended to make a vestment made from such embroidered fabric rather stiff, which tended to restricting the movements of the priest's arms. Therefore, it became the practice to apply just a wide band, an orphrey, of this *Opus Anglicanum* embroidery to a more flexible fabric rather than to have the entire vestment embroidered. The orphrey was made in the shape of the cross and was applied in place of the narrow bands of braid that had originally served to strengthen the seams at the front and back of the chasuble. The woollen or silk fabrics that were used allowed the priest to lift his arms easily, as the bulk of the chasuble fell back comfortably into folds about his arms. It would appear that the embroidered orphery of the Erpingham chasuble is made from individual panels rather than one long continuous piece of embroidery, because there is an uneven and inconsistent arrangement of the ground that the figures stand upon. The semicircular bands of colour, whether they are depicting tussocks of vegetation, rocks or a representation of hillocks, are not of the same proportion in each scene. This might suggest that they are irregular in shape along this edge because they have been cut from an older garment where the embroideries had become worn, or that the individual scenes might have been deliberately selected, again from another garment, because of the specific saints they portrayed. The outer edges of the panels are edged with a narrow braid that is carefully stitched in place.

Royalty and their retainers relied upon their own priests for their spiritual needs, particularly when travelling away from England or in exile. Several priests are known to have accompanied the expedition of 1415. A chasuble was always required, and was to be worn by the celebrant priest at Mass. Thus we may consider that this chasuble may have been

*47 and 48. The Erpingham chasuble, back, detail of the Erpingham emblem of a falcon rising and of Sir Thomas's coat of arms.*

commissioned to be worn by the priest who accompanied Sir Thomas on his travels or who served in one of the churches to which he had given his patronage. A chasuble was the principle vestment worn by the priest for the celebration of the Mass. The vestment developed originally from the practical, woollen travelling garment worn by both men and women in the Graeco-Roman world – the *paenula*. This garment was made from a semicircle or more of fabric, usually two quadrants, which were sewn together to form a conical cloak, with just a single opening for the head. This was worn with the seams to the front and back. Narrow bands of braid were stitched over the joins in the fabric; this strengthened the seams, and could also serve to decorate the garment. During the seventh century, the name chasuble became common parlance for this vestment, and in the eighth century the chasuble was designated as the distinctive outer garment to be worn by the presiding priest during the Mass. During subsequent years liturgical practice altered; namely, the practice of the elevation of the host was introduced. This required the priest to hold the bread and wine above his head so that the congregation might see the sacraments at the significant moment during the service, thus the priest needed to be able to lift his arms freely.

There can be no doubt of the high quality of the embroidery. For approximately one hundred years, English embroidery was considered the best that money could buy throughout all of Western Europe. It had come to the attention of Pope Innocent IV at the Council of Lyons in 1246, when he observed the embroidered vestments worn by English clerics. Matthew Paris, the chronicler monk of St Albans, records that they 'were embroidered after a most desirable fashion'. Pope Innocent IV had letters sent to the Cistercian abbots in England in which he requested that he be sent vestments of *Opus Anglicanum*. He noted: 'England is our garden of delight; truly it is a well inexhaustible, and from where much more may be extracted.' And the monk's report continues: 'This command of my lord pope did not displease the London merchants who sold them at their own price.' The effectiveness of the Pope's request must be measured by the fact that, in the Vatican inventory of 1295, *Opus Anglicanum* is mentioned 113 times, from which is deduced there were more vestments of *Opus Anglicanum* than of any other style of embroidery.

The embroidery on the orphrey of the Erpingham chasuble is of the first part iof the fifteenth century, which is after this 'great period' of English embroidery, but none the less it is still of a very fine quality. It is thought to have been made in London. Such was the value and respect for these English embroideries that they would be cut from worn vestments and reapplied to new fabric. In the case of Sir Thomas's chasuble, as we noted at the outset, the embroidery is of an earlier date than the style and technique of the silk would suggest. The embroidery is, as during the 'great period' of *Opus Anglicanum*, worked predominately in two types of stitches that completely cover the surface of the fabric: split stitch and underside couching. Split stitches are worked in lines. As the name suggests, this is a stitch in which the second and subsequent stitches are made to pierce, half way along the first stitch, so as to 'split' each stitch in turn. The result is a line that can be used, as if to draw on the surface of the fabric, or on top of other stitches. In this case the lines of split stitch have been used to describe the features of the faces. The quality of this English embroidery is demonstrated well in the working of the split stitch, for it can be seen that each angel has been given a different and very lively expression. Much of the rest of the embroidery is worked in underside couching, and a marked versatility and expressive quality – despite the limited repertoire of stitches that might have inhibited many a lesser workforce of embroiderers – in the production of a truly lavish embroidery.

Underside couching was the stitch through which the embroidery of English achieved such an international reputation. Whilst other centres on the Continent used the same stitch, none were able to match the fine quality of the English embroiderers' work. The underside couching stitch, when well worked, covers the entire surface of the fabric, as do many other forms of stitches, but what makes underside couching significant is that the finished couched work is so flexible. Standard couching entails securing one – usually thicker and perhaps metal – couched thread to the surface of the fabric by means of a second, securing thread. The couched thread remains on the surface. The securing thread may contribute to the decorative scheme of the embroidery through the patterns created by the spacing of the securing stitches and or, by their colour, whether through the selection of a contrasting or a toning colour. Underside couching differs from standard couching in that a small loop of the couched thread is pulled, by the securing thread, through to the back of the fabric. This acts like a hinge, creating a greater degree of flexibility for the finished work. The securing thread is not visible from the front of the work, yet the mark where the couched thread is pulled to the back can be organized so as to create a pattern, usually a chevron design. A thread couched by the standard couching method lies taut on the surface of the fabric, and when such embroidered fabric is folded, either during storage or in the wearing, the standard couched thread could soon snap or pull away from the securing threads.

The ending of this 'great period' of English embroidery is thought to have been brought about as much by changes in fashion as by the reduction in population caused by the Black

Death plagues, which must have affected the numbers of skilled embroiderers in London as much as any other section of society. The Italian weavers had implemented significant developments in their looms and weaving techniques. Complex weaves, such as that of the silk of Sir Thomas's chasuble, were the result. This silk is a lampas – a particularly sophisticated weaving technique – and woven with coloured silks and brocaded with silver-gilt thread. In the weaving technique, warp threads run the length of the fabric that is wound on the loom, whilst weft threads are woven over and under the long warp threads, across the width of the fabric. As the warp threads are adjusted to receive the interweaving weft so the pattern of the finished fabric can be formed. On Sir Thomas's chasuble the warp thread is red and this is the predominant colour of the fabric. The repeated patterns are formed on the surface of the red of the fabric as the weft threads are allowed to surface at key points of the design. White, cream, blue and green silk weft threads are interwoven with the red warp threads across the width of the fabric, so as to depict the baskets of flowers and leaves of the garden that surround the camels. The camels are 'brocaded', which means that the silver gilt thread is brought to the surface and, although it is laid across a considerable number of the red warp, the fabric remains structurally strong. A positive identification of the origin of this woven silk fabric is unlikely to be possible; Italian silks were abundantly traded across all of Western Europe, but it may be significant that Sir Thomas had travelled through Venice.

Metal weaving and embroidery threads were imported to Europe, predominately through Venice, from Cyprus, the Middle East and Asia. By pulling narrow strips of silver gilt through drawing mills, a very thin metal thread was produced. This was wound around a core of silk thread known as the 'soul' of the thread. The fabric of the Sir Thomas's chasuble has silk cores of either red or yellow. These different coloured silks give a slightly different hue to the finished thread. This type of gold thread was more expensive than that commonly used, in which a thin layer of gold or silver gilt was applied to the surface of a membrane usually made of prepared animal skin or intestine. This too was cut into narrow strips, but was not twisted onto a silk core but laid flat in the weaving process and thus bound into the fabric. The effect was a little more garish as relatively more light was reflected by this type of metal thread. It was however a cheaper thread as it was simpler to produce and contained relatively less precious metal. However, so much deterioration due to tarnish and build-up of dirt renders such comparison difficult. That this fabric is woven with the most expensive silver-gilt thread suggests that it was very valuable and such pieces are rare. There are two other chasubles in the Victoria and Albert collection which are brocaded with similar silver-gilt thread (items 935-1901 and T26-1922).

Only the back of Sir Thomas's chasuble is visible in the display cabinet today. God the Father is seated above the inscription 'INRI', whilst Mary stoops at the foot of the Cross. Five angels hold chalices to catch Christ's blood as it falls from his wounds; a sixth angel is at Mary's side. Each angel's expression and stance is different; the intense facial expression and arms crossed over the heart of the seventh angel lead us to believe this angel to be deep in prayer. In the two lower scenes, and those on the front of the chasuble, pairs of apostles and female saints stand on banded mounds that are framed by a design of an ogee arch that is supported on twisted columns, and above are leafy fronds. The colours are altered as this framed design is repeated in each scene. The saints and apostles have not been identified but the figure on the left of the lower back scene is crowned and, as she holds a spray of lilies in her hand, would no doubt represent the Virgin Mary. Perhaps it is significant that outsized lilies are the flowers that surround the silver gilt camels as they stand in their fanciful settings on the red silk fabric.

The two heraldic shields are worked in a very different simple style of embroidery and it would seem a reasonable supposition that they are domestic rather than professional embroiderer's work. Perhaps they were embroidered by some of Sir Thomas's household or family members. There are signs that repairs have been undertaken – for example the falcon's feet are of rather bright cream silk and the gold of his claws is considerably brighter than gold thread in other areas of the chasuble – but there is no documentary evidence of the date or circumstance of any repairs. Thus there is much to consider about this crimson red silk vestment. It speaks of a wealthy patron of the church: Sir Thomas Erpingham. A warrior who travelled far with his motto 'yenk', he might have knelt before a priest wearing this chasuble. As candle or sunlight was reflected from the silver gilt camels that are emblazoned across the crimson silk, he had much to look at, to consider and, as we may also, to 'think' about and 'remember'.

# 5 Chivalry at Agincourt

## Matthew Strickland

> A Knyght ther was, and that a worthy man,
> That fro the tyme that he first bigan
> To riden out, he loved chivalrie,
> Trouthe and honour, fredom and curteisie.
> Ful worthy was he in his lordes werre,
> And therto had he ridden, no man ferre,
> As wel in christendom as in hethernesse,
> And ever honoured for his worthynesse.

So begins the description of the Knight from the famous Prologue to Chaucer's *Canterbury Tales*, begun *c*.1386, the year Sir Thomas Erpingham left for Spain in the retinue of John of Gaunt, himself a patron of Chaucer. Chaucer's Knight, like his fellow pilgrims en route to the shrine of St Thomas Becket at Canterbury, is a composite figure and a social archetype, though the poet was almost certainly drawing on the crusading experiences of contemporary English nobles such as the Scrope family and possibly – since the *Tales* were still unfinished by Chaucer's death in 1400 – the knight errantry of Henry of Bolingbroke in 1390 and 1392. But his words could apply fittingly to Sir Thomas, who, as we have seen, before crowning a long and distinguished military career at Agincourt, had seen service in Spain, possibly in Ireland and earlier in Prussia, where in Henry of Bolingbroke's retinue, he may well, like Chaucer's Knight, have 'the bord bigonne above all nacions in Pruce' ('taken the head of the table before all nations, in Prussia') at the Table of Honour of the Teutonic knights.

Contradicting the traditional understanding of Chaucer's representation of the Knight as an epitome of chivalric virtues, Terry Jones argues in his challenging book, *Chaucer's Knight: Portrait of A Medieval Mercenary*, that those contemporary knights, under the guise of Holy War, were little more than unprincipled swords for hire, fighting for both Christian and Muslim paymasters alike and taking part in horrendous acts of brutality such as the sack of Alexandria in 1365. It may be easy to accept Jones' stark reminder of what expeditions such as those in Prussia really entailed; the raids or *Reysen* of the Teutonic knights involved ravaging, burning, even enslaving, and often enough the massacre of men, women and children. During the sack of Vilna in 1390, for example, in which Bolingbroke and Erpingham took part, a contemporary chronicler, John of Posilge, noted (doubtless with some exaggeration) that 'over two thousand persons were captured and slain, and the fire was so great that they perished there all together … and piteous it was how they all burned'.

Yet conversely, we should heed the warning of Maurice Keen, the doyen of the study of late medieval chivalry, that it would be a mistake to see crusading expeditions as driven primarily by profit. Whether in the Mediterranean, the Levant or the Baltic, crusading was an enormously expensive and dangerous business, and – unlike the wars in France – few came back with anything save heavy debts. This was particularly true for operations in the 'Wilderness' of Lithuania, a poor land where plunder and booty were scarce, and it was for this very reason that the Teutonic knights tried to attract knights from the west by the allure of elaborate chivalric ceremonial such as the Table of Honour or *Ehrentisch*, with its strong Arthurian overtones, by feasting and by the hunting of exotic animals such as bear and elk in the great forests of the eastern marches. Bolingbroke was fortunate indeed that his father, John of Gaunt, had both the willingness and the financial resources of the Lancastrian duchy to foot the enormous bill of his son's two Prussian expeditions. (The accounts for these expeditions of Bolingbroke show the conspicuous consumption of a great aristocrat and his retinue, with costly raiment, jewels, and luxury foodstuffs, while even the earl's hawks – an essential noble prerequisite at home and abroad – were fed on chicken during the campaign. During the privations endured by Henry V's army on the march to Calais in 1415, Erpingham may have fondly remembered these days of feeding on delicacies spiced with ginger, garlic, rice, almonds, cherries even in the depths of the Wilderness, and whiling away hours in dicing, minstrelsy, and dalliance with women.)

Nor was the crusading ideal an anachronism by the later fourteenth century. Indeed, it was not only very much alive among the English aristocracy, with families such as Lovell, Hastings, Morley, Scrope of Masham, Montague, Percy, Neville and others all boasting members who had taken the cross, but the defence of Christendom was seen by contemporaries as the ultimate duty and source of honour. In his *Livre de Chevalerie*, written *c*.1350, the distinguished French knight, Geoffroi de Charny, – who was killed at Poitiers in 1356 bearing the hallowed Oriflamme banner – provided a sliding scale of feats of arms and their relative kudos. Skill in individual jousting in the lists deserved praise, but not as much as participation in the dangerous mock-battle of the mêlée. More honourable still was service in real war within Christendom, either in siege or pitched battle, but the ultimate accolade went to those knights who had fought in distant lands (as he had) against the enemies of Christ.

Chaucer's skill and ambiguity ensures that the debate over his portrait of the Knight will not be quickly resolved. But for our purposes, the controversy helps to contextualize Sir Thomas Erpingham. He was not a *condottieri* – a professional mercenary – unlike his celebrated contemporary, Sir John Hawkwood, who fought for Milan then Florence, where his magnificent memorial by Uccello lies alongside that of Dante, and whose bones were repatriated at the request of Richard II, as a national hero, to be buried in the church at Sible Hedingham, Essex. This is a warning against the anachronistic assumption that mercenary service was dishonourable, or that it attracted only the odium of contemporaries. Nor was Erpingham a captain like Sir Hugh Calverley and Robert Knolles who fought in English armies against the French, but during peace with France led the notorious Free Companies of roving mercenaries who devastated large areas of the Midi and southern France. Rather, Erpingham was an indentured retainer, pledged to serve the greatest aristocratic family in the land both in peace as a courtier and administrator, and in war as a soldier.

And whereas Jones can point to the telling absence from the list of the Knight's campaigns of the great English victories of the first part of the Hundred Years War – Sluys, 1340, Crécy, 1346, Poitiers, 1356, and Najera, 1367, suggesting that the Knight was neglecting the war effort on the home front for gold, glory and girls (and possibly God) in more distant lands –

*49. Monument to Sir John Hawkwood, Florence Cathedral.*

such a charge could hardly be levelled at the commander of the archers at Agincourt. In this capacity, we can safely say 'ful worthy was he in his lordes werre' ('worthy' here meaning primarily 'pre-eminent for one's military skill') and, as his distinguished career shows, he clearly was 'ever honoured for his worthyness'.

Chivalry, Maurice Keen has written, is 'a word elusive of definition, tonal rather than precise in its implications', whose meaning could range from simply a body of knights ('the king with all his chivalry') to a complex set of social and ethical values. It was primarily an aristocratic code, at once both military and courtly, but essentially timeless in many of its core values. As Malcolm Vale, another leading historian of late medieval chivalric culture, has written:

> There can be no doubt that the ideal qualities of chivalry – honour, loyalty, courage, generosity – have fulfilled a fundamental human need, felt especially among warrior elites whose social function has been to fight. Chivalry was often no more, and no less, than the sentiment of honour in its medieval guise. That sentiment has been confined neither to the Middle Ages, nor to Western

Europe, and is found in Ancient, Asiatic, African and Oriental civilizations. Among warrior classes, it possesses a universal and perhaps, an eternal validity.

The chivalry of Western Europe in the Middle Ages was, of course, more culturally specific. It had, as we shall see, a powerful Christian dimension, and was essentially Franco-centric if not Francophile; despite the political tensions of the Hundred Years War, men still looked to the courts of France, and by the early fifteenth century above all to the courts of Burgundy, as the mainsprings in the development of the cult of chivalry.

Yet if we ask what Erpingham and his fellows understood by chivalry and the essence of knighthood, we can scarcely do better than turn to the Norfolk village of Elsing, and to the brass of Sir Hugh Hastings, one of the finest of its period in the country, and which Erpingham himself very probably saw and admired. Sir Hugh had been one of Edward III's captains who had fought in the great naval battle of Sluys in 1340, had taken part in the Crécy campaign (though not in the battle), and had died at the siege of Calais in 1346, probably of disease, as so many were to do before the walls of Harfleur in 1415. Of gentle but obscure birth, Hastings had risen to prominence through feats of arms as had his fellow Norfolk men, Sir Oliver Ingham and Sir Thomas Dagworth, forcefully reminding us that war was a key means of social advancement. As a young man, Erpingham would have grown up hearing stories of the exploits of these men, warriors of the first generation of the Hundred Years War, and seen the building or beautification of churches throughout the county raised as thank-offerings with new found wealth from the spoils of war, such as the fine church at Elsing itself built in the Decorated style with its great aisleless nave boasting a great single-span roof over 40ft.

Hastings' brass is an unabashed proclamation of his affluence, status and martial pride. He is portrayed in full armour of the very latest fashion for the 1340s, which, though outmoded by the time of Agincourt, symbolized both his rank and the essential raison d'être of a warrior aristocracy. The aristocracy was itself stratified from the greatest lords to the lesser gentry, but in time of war all these men are described in contemporary texts as 'homines ad arma' – men-at-arms – whose ability to afford the full suit of armour or 'white harness' as it came to be called, marked them out from the other ranks. Much has been made of the yeoman status of the archers at Agincourt, and certainly there was vital distinction between the manner in which the French and English nobility viewed their infantry. The proportions of archers to men-at-arms in English armies of the Hundred Years War is in itself eloquent testimony to the value commanders placed on their bowmen, while the system of indentured retinues ensured smaller numbers but the pick of well-trained men with strong esprit de corps. By contrast, the French knights at Crécy had not scrupled to ride down their own Genoese crossbowmen, and when, before Agincourt, the citizens of Paris offered the service of 6,000 well-armed militia, one of the duke of Berry's retinue supposedly exclaimed, 'What do we want of the assistance of these shopkeepers, for we are three times as many as the English?'. Whether or not this tale is apocryphal, the French were to pay a terrible price for pushing their numerous infantry to the rear where they were useless, thereby ignoring Marshal Boucicaut's original plan to provide effective supporting fire by positioning units of archers in the French front rank.

Yet it would be naive to deny that there was still a wide social gulf fixed between English lords such as Erpingham and the majority of their archers, many of whom, noted the

*50. Brass of Sir Hugh Hastings, Elsing church (Norfolk).*

chronicler, Jean Le Fèvre, sire de St Rémy, 'were without armour in their doublets, their hosen loosened, having hatchets and axes or long swords hanging from their girdles, and some with their feet naked'. Erpingham was a man of his age, and had aided the suppression of the Peasants Revolt in Norfolk in 1381. At that time, he may well have been mindful of the excesses committed during the French peasant uprising of 1358 known as the Jacquerie, when, according to Froissart, French and English nobles buried their differences and attacked the villains 'small and dark' who had dared to challenge the social order.

Hastings' nobility of birth is proclaimed not only by his martial attire, but by his arms or a *manche gules*. There can be no better indication of the importance of such displays of lineage than the fact that this very tomb was used in the case of Grey vs. Hastings brought before the Court of Chivalry over right to bear these arms. Erpingham himself gave evidence to the

*51. Elsing Church (Norfolk).*

court, telling how, when he was in Prussia, he had seen Hastings' arms in the Marienkirche of the Teutonic Knights at Königsberg – for it was the custom of knights to leave a depiction of their arms in painting, carving or in stained glass as a permanent reminder of their visit and feats of arms. Arms on their surcoats and shields, originally of enamel or painted glass, identify the 'weepers' who surround Hastings on his brass, and a very distinguished group they are: Edward III; the earls of Lancaster, Warwick, and Pembroke; Ralph, lord of Stafford and Amaury, lord of St Amand. There could be no more striking expression of the concept of a brotherhood-in-arms. Though Sir Hugh was only a minor noble, he here claims comradeship with the greatest in the land through their shared service in the French wars.

Erpingham doubtless felt a similar sense of comradeship-in-arms with those who had served on the Agincourt campaign. Equally, shared experiences on the expeditions to Prussia may well have played an important part in developing ties of mutual loyalty between Bolingbroke and those knights such as Erpingham, Staveley, Swinburne, Norbury, Waterton, Bucton and others who were to support the future Henry IV in his coup of 1399 and to serve him thereafter. But such expeditions also had an international dimension. Froissart tells of how, during the sack of Caen by Edward III in 1346, a group of French nobles sheltering in a tower and in fear of their lives at the hands of the English archers were relieved to see the English knight, Sir Thomas Holland, 'whom they recognized because they had campaigned together in Granada and Prussia, and on other expeditions, in the way in which knights do meet each other'. He willingly accepted their surrender, and, adds Froissart, 'was delighted, not only because he could save their lives, but also because their capture meant an excellent day's work and a fine haul of valuable prisoners, enough to bring in a hundred thousand gold moutons'. Such a remark by the self-proclaimed chronicler of chivalry remind us that war was a business, and that contemporaries saw nothing incongruous in the often inseparable fusion of honour, chivalry and profit. The incident also heightens the tragedy of the great

*52 and 53. Tomb of Sir Oliver de Ingham, d.1344, Ingham Church (Norfolk).*

battles of the Hundred Years War, in which many of the opponents were well known to each other as erstwhile brothers in arms and members of common chivalric community. Many of the knights who had fought with Marshal Boucicault in an international Christian force against the Turks at the disastrous battle of Nicopolis, in 1396, were to die on the field of Agincourt.

As a younger man, Erpingham would have known the comradeship, fostered through military training and the tournament, of John of Gaunt's household and affinity, and basked in the 'associative honour' of serving so great a lord and his royal heirs. Had we an extant brass or funerary effigy of Sir Thomas, it may well have displayed the famous Lancastrian collar of linked SS, as does that of another of Henry V's commanders, Sir Edmund de Thorpe at Ashwellthorpe, Norfolk, who was killed in 1418. As an additional badge of livery, Sir Edmund bears a white swan, strongly reminiscent both of the superb Dunstable swan of white enamel and gold of *c*.1400, which has Lancastrian associations, and of the famous Wilton diptych, in which the court of heaven – all save the Virgin herself – bear the white hart livery badge of Richard II.

Erpingham was further honoured in 1400 by admission to that most striking of all expressions of a brotherhood-in-arms, the Order of the Garter; an elite association of knights conceived by Edward III in 1344 as 'The Order of the Round Table' but refounded in 1348. With their base at Windsor Castle, the Garter knights wore elaborate ceremonial costume at their annual gatherings, and at all times bore the blue and gold garter insignia, as seen for example on the fine brass of Sir Simon Felbrigg, made the year after Agincourt (although Sir Simon himself did not die until 1442). The functions of the Order of the Garter fused pragmatism, idealism and romance. As a political institution, it served to foster vital bonds of loyalty between the aristocracy and the royal family, but in so doing consciously drew on

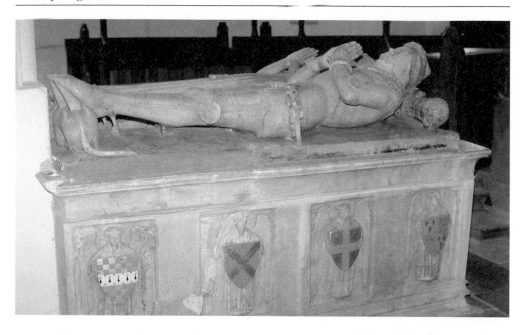

*54 and 55. Tomb chest and effigy of Sir Edmund de Thorpe, d.1418, Ashwellthorpe (Norfolk) .*

Arthurian models to reinforce the prestige of king and nobles alike. Erpingham's associations with the Order remind us of the extent to which Arthurian legend pervaded chivalric consciousness not merely in literature and art, but in political life. Arthur was perceived as a historical figure; the chronicler Jean Froissart, for example, believed that Windsor Castle was on the site of Camelot itself, while tournaments, such as the great jousts at St Ingelvert held near Calais in 1390 (which Erpingham may well have witnessed), were suffused with Arthurian imagery. It is a mistake to dismiss the Arthurian role play so central to the cult of late medieval chivalry as merely fantasy make-believe or hollow escapism. For not only was the imperial symbolism of Arthur ruthlessly exploited by English kings, but knights of all countries strove both to emulate the deeds of Arthur and his paladins and to be compared to these epitomes of chivalry.

Mention of the Garter and its patron, St George, brings us back to a central feature of the Hastings brass. Above the earthly canopy containing Sir Hugh, his hands in the gesture of prayer and feudal supplication, sit Christ and the crowned Virgin, whilst below angels hold the knight's pillow and carry his naked soul heavenwards with St George, fittingly armed and mounted as a knight, standing guard. Long gone is the view of earlier churchmen that by his very profession the knight endangered his soul, and that the only sure way to gain salvation was to lay aside arms and assume the habit; here is a confident assertion of the validity of knighthood as a Christian vocation. The statement is re-enforced by the figure of St George, centrally placed between the earthly and the divine, one of the military wing of heaven, interceding for and guarding the knight who has fought under his banner.

A saint of eastern origin, St George enjoyed widespread veneration throughout Western Europe from the later eleventh century, but in England his cult reached its apogee in the fourteenth and fifteenth centuries. Embodying the ideal virtues of Christian chivalry, he became patron of the Order of the Garter, with the chapel of St George at Windsor housing the stalls of the Garter knights. His name was the war-cry of English kings – 'Cry God for Harry, England and Saint George' – and at Agincourt, his banner was born by an esquire, one Thomas Strickland, who years later petitioned Henry VI to be rewarded for his services in that battle. The victory at Agincourt further enhanced the saint's prestige, for at Henry V's personal request, the archbishop of Canterbury, Henry Chichele, ordered on the 23 April the feast of St George, 'the special patron and protector of the English nation', to be kept as 'a greater double' – a special feast day, celebrated with elaborate liturgy and choral antiphons, upon which all servile work was banned and attendance at church required as if Christmas day.

In Norwich Cathedral, with its regimental chapel and colours hanging as silent witness to past struggles, fusing invocation, remembrance and thanksgiving, we perhaps get closer than is possible elsewhere to the spirit of Erpingham's age, in which the military and the divine fused so inextricably. Men believed in the physical intervention of God and the saints in battle. The French war-cry, 'Montjoie! St Denis!', called upon the patron saint of France, whose deep-red Oriflamme banner, symbolizing mortal war against the enemy, was ritually taken from the altar of the royal abbey of St Denis, infused with divine power. At Agincourt, on the English side, the banner of St George was joined by those of two other great patrons of England, St Edmund and St Edward the Confessor, together with the banner of the Trinity, while at the time of the battle, holy oil was seen to have oozed from the tomb of St John of

Beverley, signifying his aid for Henry's army. And throughout the battle, the priests, who were stationed at the rear with the baggage train, including a relic of the True Cross, offered up prayers and intercessions.

It has been said that there is no atheist on a battlefield, and in an age of faith, spiritual preparations for battle were often intense. Armies might undergo ritual fasting to obtain spiritual purity and God's favour, though in 1415 the march from Harfleur had already left the English half-starved. For men facing the prospect of imminent death, it was vital to confess and be absolved so as to die shriven, and if possible to be fortified by taking mass. The chronicler of the *Gesta Henrici Quinti*, known as 'the Chaplain', notes that on the eve of the battle in the English camp 'there was no shortage then save only one of priests'. And on the morrow, at the command 'Banners advance', the English knelt and beseeched the protection of God, kissing the ground three times and each putting a small piece of earth in his mouth signifying humility, mortality, and man's creation from and return to dust. Knights' armour often bore talismans invoking protection; besagews, guarding the vulnerable arm joints, might be painted with the cross of St George, while bascinets might carry the sacred monogram *IHS* or 'Jesus of Nazareth' on the brow. A famous Italian armour from a slightly later period (*c.*1455), and now in the Kelvingrove Museum, Glasgow, bears a series of invocations such as 'Ave Maria' at the most vulnerable parts of the armour. Even swords, which like banners might well be blessed, likewise carried mottoes such as 'In Nomine Domini' – 'in the name of the Lord'.

Battle itself was regarded as a judicial trial by combat on a grand scale, in which God would judge and award victory to the side whose cause was most just. Henry V's triumph at Agincourt against seemingly impossible odds served to reinforce his deeply held belief in the justice of his war against France to win back what he regarded as his rightful inheritance. The view was widely shared by his subjects. As a contemporary English chronicler wrote, 'Thus Almyghty God and Seynt George brought oure enymies to grounde and yaf us that day the victorie…God that day faught for us'.

What then did chivalry mean in battle itself? It is common for modern commentators to juxtapose chivalric ideals with the brutality of medieval warfare, in which the great harrying raids or *chevauchées* deliberately targeted the peasantry and most vulnerable sectors of society, and to suppose thereby that chivalry was at best ineffectual and at worst a tinsel gloss deliberately masking the cruelty and profiteering of the nobility in war. But such a view is anachronistic. To be sure, much of medieval warfare involved burning and laying waste the enemy's countryside, which brought misery and suffering to many non-combatants, but such tactics were a commonplace in almost all wars. 'War without fire', Henry V is supposed to have remarked according to the French chronicler, Jean Juvenal des Ursins, 'is like sausages without mustard'. Chivalry sought to mitigate the worst horrors of war by establishing a code of honourable conduct between the knights – the men whose social raison d'être was to fight – and to foster concepts of ransom and the honourable treatment of prisoners.

Few if any questioned the assumption that it was a code which applied only to members of the nobility: the one major charge that we might choose to bring against the chivalric ethos. Indeed, it was partly this very recognition that led to such appallingly high casualties among the French at Agincourt. For the English archers had neither opportunity nor inclination to spare French nobles. In his address before the battle, the king had reminded them of the

*56. William Wilcotes (d.1411). Detail of monument in North Leigh Church (Oxon.), showing the name 'Jesus of Nazareth' above the forehead.*

French boast to cut three fingers from the right hand of every English archer caught, and they were well aware that if the tide or battle turned, they would cut down without mercy. Once they had poured volleys of arrows into the flanks of the French ranks, they downed their bows and worked terrible execution upon the encumbered French with swords, daggers, axes and leaden mauls.

But if Agincourt shows us the combat between archer and aristocrat, it also reminds us that in the thick of battle – as contemporaries were all too well aware – a code of honour had practical limitations. In theory, a knight could surrender – if at all possible to a man of equal or higher rank – by presenting his captor with his right gauntlet, thereby initiating what was in effect a personal contract for the payment of ransom in return for safety. He was then put on parole, escorted to the rear, and if wounded, his captor might even have him attended to; not only was he a fellow knight, but was now a very valuable financial asset. But at Agincourt, being so heavily outnumbered, the English were preoccupied with the grim business of bitter hand to hand fighting with lances, poleaxes and swords, in which knights perforce delivered deadly blows, fatally wounding or killing opponents outright. In such circumstances, accepting parole was often a practical impossibility. The duke of Alençon, for example, who had wounded Humphrey, duke of Gloucester, and had struck off part of the crown from King Henry's bascinet, attempted to surrender to the king's bodyguard who had surrounded him, crying, 'I am the duke of Alençon, and I yield myself to you'. But even as the King reached out to accept his gage, Alençon was slain. Some French nobles, noted the *Gesta Henrici Quinti* doubtless with some hyperbole, 'surrendered themselves more than ten times. No one, however', he continues, 'had time to take them prisoner, but almost all, without distinction of person, were, as soon as they were struck down, put to death without respite, either by those who had laid them low, or by others following after'. Many French knights, moreover, fell and were either suffocated or crushed in the press, as the French line disintegrated into a heaving mass, pressured by comrades from behind but held to the front by the English. Prisoners could thus only be effectively taken in large numbers once it was felt that the battle had been won and the was retiring from the field. It was the fear that the French were regrouping to attack again, coupled with an attack on the English baggage train in the rear, which caused Henry to order the killing of the French prisoners already taken. This order was resisted by many of the English knights, who feared for both their honour and their purses, and was carried out by a body of archers. Yet Henry received little censure from the French for this deed. Contemporaries, unlike some modern commentators, accepted this as the reality of war, and some writers, like St Rémy, rather blamed the French knights who attacked the baggage for provoking this action. Nothing could explode better than the battle of Agincourt the myth that, for the knighthood, war was some form of lucrative game, devoid of real danger to themselves, and cloaked in the fantastic trappings of Arthurian role play.

Nor, despite the appalling casualties suffered by the French, were battles such as Agincourt the nemesis of chivalry. Men-at-arms still remained dominant both socially and militarily. Dismounted knights formed the key units on both sides at Agincourt, and for all the enormous value of the English archers, the lightly armed bowmen would have been extremely vulnerable without the solid support of Henry V's men-at-arms on foot. As already noted in Chapter Two, it was the interdependence of the two typed of troops which was crucial. Let us remember that after arraying the archers, Sir Thomas Erpingham dismounted to join the king's battalion. Participation in such battles, moreover, was regarded as the pinnacle of a chivalric career; the ultimate test of prowess and courage. The victories of Crécy, Poitiers and Najera assured the lasting fame of the Black Prince, whereas his younger brother, John of Gaunt, who never commanded in such triumphs, is remembered essentially as a politician, despite a long military career. We remember Henry V as the victor of Agincourt rather than as the conqueror of Normandy. Likewise, it was as the commander of the archers at Agincourt, not as a crusader in Prussia in 1390 and 1392, that Sir Thomas, in Chaucer's words, was 'evere honoured for his worthynesse'. Geoffroi de Charny, who regarded participation on crusade as the ultimate accolade in his sliding scale of honour, would not have approved of this prioritization, which elevated national wars over the international defence of Christendom. But if he had been able to look over Erpingham's long and distinguished career, Charny would doubtless have agreed that, like Chaucer's knight, Sir Thomas 'loved chivalrie'.

# 6 The Heraldry of Agincourt

## Heraldic Insights into the Battle of Agincourt
Elizabeth Armstrong

When considering any medieval battle, heraldry must be given its place as it had such an important part to play on the actual battlefield. This chapter concentrates on aspects of heraldry which are relevant to the battle of Agincourt with the intention of proving how vital it is to appreciate the heraldry in order to fully understand a medieval battle. It is followed by a discussion of those most closely linked to the development of heraldry in both military and civil contexts: the heralds.

Heraldry came into existence because it was necessary to show who was who in a battle situation. It was essential that heraldry should be hereditary so that arms became well known. What makes medieval heraldry so attractive is its colour and distinctiveness. These attributes arose because coats of arms by their very nature had to be clearly discernible. Rules were formulated to ensure that this was achieved. The main heraldic tinctures divided into metals ('or' for gold, 'argent' for silver or white); colours ('gules' for red, 'vert' for green, 'azure' for blue, 'purpure' for purple, and 'sable' for black); 'vair' represented squirrel fur and ermine. Rarely did a metal object appear upon a metal field, or a coloured object upon a coloured field, because clarity was so important. There are exceptions, for instance, where a field consists of both a metal and a colour, a charge of either a metal or a colour may be placed on the whole field, and the rule is not vigorously applied to bordures, chiefs, furs, charges blazoned as proper or to a charge surmounting both the field and another charge.

The problem of how to achieve clarity had therefore been overcome, but how to show who was who in a family situation? Examples relating to Agincourt show the subtle differences which distinguished different members of the same family. First let us look at the shields of Henry V's three brothers who all bore the royal arms, France (azure three fleurs-de-lys or) quartering England (gules three lions passant guardant or), 'differenced' in some way. The eldest, Thomas, duke of Clarence, who was invalided home from Harfleur, had a label ermine charged on each point with a red canton. John, duke of Bedford, lieutenant of England in Henry V's absence, bore a label of five points, two ermine and three azure, each charged with three fleurs-de-lys or. The two ermine points denoted his descent from his grandfather, John of Gaunt, but they also had a relevance to his earldom of Richmond. Humphrey, duke of Gloucester, who was a commander of the main body on the march to Agincourt, and was felled during the battle but saved from death by Henry V, differenced his royal arms with a plain white bordure. Thomas Beaufort – earl of Dorset and Henry V's uncle as the natural son of John of Gaunt by Catherine Swynford – who was admiral of the fleet which sailed to France and later governor of Harfleur, on legitimization bore the royal arms with a bordure compony ermine and azure. The treacherous

Richard, earl of Cambridge (the grandson of Edward III and son of Edmund of Langley, duke of York), who was behind the Southampton plot prior to the fleet sailing for France, bore a label argent charged on each point with three roundels gules, plus the Leon bordure argent charged with eight or twelve lions rampant purpure derived from Richard's mother, Isabella of Castile and Leon. Finally his elder brother, Edward, duke of York, who was a commander of the rear guard on the march to Agincourt and in charge of the right wing at Agincourt itself, bore a label argent charged on each point with three roundels gules. Such differences enabled soldiers to follow their own particular lord on the battlefield.

A similar situation arises with regard to French royal differences, where princes of the blood royal bore the French royal arms ('modern', that is, bearing three fleurs-de-lys), similarly 'differenced'. The Dauphin Louis, who was not at the battle, bore the arms of France quarterly with the arms of the Dauphiné (or a dolphin hauriant and embowed azure). Charles, duke of Orléans, nephew of King Charles VI, captured at the battle, bore France modern a label argent. John, duke of Bourbon, France modern a baston gules; John, duke of Alençon, who died at the battle, France ancient within a bordure gules charged with eight roundels argent. John, duke of Burgundy, who was not at the battle, quarterly 1 & 4 France ancient within a bordure compony argent and gules 2 & 3 bendy of six pieces or and azure within a bordure gules. His brother, who met his death there, Anthony, duke of Brabant, quarterly 1 & 4 France ancient within a bordure compony argent and gules (Burgundy) 2 & 3 sable a lion rampant or (Brabant). Another brother of Burgundy killed in the battle was Philip of Burgundy, count of Nevers, who bore France modern within a bordure compony gules and argent. Prior to the battle, he had been knighted by Marshal Boucicaut for his handling of a scouting party. Charles of Artois, count of Eu, bore France ancient a label of three points gules each charged with three castles or. He was captured and imprisoned for twenty years. The constable, d'Albret, bore arms of quarterly France modern and gules, with a banner of plain gules.

Great importance was placed on coats of arms. They were a matter of family pride and a motivation for bravery on the battlefield. They sometimes inspired honourable acts. Two nights before Agincourt, Henry V had ridden half a league beyond the place fixed for his night's lodging, but he would not turn back because he was wearing his coat of arms. He perhaps considered it a matter of honour not to retreat because of that apparel. Coats of arms also had an important part to play with regard to ransoms. They were indications of who was worth saving in monetary terms. During the butchery of the French prisoners at Agincourt, some of the buildings housing the wounded French were set on fire. Hibbert notes the case of Gilbert de Lannoy, who, in spite of his injuries, crawled out and surrendered to Sir John Cornwall, presumably realizing that he was a commander or man of substance. Surprise was expressed at the shedding of noble blood so far as prisoners were concerned. Indeed when the order was given to slaughter the prisoners, there was a reluctance to carry it out, not on humanitarian grounds, but because it would lead to less ransoms. Duke Anthony of Brabant lost his life at Agincourt partly as a result of not wearing his proper surcoat (in his haste to fight he arrived on the battlefield in advance of his armorial accoutrements) and partly because members of his retinue avoided him when he was captured during the battle because they did not wish to reveal his status. Alas these factors led to him being butchered instead of ransomed.

Coats of arms were displayed on surcoats, horse bardings and pavons (pavons were triangular pieces of cloth which were attached to lances by their long straight sides with their narrow ends at the top – they were the precursors of pennoncels and pennons and were not really suited for complete displays of arms), pennoncels (longer triangular pieces of cloth attached to lances), and pennons (swallow-tailed pieces of cloth larger than pennoncels) and banners. Sometimes the word pennoncel was used to denote a pennon and vice versa. In the Lutterell Psalter (*c.*1320 to 1340) the splendid illuminated miniature of Sir Geoffrey Lutterell, who died in 1345, shows that arms might also appear on the shield, helmet, crest, saddle, ailletts, horse's chanfron and horse's fan crest. However such full displays were more applicable to a tournament than a battle situation. A pennoncel seems to have been carried by a knight commanding a unit of between twenty-five and eighty cavalrymen. When this unit was grouped with other such units, it made up part of a large formation under a knight flying a pennon. If that knight distinguished himself in battle, he might be made a banneret. A group of bannerets with their respective units formed a 'battle'.

Sometimes promotion from knight pennoncel to knight banneret was evidenced by removing the pennon's swallow tail leaving a banner shape. According to Froissart, although he is not always a reliable witness, such a ceremony took place during the Black Prince's Spanish campaign of 1367. Sir John Chandos is said to have proffered his pennon to the Black Prince, at the same time indicating that his possessions were sufficient to justify advancement to knight banneret. He then received it back from Pedro II of Castile, presumably with its tails removed. Bannerets were men of considerable standing who were entitled to display their own banners. Although a knight rarely served under another knight, he was willing to serve under a banneret. All hereditary barons served as bannerets by prescription. When a baron was represented by a son, the son as a rule displayed his father's banner. The question of whether a man served as a banneret or as an ordinary knight bachelor might depend upon how wealthy he was. When a king created a banneret who had little wealth, he generally gave him an annual pension. A banneret also received four shillings wages per day if serving in the army, whereas a knight bachelor received two shillings. (Mounted men-at-arms who were not knighted received one shilling per day, and archers, 6d.)

In addition to the personal banners carried by the bannerets, national and spiritual banners appeared on the battlefield. At Agincourt, the banner of St. George (argent a cross gules) would have been unfurled and it was ordained that Henry V's soldiers should wear a large red St George's cross on both the chest and back. The banner of St George was carried by Thomas Strickland esquire whose own arms were sable three escallops argent. Clause eighteen of the 'statutes and ordinances to be kept in times of war', which Henry issued at Mantes in 1419, expressly stipulated that a banner or pennon showing the cross of St George should not be raised unless authorized. Banner discipline was essential if a battle was to be fought efficiently. Other banners used in the English army at Agincourt included those of the Holy Trinity (gules an orle and pall argent inscribed with the Trinity in unity), the sainted kings Edmund (azure three crowns or) and Edward the Confessor (azure a cross flory between five martlets or), and the royal arms. The banner of the Holy Trinity demonstrated Henry V's belief that the invasion of France had a spiritual dimension. Presumably it was also waved aloft to attract helpful intervention by the Almighty. St Edmund was held in high regard in the Middle Ages and the banner showing his attributed arms was displayed both by Richard II during his Irish campaigns and by Henry V at Agincourt. As for the banner of Edward the Confessor, Richard II, on his banner and on display about his court, had impaled the royal arms with those attributed to Edward the Confessor. On the battlefield it was a natural progression from displaying the arms of Edward the Confessor separately to combining them with the royal arms. Henry V seems to have felt some affection for the unfortunate Richard II (after all, although Richard II took him as a hostage on his Irish expedition, he was knighted by Richard II during it) and a degree of guilt because of the part his father had played in Richard II's deposition and death. In this context, perhaps, the display of King Edmund's and Edward the Confessor's attributed arms is understandable. In any case, grants of Edward the Confessor's attributed arms were made to Richard II's two Holland half brothers, and Henry V's father, Henry IV, had also impaled his own arms with Edward the Confessor's attributed arms, so there were plenty of precedents for such display.

On a march, banners had a vital part to play. Marshals carried them on horseback in front of an army for the purpose of giving direction. We know that Henry V's great-grandfather, Edward III, when moving his army over long distances, ordered his knights not to leave their positions in their lords' formations and not to advance in front of their lords' banners, such was his appreciation of the importance of banner discipline. On battlefields, banners directly indicated changes of direction. Forward indicated attack. They were used to halt the army, withdraw, set up camp, act as a rallying point or mark the different commanders' positions.

Among the French host at Agincourt it is likely that there were the banners of St. Denis (azure a cross argent), St. Martin (azure a cross or), and possibly Brittany (or a cross sable), although we know from the chronicles of Enguerrand de Monstrelet that the duke of Brittany did not participate in the battle. Later sources suggest that the duke of Orléans had a banner bearing argent a hedgehog sable, and the duke of Bourbon a standard bearing the cross of St Denis, parted white and green and charged with a flying stag with the collar bearing the word 'Esperance' above flames of fire, three thistles counterchanged, and the cry 'Esperance, Esperance'. At Agincourt too, the French flew the oriflamme. This may have developed as a standard from the embroidered coverings which had originally enclosed the shrine of St Martin at the abbey of Marmoutiers. When the kings of France decided to reside at Paris, they switched their devotion from St Martin to St Denis, and St Denis became France's patron saint. The kings of France thus fought under the banner of St Denis. In peace time this banner was kept in the treasury at the abbey of St Denis to the north of Paris. By 1088 it was known as the oriflamme. When a war situation arose, it became the custom for the oriflamme to be taken from the altar at St Denis by the king himself after a solemn service. With one exception, its presence in an army denoted that the

*57. Manuscript illumination showing the duke of Orléans imprisoned in the Tower of London.*

king of France was present also. The exception was the battle of Agincourt where the king of France was not with his army as a result of his mental frailty. Its bearer at that battle, Guillaume Martel, Sire de Bacqueville, was killed. (His own coat was or three hammers gules within a bordure compony azure and argent.) The original oriflamme (or, as it is sometimes given, oliflamme) must have been replaced again and again and possibly its design altered from time to time. For instance, the oriflamme was abandoned at Crécy and yet Philip VI collected it again (presumably a replacement for the one lost) from St Denis on 18 March in the following year. It has been suggested that when the oriflamme was flown, it may have indicated that no quarter was to be given and that Henry V took this to be so at Agincourt, when he ordered the killing of the French prisoners. This supposition is borne out by Geoffrey le Baker's chronicle written *c*.1357-1360, which states that King Philip at Crécy 'fearing that his men would spend their whole time trying to capture nobles for ransom and would only fight half-heartedly for a general victory, ordered the standard called the oriflamme; when this was raised, no-one was to take prisoners on pain of death. It was called the oriflamme to imply that the mercy of the French was entirely consumed and no-one's life could be spared, just as flaming oil destroys everything that can be burnt.'

Standards, as well as banners, appeared on medieval battlefields. They were narrow flags divided into two rounded or sharp ends and were never furled during a battle. They were used as rallying points. The length depended on the rank or status of the owner. They were flown by the sovereign, peers, knights banneret, and by those of lesser rank. At the battle of Agincourt, English standards bore the cross of St George and French standards the cross of St Denis. To lose a banner or standard was a mark of dishonour. According to Tudor authorities, Henry V had at the battle two standards: one bearing the cross of St George, parted argent and azure and fringed of the same, with the antelope and red roses of the House of Lancaster, bearing the motto 'Dieu et mon droyt'; and another bearing the cross of St George, parted argent and fringed of the same, with the white swan of Bohun and the tree stocks of Woodstock, and bearing the same motto.

At Agincourt, Henry V's arms showed the French arms quartered with the arms of England. This practice had originated as a result of Edward III claiming succession to the crown of France through his mother, Isabella of France. In 1328, Edward, through his mother, was the closest male relative of Charles IV, being the only surviving male descendant of Philip IV (the Fair). But this was through the female line. The French preferred as Charles IV's successor his heir through the male line, Philip of Valois (Philip VI), who was descended from the brother of Philip IV. Although Edward paid homage to Philip VI for Gascony and Ponthieu in June 1329, thus accepting Philip's kingship, he was most reluctant to do so, which was an indication of the problems to come. At the start of Edward's reign in 1327, he bore the arms of England alone, but in January 1340, to illustrate what he claimed was his right to the French throne, he incorporated in his shield the arms of France ancient (with many fleurs-de-lys), placing the arms in the first and fourth quarters of his shield, the previous arms of England being retained in the second and third quarters. The fleurs-de-lys, which appear on the arms of medieval French kings, conceivably originated from iris flowers or 'the flowers of Louis'. Louis VII (1137-80) may have been the first French king to display them. One heraldic argument advanced to support the view that Salic Law excluded from the French royal succession those who were descended through a woman. This was that the crown, of which the fleurs-de-lys were the emblem, could not pass through the female line because it was written of the lilies 'they toil not, neither do they spin'. Charles V of France (1364-80), in whose reign the notion of the Salic Law was much developed, reduced the number of fleurs-de-lys to three to symbolize the Trinity. This coat, probably introduced in 1376, is described as France modern. It has been suggested that Charles V may have wanted to make the French arms different from those shown on England's shield, but surely he would have realized that there was a strong danger that the King of England would again be a likely copycat. Indeed around 1405, Henry IV adopted the example of France modern, with only three fleurs-de-lys in the French quarters, and that form continued to be used by Henry V and his successors, quartered, as before, with the arms of England.

The English royal motto 'Dieu et mon droyt' (God and my right) was adopted by Edward III in 1340, quite probably with his claim to the French throne in mind. He may even have founded the Order of the Garter in 1348 with a view to gaining support for this claim. The motto 'Honi soit qui mal y pense' (Shame to him who thinks ill of it) could have been aimed at opponents of his aggressive attitude towards France. The colours of the garter – azure and or (blue and gold) – are, of course, those of the French royal arms. Both the motto and the Order of the Garter have a relevance therefore to Henry V's French adventures. He continued to use the motto and the Order, both of which remain to this day.

Heralds had an important part to play at Agincourt, as will be explained further. They were clearly recognisable on the battlefield because they wore tabards bearing their sovereign's arms. For example, Montjoy, King of Arms for the French, so named because of the French war cry, 'Montjoie, St Denis', bore the arms of France. Among the battlefield duties of such heralds was the duty of assisting the marshal and constable to draw up the knights in battle order, taking into account the order of precedence. They also had vital roles in connection with identifying and estimating the number of the dead and acting as messengers. In the chronicle of Jean Le Fèvre, Sire de St Rémy, Henry V calls for Montjoy, 'the principal herald of France and in the presence of his own heralds asks him formally whether the victory belonged to him or to the King of France, reminding him that the slaughter was not of his doing, but had been forced upon him by the intractability of Montjoy's countrymen. The French herald conceded the victory'. Le Fèvre was actually at Agincourt with the English army. It is not clear why, but he seems to have had some heraldic function, perhaps even as Henry V's pursuivant. We learn from him that the English and French heralds remained side by side at their common observation post, keeping count of those whose deaths were worthy of recording. Afterwards he took up service with the duke of Burgundy, and in 1431 was appointed king of arms of the order of the Golden Fleece (*Toison d'or*), the order which the duke had founded in 1429.

Sir Thomas Erpingham, a major player on the national scene and at the battle, was a great benefactor of both Norwich and Norfolk. He had a particular fondness for Norwich Cathedral and was buried there at his wish. It has been mooted that some of the cathedral's misericords may have been carved to commemorate men who were involved in the Agincourt campaign, including Sir Thomas himself (vert an escutcheon within an orle of martlets argent), the two earls of Suffolk, father and son, one dying at Harfleur, the other at the battle (azure a fess between three leopards' faces or), Richard Courtenay, bishop of Norwich (or 3 torteaux and a label of three points azure each charged as the field), and Sir Thomas Morley (argent a lion rampant sable crowned or). Maybe Sir Thomas organized the raising of funds from his fellow campaigners. The misericord of Richard Courtenay, the bishop of Norwich who died from dysentery at Harfleur, incorporates his initials, showing beyond doubt whom the carving portrays. The misericord carving of a swan ducally gorged was originally the badge of the family of the mother of Henry V, namely the Bohuns, and was used by both Henry IV and Henry V. As we have seen, Sir Thomas Erpingham was a loyal and courageous supporter of the House of Lancaster, unswervingly serving John of Gaunt, his son Henry IV and grandson Henry V. It would not be unlikely that he would have wanted to ensure that the new choir stalls included a suitable reference to the Lancastrians, following Henry V's success at Agincourt. One of the misericords portrays a king's head. Perhaps it was meant to represent Henry V, although it was suggested by A.B. Whittingham (in his publication of 1981, 'Norwich Cathedral Bosses and Misericords') that it was the head of Henry IV.

Heraldry had a definite part to play with regard to the fleet which brought Henry V's army to Harfleur. A number of sails were decorated with heraldic emblems. The *Trinité Royale*, the ship which carried Henry V, displayed the royal arms on its sail. It flew at its masthead banners displaying the Trinity, the Virgin Mary and the arms of St Edward, St George and England. At its deckhead appeared a leopard carved in gold-painted wood. It also bore four shields of the king's arms within a collar of gold and two more with the cross of St George within the Garter. The *Katherine of the Tower* had an antelope climbing up a gold beacon painted or embroidered on its sail. The sail of the *Nicholas* bore a swan and that of another unnamed ship bore ostrich feathers and stars. The antelope, beacon, swan and ostrich feathers were all badges of Henry V.

The arms of the traitor Henry Lord Scrope of Masham (azure a bend or and a label argent), who was involved in the Cambridge plot and executed after a trial by his peers, have a relevance to the concept of honour, which played such an important part in a medieval knight's mental make-up. It was felt that as Lord Scrope was a Knight of the Garter, his disgrace might affect the way people viewed the Order of the Garter. In Belz's *Memorials of the Most Noble Order of the Garter*, he writes,

> it appears to have been thought necessary to absolve the Order from any disgrace that might attach to it in consequence of the offence of one of its companions. The record of Scrope's attainder in Parliament, therefore, recites that 'whereas he was a knight of the renowned and excellent military Order of the Garter, which had been laudably instituted in support of the faith, the king, the realm, and the law, no person shall presume to vilify or reflect upon those who are worthy members of that venerable body, because the said Henry Scrope has dishonoured himself by the crime he has committed'.

The concept of honour also has a relevance to the episode of Sir John Fastolf's alleged cowardice at Patay. Sir John took part in the campaign of 1415, but was one of those left to garrison at Harfleur. His arms were quarterly or and azure a bend gules charged with three cross-crosslets argent but also attributed to him as his arms are quarterly or and azure a bend gules charged with three escallops argent. Fastolf became a Knight of the Garter, but later John, duke of Bedford, deprived him of the Garter for deserting Lord Talbot at the battle of Patay in 1429. However the Garter was restored because it was proved that he retreated only after Talbot's capture and therefore had not acted dishonourably after all. Interestingly it seems that although the Garter appears on knightly effigies it was not actually worn on the battlefield.

War cries had an important part to play on the medieval battlefield with regard to bolstering morale and helping to identify fighters. A war cry was considered to be an attribute of nobility. For instance, of Sir Simon Felbrigg, who was Richard II's standard

58. *Brass of Sir Simon Felbrigg and his wife, Felbrigg Church (Norfolk).*

bearer and who took part in the Agincourt campaign, we learn from later traditions that 'he was a gentleman de nom, d'armes et de cry'. Sometimes the names of patron saints were used as war cries, such as St George and St Denis. Burgundian cries included 'Bourgogne, Bourgogne', 'Montjoie, Notre Dame, Bourgogne', 'Monjoie St Andrew'. The count of Eu's cry is believed to be 'Montjoie au blanc épervier'. Others may have used family names, such as 'Ailly' for Baldwin d'Ailly, and 'à Créquy, Créquy le grand Baron', for Jacques, sire de Créquy. Many more are included in Palliser's *Historic Devices, Badges and War Cries*, although there are always problems in establishing their authenticity.

One further aspect of battlefield heraldry needs to be touched upon, namely how individuals' participation in battles on occasions had an effect on their families' heraldry. Richard Waller's coat was sable three walnut leaves or between two bendlets argent. After the battle his family added the shield of Charles, duke of Orléans, to its crest of a walnut tree to evidence the fact that Richard Waller took the duke prisoner at Agincourt. The family of Sir Roland Lenthale, one of the commanders at Agincourt, adopted the motto 'Agincourt'. (His coat was argent on a bend cotised sable three mullets or.) John de Wodehouse bore the coat sable three ermine cinquefoils between an ermine chevron. It is claimed that after the battle his chevron was changed from ermine to or scattered with drops of blood, and that his family later adopted the motto 'Agincourt'.

In conclusion, heraldry evolved as a result of its importance on the battlefield. It had a vital role there and also a part to play in the realm of politics and foreign affairs as has been seen already with regard to England's former French interests. In the medieval period, heraldry retained a simplicity and thus a beauty which it lost later on when it became principally a matter of status, instead of being used for practical purposes, including battlefield display. The design and colour of medieval heraldry is superb because the need for clarity on the battlefield was uppermost. When forged for battlefield use, it had none of the ostentatious vulgarity of later periods. It is fascinating to study it in the context of the battlefield and in that context it has many interesting facets. To the medieval man his heraldry was a matter of great importance; on occasions he was prepared to die in the heat of battle determined that his arms should not become objects of dishonour. We must admire the thought and skill which produced exquisite arms and the bravery of those who bore them.

# The Heralds at the time of Agincourt

Henry Paston-Bedingfield

Heralds have existed since about the 1170s. It is thought that the first part of the word may derive from the German word for army, 'heer'. The second part is linked to the English word 'wield', meaning to exercise control. Heralds were, and still are today, those with specialized knowledge of coats of arms, ceremonial matters, general matters of honour or of a chivalric nature. They used to oversee tournaments and were employed on diplomatic missions. In this capacity, they had what we call today 'diplomatic immunity'. It was treason to buffet a herald – and it still is! W.H. Godfrey suggested that 'the heralds of the kings of England formed a part of the household establishment from the reign of Edward I or earlier, and from that of Henry V at least functioned in some measure as a corporation'. The heralds certainly had robes provided for the coronation of Henry V in 1413. Two years later, Henry drew up a list of the heralds to go with him on the Agincourt campaign, and this passed the privy seal on 22 June 1415, four months before the battle. They were Leicester, Guyenne, and Ireland kings of arms, and Hereford herald, who was marshal of arms in Lancaster king of arms' place. In effect, they were the four kings of arms of the English obedience.

Leicester was the king of arms of the southern province of England (i.e. south of Trent); Henry Grene seems to have held the office from about 1380 to 1419. He had initially been a herald of John of Gaunt who was earl of Leicester as well as duke of Lancaster. In that capacity Grene went to Portugal in 1380 and Spain in 1386. He then became a herald of King Richard II and was present on the Irish campaign of 1399. He continued in office under Henry IV who made him king of arms for the southern province. We later find him at the siege of Coity in Wales in 1405. He died in 1419.

Ireland was the king of arms of the dominion of Ireland but none of the incumbents had much to do with that island and were counted as members of the office of arms in England. The title lapsed in 1487, and in 1552 it became Ulster king of arms. In 1415 Ireland king of arms was Thomas Collyer, but nothing more is known of him, except that in 1417 the King confirmed to him an annuity of 10 marks which had previously been granted by Edward, duke of York. Perhaps Collyer had earlier served the duke as pursuivant: the duke, of course, met his death in the battle.

Guyenne king of arms in the list was William Bruges, who had been in this position since March or April 1413 (i.e. around the time of the accession of Henry V), and who had served as Chester herald since 1398, in which capacity he would have been closely connected with Prince Henry when earl of Chester. Remember that the list was dated 22 *June* 1415. In fact, William Bruges may have been created Garter king of arms between that date and 4 July, when his father made a will which mentioned him. It is now generally considered, however, that the creation as Garter dates to 1417 rather than to 1415. Whatever the definite date of creation of William Bruges as Garter, this was the first time that a king of arms was named after an order of chivalry. At the same time he was specifically made the chief of the English heralds; Garter still holds that position today. Bruges was prominent throughout Henry's reign and also served on many diplomatic missions under Henry VI, dying in March 1450, by which time most of the conquests in France had been lost.

The last name on the 1415 list is Hereford herald, marshal of arms of the northern province. Hereford herald had originally been associated with Humphrey de Bohun, earl of Hereford, but after his death in 1372 he became a royal herald and remained so under the first two Lancastrian kings. (Hereford was, of course, one of the titles borne by Henry Bolingbroke by virtue of his marriage to Humphrey's daughter, Mary.) We do not know the full name of Hereford herald in 1415 (his Christian name was Richard) but he had also attended Henry V's coronation in 1413 alongside William Bruges, went overseas on a diplomatic mission in 1414, and attended the Agincourt campaign in place of his master, Lancaster king of arms, of the northern province, because of the latter's indisposition. Lancaster was Guyenne's father, Richard Bruges, and William Bruges was himself succeeded as Garter by his own son-in-law, John Smert. Richard Bruges had earlier been Lancaster herald to John of Gaunt, and had been made king of arms of the northern province at the accession of Henry IV. He probably died in 1419.

The French heralds were Montjoy king of arms, and at least three others, possibly including Berry king of arms. The three that have been mentioned were those sent by the dukes of Orléans and Bourbon to parlay with Henry V a little while before the battle to find out King Henry's intention. The King told them that he intended to march straight to Calais, trusting that no one would try to stop him. Jean Le Fèvre states in his chronicle that the English and French heralds stood together as observers during the battle. This has been taken as a sign of the international brotherhood of heralds acting in their professional capacity. After the battle, when asked by Henry V, Montjoy told him the day was his and that the nearby castle was called Agincourt. Henry V thus named the battle. Le Fèvre is sometimes referred to as a herald during the Agincourt campaign, though there is no actual evidence. He certainly accompanied Henry V throughout and returned to London with him. His account is an eye-witness chronicle of the events that took place. He was a subject of Henry V as he was born in *c*.1395 in Abbeville in the county of Ponthieu, which was later ceded to Burgundy. In 1425, he was appointed Charolais herald by the Duke of Burgundy and in 1431 he became the first king of arms of the order of the *Toison d'or* (Golden Fleece).

As has been discussed, the chief function of the heralds at the battle, apart from carrying messages, was to identify the dead and wounded by the surcoats worn by the combatants. This is well evidenced in the chronicle of Le Fèvre. He gives a list of those slain, adding 'so many noble and esquires died there and other valiant men whom I myself saw, which was a pitiful sight to see and to hear told by the officers of arms who were present at the battle, both on the English and the French sides. For during the battle all the officers of arms, of one side and the other, were grouped together and afterwards those of the French side went off to where it seemed best to them and those of the English stayed with their masters, who had won the battle. But as for me, I stayed with the English'. Soon after the battle, Henry created Agincourt king of arms, whose title occurs several times down to 1419 but whose name we do not know. Was it an honorary rank or did he have a province in France? We do not know.

*59. The earl of Warwick being created a knight of the Garter. (Pageant of the Birth, Life and Death of Richard Beauchamp, earl of Warwick, d.1439).*

Apart from those already mentioned, there were a number of other heralds in existence during Henry V's reign; some royal, others private. William Boys was, in 1413, Dorset herald to Thomas Beaufort, earl of Dorset, and then Exeter herald on Beaufort's promotion to be duke of Exeter in 1416. His elder son, also William Boys, was Blanchlyverer pursuivant by 1418, the name being derived from the white greyhound badge of Edward III. His younger brother, Thomas Boys, was Antelope pursuivant, his name being derived from the Antelope badge of Henry IV's first wife, Mary de Bohun. He also attended Henry V at the battle. John Cosoun was Arundel herald (*c*.1413), who attended Thomas Fitzalan, earl of Arundel, at the siege of Harfleur and on his fatal illness in October 1415. Thereafter, he was engaged by John Mowbray, duke of Norfolk, as Mowbray herald. Cadran herald (name unknown) was engaged by Thomas Beaufort, earl of Dorset, in 1415. In 1416, he was in trouble for running off with four silver cups entrusted to him by a pursuivant of the chancellor of France, one Septfaux. Clarence herald (not to be confused with Clarenceux king of arms), John Haswell or Ashwell, was retained by Thomas, duke of Clarence, brother of Henry V, and attended the chapter of the English heralds at Rouen in 1420. Cornwall herald was instituted by Richard II, presumably for the prince of Wales as duke of Cornwall. He attended the coronation of Henry V in 1413. John, a herald to the earl of Derby from 1393 (Henry IV) attended Henry V's coronation. Gloucester herald, one Rowland, was probably in the retinue of Humphrey, duke of Gloucester, in 1415. Leopard herald was a title under Henry V and VI. His name recalls the beast in the royal arms of England, for a time called leopards rather than lions. Nicholas Serby was Leopard around 1404 and attended the chapter in 1420.

Ireland king of arms, 'Jehan Kyrkeby autrement dit Irland Roy d'armes des Irlandois', also attended the chapter meeting of 1420 at Rouen, and was at the coronation of Queen Katherine in 1421. William Horsley was Clarenceux king of arms at the chapter of 1420. Although this was not a completely new title, it seems that from his creation, which was probably in 1419, Clarenceux king of arms ruled the northern province in place of Lancaster king of arms. Finally, John Mowbray, earl of Nottingham and earl Marshal (later the duke of Norfolk) had two heralds. One was Giles Walter, Mowbray herald at the chapter meeting in 1420, and John Kyndale, Nottingham herald, who attended the coronation of Henry V, and later of Queen Katherine. So, Henry V created Garter, Clarenceux and Agincourt kings of arms and probably also Rouge Croix pursuivant, not yet mentioned, but who occurs in 1418/19 at Caudebec in Normandy, and Antelope pursuivant. Noblemen's officers in Henry's time were Arundel, Cadran, Dorset and Exeter, and possibly Richmond heralds, and Blanchlyverer, Bonespoir (perhaps a pursuivant of John Holland, earl of Huntingdon, in 1419) and Bellême pursuivant of Thomas de Montagu, earl of Salisbury and lord of Bellême, near Alençon. The last named pursuivant was slain by brigands before 21 June 1421.

By 1400, as Anthony Wagner notes, 'the heralds were the acknowledged experts on armorial bearings'. As has already been shown, it was important for coats to be distinctive and easily recognisable, and it is not surprising that there needed to be some regulation, by the officers of arms on behalf of the crown, culminating in the court of chivalry itself. Writing around 1440, Nicholas Upton, in his *De Studio Militari*, noted men who had assumed arms based on their service in the war in France. A French chronicler, Jean Juvenal des Ursins, writing in the 1430s or 40s, also claims that Henry V promised to ennoble all those who were serving with him at Agincourt if they were not already noble, and that they might wear his collar of SS to show their nobility. In this context, therefore, it is important to review what is known as the 'Agincourt exemption'. This was a royal order sent out on the eve of Henry's campaign to Normandy in the summer 1417. I cite here the text as translated by Harris Nicholas in his *History of the Battle of Agincourt*:

> 'Forasmuch as we are informed divers persons, who in our expeditions heretofore made, assumed, and in our expedition to be forthwith made, (God speeding) do purpose to wear Arms and Coats of Arms, called Coate-armures, although neither they nor their ancestors bore Arms in times past. And as the Almighty disposes his grace as he pleases to mankind, equally to rich and poor, so we willing that each one of our aforesaid subjects be duly

treated and respected according to his rank, do command you that in all the places within your bailiwick where by our writ we lately caused proclamation to be made for musters, you cause it to be publicly proclaimed on our part, that no one, of what estate, degree, or condition soever he be, do take upon himself such Arms or Coats of Arms, unless he possess, or ought to possess them, by right of ancestry, or by grant of some person having sufficient power thereunto: And that on the day of his muster he do openly shew to the persons by us hereunto assigned to be assigned, by whose grant he obtained the said Coats of Arms, excepting those who bore arms with us at the Battle of Agincourt, under penalty of being refused to proceed in the aforesaid expedition in the retinue of him by whom he is retained, and of the loss of his pledges taken on the aforesaid account, and moreover of the erasure and seizure of the said Arms and coats, called Coate-armures, at the time of his said muster, if they shall be seen or found upon him. And this do you in no wise omit.

> Witness the King at the city of New
> Sarum, the second day of June 1417.'

Similar writs were issued to the sheriffs of Wilts, Sussex, and Dorset.

I found this rather puzzling when I read Anthony Wagner's *The Heralds of England*, and indeed it is still somewhat of a mystery how grants of arms were made precisely at this date. But the matter is much assisted by the commentary made on it by Nicholas.

> The subjoined translation of a writ relative to coat armour allows of the inference that Henry was desirous of rewarding, in an especial manner, those who served under him in the battle, and it was probably with that view that their names were placed upon record; but what other privileges they received has not been ascertained. It is a common error to suppose that every person who was at Agincourt was allowed to assume whatever armorial bearings he pleased, which may be traced to Shakespeare having made Henry exclaim,
>
>> 'For he, today that sheds his blood with me,
>> Shall be my brother; be he ne'er so vile
>> This day shall gentle his condition.'

The fact was, that when the King upon the occasion of another expedition, in 1417, found it necessary to restrain the assumption of coats of arms, he specially excepted such as had borne them at Agincourt, thus making the circumstance of their having used them on that day a sufficient title for their being continued; but he did not create any privilege to others to adopt them in consequence of their services on that occasion.

Two further things that exist today emanate from the reign of Henry V. One is the collar of SS, created as an honour by the Lancastrian kings. This is not the place to discuss it, and in any case there is not enough time, but suffice it to say that heralds and kings of arms, amongst others, wear this collar to this very day. I wear it with tabard when in attendance on Her Majesty at the State Opening of Parliament. The other is a chapter meeting, held at Rouen on 5 January 1420. Those in attendance at that meeting were: Garter, Clarenceux, and Ireland kings of arms, with Leopard, Clarence, Exeter (who was also by this time marshal of arms of the northern province of England), and Mowbray heralds. It is clear that this was the beginning of an incorporation of the English heralds as a constitution was discussed, so too a corporate seal and oaths of allegiance. It is also clear that this was all based on the previous incorporation of the French heralds in 1408. King Henry V died two years later in 1422, having given a big boost to the herald's profession. Later in that century a civil war broke out, which is now called the Wars of the Roses, which must have prevented the realization of a corporate body of heralds. This eventually took place by charter of Richard III on 2 March 1484, and we have had regular chapter meetings ever since. But that is another subject.

# 7 Shakespeare's Agincourt
## Sir Thomas Erpingham and the Missing Archers
### Christopher Smith

> Agincourt, Agincourt,
> Know ye not Agincourt?

The question is, of course, rhetorical, like much in Shakespeare's *Henry V*, and, just as our modern responses to the theme have been shaped and, in large measure, even fixed by two widely admired film versions, by Lawrence Olivier for Two Cities in 1944 and Branagh for Renaissance in 1987, so too Shakespeare's early audiences (the play was first performed in 1599, appearing in print in the following year) went to the theatre with the ballads echoing in their minds.

> Agincourt, Agincourt:
> Know ye not Agincourt?
> Where English slu and hurt
> All their French foemen?
> With our pikes and bills brown
> How the French were beat down
> Shot by our bowmen.

Or again,

> Our English archers discharged their shafts
> As thicke as hayle in skye
> And many a Frenchman on the feelde
> That happy day did dye.

More serious readers would have gained a similar impression from Roger Ascham's treatise on archery, *Toxophilus*, first printed in 1547, republished in 1560 and again, a dozen years after his death, in 1583, and evidently read by Shakespeare about the time he was writing *King Lear*. Eulogizing the longbow not only as a weapon but also as a factor in the moral rearmament of the English people, Ascham not unnaturally picks out Agincourt for a historical summary that is as explicit as it is brief.

> Kynge Henrie the fift a prince pereles and most vyctoriouse conqueroure of
> all that euer dyed yet in this part of the world, at the battel of Dagin court

with vii. M fyghtynge men, and yet many of them sycke, beynge such Archers as the Cronycle sayeth that moost parte of them drewe a yarde, slewe all the Cheualrie of Fraunce to the nomber of XL. M, and moo, and lost not paste xxvi Englysshe men.

As Ascham himself indicates, historical sources underpinning popular memories of the great victory in 1415 were also readily available. Those members of Shakespeare's audience who had the intellectual curiosity could, like the playwright himself, of course, consult the records in the attractive form given them by Raphael Holinshed in the *Chronicles of England, Scotland and Ireland* (1586-7). It is hardly less certain that Holinshed's *Chronicle* shaped the thinking of many of Shakespeare's contemporaries than that it left its deep mark on his play. If these points are allowed, then it becomes particularly interesting to note not only the similarities between *Henry V* and its historical sources, as scrupulous scholars and editors have done with such acumen, but also certain divergences and discrepancies. They cannot, it would seem, have passed unnoticed in the Elizabethan age; in fact, they are so marked that they invite interpretation not as mere differences but as significant transformations. We moderns should heed them too, even though we may, in order to do so, find ourselves obliged to reject the persistent beguiling and colourful images created on the screen particularly by Olivier, but also by Branagh too, who went beyond the play back to history to recreate a version of events that cannot but appear, after due comparisons, more populist in orientation than Shakespeare's.

Yet where in Shakespeare's *Henry V* are the archers? The simple question serves to focus the problem. Modern historians endorse the chronicles: English longbowmen played a crucial role at Agincourt, as they did virtually throughout the Hundred Years War. Yet it is quite in vain that we look for them in the play. Their absence is perhaps all the more surprising since Shakespeare has found a role for Sir Thomas Erpingham. This chapter will concentrate mainly on the issue of the 'missing archers', but first let us say a few words not only on Shakespeare's portrayal of the old knight, but also on the ways in which our two directors, Olivier and Branagh, sought to use him in their own distinctive fashion.

## Shakespeare's Erpingham

In the play, Erpingham appears in Act IV only – an act which takes us through the English and French camps on the eve of battle and then onto the field itself on Saint Crispin's day. Erpingham emerges, however briefly, as a counterpart to Falstaff. Indeed, the very brevity of his appearance may constitute a meaningful comment on the other character, who had long loomed too large in Prince Hal's life. Filling the part of what has been characterized by Thomas Cranfill as one of Shakespeare's 'old heroes', Erpingham is presented as the elderly but worthy embodiment of steadiness and loyalty. When the character first appears on stage, Shakespeare immediately directs our responses to him by making the king greet him as 'old Sir Thomas Erpingham'. This reinforces an impression the audience will have already gained from his body language and his 'good white head', and when the king, strictly unnecessarily, mentions his hair the point is stressed yet further. Then the king goes on to comment that the knight might prefer a more comfortable bed than the hard ground, and this very considerateness hints once again at old age and the weariness of the flesh that often goes with it. In this context the language of Henry's generalizations about the way the mind can revive the body keeps up the insistence on the theme: '...when the mind is quicken'd, out of doubt the organs, though defunct and dead before, break up their drowsy grave'.

It is as if the king, with Erpingham before him, can hardly avoid the vocabulary of mortality. After this, not only does the episode end, as Erpingham departs, with the king describing him as 'old heart', but a little later, the soldier Williams also uses, as if no other were available, the adjective 'old' when speaking of the knight. The theme of age goes, however, hand in hand with that of honour. Erpingham is invariably referred to by his full name and title. Moreover, it is notable how many times the adjective 'good' is used in speeches addressed to him or concerned with him. Cumulatively the effect is to create an impression of praiseworthiness.

> Good morrow, old Sir Thomas Erpingham:
> A good soft pillow for that good white head
> Were better than the churlish turf of France

And 'good' will be the second word Henry uses in his next speech in which the knight is praised in a generalization: 'Tis good for men to love their present pains'. In the context of so many repetitions of 'good', Erpingham's own use of the comparative degree of the same adjective in a reply that in any case redounds to his credit is all the more striking: 'This lodging likes me better, since I may say, 'Now lie I like a king''. Shakespeare, as if intent on stressing the link between goodness and age in the knight that we have already noted, gives the following words to Henry when, later in the scene, Erpingham informs him that his nobles are looking for him: 'Good old knight, collect them altogether at my tent'. And it is tempting to interpret 'I'll be before thee' as a hint that the young monarch can walk more quickly than his interlocutor.

The theme of goodness is, moreover, reinforced by being contrasted with the 'churlish' in 'the churlish turf of France'. In the circumstances of a play filled with praise for English chivalry, Erpingham will, then, rise as nobler yet when compared with the 'churlish turf' of France. The impressions gained when first we see Erpingham are strengthened when Williams, in simple tribute, echoes his monarch's estimation by calling the knight, 'a good old commander and a most kind gentleman'.

Many have been content to see Erpingham simply as the embodiment of the view that old age has, in Tennyson's phrase, 'yet his honour and his toil'. There are, however, some puzzles in his role. This may be seen even in a simple piece of stage business. Henry's borrowing of Erpingham's cloak is, of course, a homely realistic detail that readily yields symbolism in a Judaeo-Christian tradition stretching back to the Second Book of Kings, and is an apt emblem of Henry's readiness to slough off his old self and assume a new, more responsible persona. But is not a reciprocal piece of business needed too? For the king simply to take Erpingham's cloak – and his request is not, in all conscience, one that could readily be refused – and not to hand the knight his in return would be an action bespeaking an indifference to the welfare of the aged captain at dead of night that would have been entirely at odds with the solicitude

*60 and 61. Views of the tomb and chantry chapel of Henry V in Westminster Abbey.*

that has just been expressed verbally. With modern actors an exchange of cloaks might cost a valuable moment of stage time, but in Shakespeare's age the players would have been more adroit at handling these garments, so the action would not have been unduly delayed for what would appear to be a necessary gesture.

If this is detail, the interpretation of Erpingham's most famous line is quite an important issue: 'I may say, "Now lie I like a king".' Generally this is interpreted as the witty riposte of an indomitable old fire-eater turned courtier who, in a way that is often thought typically English, copes with a tense and difficult situation with a laugh. When Williams enquires what Erpingham thinks of the army's 'estate', Henry replies unhesitatingly: 'Even as men wrecked upon a sand, that look to be washed off the next tide'. That could scarcely be more explicit: he admits readily that this veteran with experience that is more valuable than some of his fellows' displays of book learning, can recognize full well that the situation is very dangerous indeed. When Bate asks whether Erpingham has 'told his thought to the king', the very form of his question indicating that he is expecting the strongly negative reply he is given: 'No; nor it is not meet he should'. In the light of these exchanges we may return to Henry's remark on Erpingham's exit: 'God-a-mercy, old heart, thou speak'st cheerfully'. The conclusion cannot be avoided that the king knows there is a gap between what Erpingham appears to be saying and what he really means. But such disingenuousness would quite undermine the honest character of 'good' Erpingham. He *lies* like a king in that he too does not tell the truth about the dangers that await the English army: we have a moment of covert understanding between the experienced captain and his youthful commander when both of them appreciate the need to cloak the truth from those whose hearts are not so stout.

Erpingham's role is so short it is difficult to trace any particular trends in its interpretation on stage. Thomas L. Berger, after showing most interestingly how the drama might have been performed with a cast of a bare thirteen actors, suggests the actor playing Erpingham might also have doubled as Fluellen, the French king and Beaumont. Even if that conclusion is accepted – and, as Berger himself scrupulously admits, it has been challenged – there are arguments against accepting the view that any particular dramatic impact would have been made. Doubling was so common a practice in Shakespeare's theatre that comparisons, possibly of an ironic nature, might well have not been made in the way that they sometimes are in modern productions, where the audience will tend to think that the director is seeking to make particular points by deciding to double certain roles. Besides, cloaked, in a white wig and doubtless bearded to emphasize his age, and adopting suitable body language, Erpingham would hardly have been recognisable as the actor taking other parts in the play. If, for authenticity or experimentally, doubling were essayed in a modern production, the dimming of the lighting for the first part of Act IV would, of course, again tend to militate against recognition.

Theatrical performance is notoriously evanescent, and there have, it may readily be granted, been few playgoers who have concentrated their attention on Erpingham when watching or recording their impressions of *Henry V*. This gives especial interest to two highly regarded film versions, Lawrence Olivier's of 1944 and Kenneth Branagh's of 1987. Following Shakespeare, Olivier does not bring on Erpingham until the night before Agincourt. The role is entrusted to the paunchy Morland Graham, and his arms, on the left shoulder of his cloak, serve to identify him visually in the film almost as well as they might have done in the fifteenth-century campaign. His 'now lie I like a king' is accepted at face value and with a ready laugh by monarch and his nobles alike. But Henry's commentary, like his remark 'thou speak'st cheerfully', is omitted, and though he borrows Erpingham's cloak, the possibility of monarch and knight exchanging them is not envisaged. Not only is the appreciation of Erpingham preserved in the later exchanges with the soldiers, but after the knight has summoned Henry back to join his nobles, he accompanies him as he returns through the camp, looking in at the tents where mass is being celebrated. This involves some slight departure from the implications of Shakespeare's text, but there are significant corresponding benefits. Silent, as in the play, but very much in evidence as a background figure with what, in this situation, we may call the English host, Erpingham is part of the audience for the battle speech. Finally we see him again, identified by his arms, as the soldiery marches off after the fighting.

All this is worthy enough but Branagh is notably more inventive in a manner that is, moreover, entirely responsible both to Shakespeare and to history. While Erpingham is given no words that Shakespeare had not assigned to him in the original play, his part is developed plausibly and consistently in the light of an awareness of Sir Thomas's place in history. Much is in fact added by making Erpingham's not just a walk-on part late in the play, but by showing the knight rather as a character who is present throughout and who shares in the responsibility for what takes place since he has lent tacit support to the plan to invade France. Erpingham, played by Edward Jewesbury, is first seen in the play in the presence chamber. With his full head of white hair, though no beard, with a trimmer

62. *The earl of Warwick received at Venice. Sir Thomas Erpingham also visited Venice when in the service of Henry Bolingbroke.*

figure than Morland Graham's and with his chain of office as steward of the household conspicuous against his smarter costume, he is an elder personage in an assembly where others are younger and emphasis is placed upon Henry's youthfulness. The courtiers are seated in stalls on the king's left and right; Erpingham's place, not insignificantly, is on the right-hand side, and only Exeter and Westmoreland are seated higher. As the Archbishop expounds his case, Erpingham turns to the two nobles and nods his head in vigorous approval. Plainly he sides with the war party. Later, after the dismissal of the French ambassador, Branagh conveys Henry's determination by striding off. As the courtiers follow him, the aged Erpingham has to bestir himself to keep up the pace.

It is in the Southampton council chamber that Erpingham is next seen. Throughout the early discussions he stands behind Exeter, grave, tense, but approving. In the moment when it seems the traitors may resist arrest, Erpingham does not advance to take part in the scuffle. Instead, he stands, protectively, by the king. For this scene, Erpingham, like the others, has donned his coat of arms, and though the tinctures are distorted by a quirk of studio lighting, so that the vert is shown correctly only towards the end, armorial bearings will henceforth reinforce the identification of the character. At Harfleur, Erpingham is first seen standing beside the king as he returns from the breach on his white charger. Next we espy him standing behind Exeter and Westmoreland, clearly inspired by the monarch's rallying cry. No doubt in order to facilitate character recognition, Branagh has the entire cast bare-headed throughout this episode (apart from Fluellen), though historically it seems unlikely those engaged in the fighting would have

*63. The earl of Warwick in Jerusalem. Sir Thomas Erpingham may have accompanied Henry Bolingbroke to the Holy Land.*

been so ill-advised as to have dispensed with the helmets about which there is so much talk in the play.

The fourth act is naturally Erpingham's high point in Branagh's film. We first glimpse him sitting on the ground beside Exeter by a camp fire while the Chorus is still setting the scene. The episode in the English camp at Agincourt opens with the king's greeting to Erpingham which is followed by the exchange about the churlish turf. Next, the lines of Henry's response are, however, cut: he responds only with 'Humph' before asking the knight for the loan of his cloak. Erpingham volunteers to accompany the king through the camp, but the offer is declined. Erpingham then pronounces the line 'The Lord in Heaven bless thee, noble Harry' with deep emotion. Indeed, it is so profound that some may sense something of an incongruity when Henry replies: 'God-a-mercy, old heart! Thou speak'st cheerfully.' Then the king wanders away through the camp. The exchanges about Erpingham between Bates and Henry are retained in their entirety. A little later, during his soliloquy, Henry walks past a cart. On it we see first a shield with his arms, next another with Erpingham's; then we realize that the cart (like those we have seen after Mountjoy's departure) is loaded with arrows.

As the day dawns, Erpingham tells the king that his nobles are seeking him, and, calling him 'good old knight', the king asks that they should be told to assemble at his tent. A nod of acquiescence, in lieu of the prosaic 'I shall do't, my lord', saves a few moments. Just before the battle, Erpingham is seen again, once more beside Exeter and Westmoreland, and at the end of the St Crispin speech he joins with nobles and common soldiery alike in the cheer. But after all have knelt and crossed themselves before the combat begins, it is noticeable that he is less athletic than his comrades in arms. Perhaps following Olivier rather than Shakespeare, Branagh makes good cinematic action out of the archers' preparations, with Erpingham bustling about, plainly concerned if not obviously in charge, as stakes are driven and sheaves of arrows are distributed. When Erpingham hands Exeter his mace we have, in the invention of a little bit of business, an emblem of the knight's role in the play. Then, as battle commences, comes Branagh's major and most significant piece of apt inventiveness. There is tension as the French charge, and the most striking expression of it comes with a shot of Erpingham's face in extreme close-up, filling the entire screen. One interpretation might be that he is simply frightened, but there is another that is a richer and more rewarding hypothesis. It is that this old soldier, who has seen much fighting in a long career, and has no illusions about the extent of his own involvement in the questionable decisions that led up to the campaign, and who is deeply concerned for the welfare of the house he serves, has a true appreciation of the horrors that are to come. That the play contains Harry's great moment of anagnorisis in his personal agony in the night is a commonplace. With fine help from the actor Michael Williams, Branagh makes Bates' intervention into something hardly less powerful. And now, in a powerful piece of what is in effect silent cinema, Erpingham too is shown to have come to a full realization of a situation for whose creation he is to a degree responsible and from which it is questionable whether there can be any escape.

Branagh's inventiveness is not yet exhausted. He has Erpingham go at the king's behest to succour the duke of York, appear to hear Llewellyn [Fluellen] lament over the slaughter of the boys and listen with emotion to the tally of slaughter. More strikingly still, and fully in keeping with his position in the household, Erpingham joins with Westmoreland and others to bear York's corpse from the field. At the conference at Troyes, Erpingham appears once more, in what we come to see more than once is his normal position, as a senior presence respectfully backing up the royal family. All in all, Branagh has developed Erpingham's role from a bit part to quite a central one, not by distorting the Shakespearean material but by developing it imaginatively in the light of the role Sir Thomas played in history.

## The Missing Archers

Yet, though Shakespeare has created a vivid cameo role for Erpingham in the eve of battle scene, he has deprived him of the part that history accords him as commander of the archers. Nothing could be more vivid than Holinshed's snapshot of this 'man of great experience in the warre' casting up his 'warder' into the air as a sign that longbowmen had taken up their position on the flank in a meadow and were ready to engage on the enemy. But Shakespeare makes nothing of a moment that the actors-turned-film directors just could not let slip. Instead, in the play, Erpingham simply makes a final appearance with 'his host', entering with Gloucester, Bedford, Exeter, Salisbury and Westmoreland for the scene which contains Henry's Crispin day speech. But a host of what manner of soldiers we are not told. Erpingham says not another word and, apparently needed to double other roles, is not seen again in the play.

146

*64 and 65. Equestrian figures, probably of Henry V, from the king's chantry chapel, Westminster Abbey.*

Shakespeare's treatment of Erpingham, particularly his disinclination to make anything of the archers in relationship with him, becomes all the more intriguing when we turn from the chronicle to another major source of *Henry V*, this time a dramatic one. *The Famous Victories of Henry the Fifth* was registered as a play in the Stationers register in 1594 and printed in 1598, but is believed to have been produced as early as 1588. The first half deals with the riotous youth of Henry V (which Shakespeare placed in his *Henry IV*), but the second deals with the invasion of France and battle of Agincourt. There are some similarities of words and action with Shakespeare, but *The Famous Victories* is much less impressive in language and style. In *The Famous Victories*, Erpingham is excluded from the cast. This suggests, on the one hand, that Shakespeare must have found something attractive in the account of the knight furnished by Holinshed which led him to prefer to follow the chronicle rather than the anonymous history play, yet did so, to all appearances, only so that he could draw quick profit from this character. For, if *The Famous Victories* banishes the old knight, it finds a place for the archers, albeit off-stage, as they erect their impromptu *cheval-de-frize*, which the king describes in enough detail to make clear how the barrier was improvized and what function it would serve:

> Then I wil, that every archer provide him a stake of
> A tree, and sharpe it a both endes,
> And at the first encounter of the horsemen,
> To pitch their stakes downe into the ground before them,

> That they may gore themselves upon them,
> And then to recoyle back and shoote wholly altogither,
> And so discomfit them.

The verse may be halting, the confusion of pronouns distressing, but the account is historical, explicit and in fact quite lengthy in a play that has to move fast as it covers a great deal more ground than *Henry V*. It is also worth noting, for future reference, that though this information about the archers' defensive barrier is included in *The Famous Victories*, command of the bowmen is allocated, not to Erpingham, who does not appear at all, but to a nobleman who also fought at Agincourt, Richard de Vere, 11th earl of Oxford. Shakespeare did not, however, choose to include these details, notwithstanding that this source, despite its generally unprepossessing stagecraft, demonstrated at this juncture a fairly conventional way of handling it in the theatre without causing any particular problems.

The evidence suggests, then, that it is not just that the archers do not figure in *Henry V*, but that Shakespeare was avoiding allowing them any part in the play. Arguing for a negative is always especially difficult. So it is worth emphasizing that Shakespeare ignored the archers, to all appearances, despite the fact that history which remained alive in the popular imagination and in scholarship granted them their due role and indeed liked to magnify it, and even though staging need not, as we have seen, have been problematic. The matter becomes even more intriguing when we recall that Shakespeare turned to his historical sources to reinstate the commander of the archers in a freshly fashioned part without following the anonymous history play in ennobling the role.

But, if not with longbows, then with what weapons does Shakespeare cram his 'wooden 0'? There is, in fact, some use of imagery from archery. For instance:

> Therefore doth heaven divide
> The state of man in diverse functions
> Setting endeavour in continual motion,
> To which is fixed, as an aim or butt
> Obedience.

But the lines are spoken by the Archbishop of Canterbury, hardly a man of war, if not exactly a man of peace either, and most likely thinking less of battlefields than of target practice in churchyards. A similar remark applies when, opening a cluster of analogies, he continues:

> I this infer,
> That many things having full reference
> To one consent may work contrariously,
> As many arrows loose several ways
> Come to one mark.

Perhaps the image that evokes the butts could be made applicable to battle tactics, but no effort is made to develop it that way, any more than in Henry's 'we will come to them

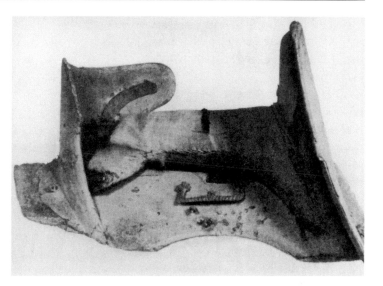

*66. Saddle of Henry V, part of the funeral achievements of Henry V, preserved in his chantry chapel in Westminster Abbey.*

and make them skirr away as swift as stones enforced from the old Assyrian slings', it is turned into a comment on fifteenth-century missiles. Orléans and the Constable quibble in proverbs about overshooting with one's bolt. Even if the reference is not to the crossbow, which would, of course, be more appropriate for Rambures's comrades in arms, it is, however, hardly in the French camp that we should be listening out for anything like appreciation of the longbow.

In fact, far from dwelling on archery and the longbow, Shakespeare either turns to the common stock of images to describe warfare or else mentions other weaponry. An inventory yields the somewhat surprising discovery that if one were to ask what is drawn to our attention as the weapon most characteristic of the English it would in fact turn out to be nothing other than the homely cudgel. The sword, like fire on many occasions, comes across as a commonplace image of conflict. Just as the latter becomes actual when the camp is torched, the sword not unexpectedly may become a literal weapon too, but not so frequently as might have been expected, while the king's, which is bent in battle can, like that of Essex, take on symbolic qualities again when put to exemplary use. The traditional view of how wars are fought and what are the due rewards finds expression in the Boy's ditty:

> And sword and shield
> In bloody field
> Doth win immortal fame.

Daggers are mentioned too, though on occasion they are wooden. Whether or not it is a tribute to the anticipated effectiveness of Constable's naked curtle axe, Williams brings home the horrors of combat by referring to 'all those legs and arms and heads chopped off in a battle'; the vivid line certainly creates an impression that what was most to be feared in the awaited battle was hand to hand combat, where the 'puissant pike' could also make its due impression, as it might too in the atrocities after the storming of a city.

Just as Katherine's bilbow reveals a readiness to expand the field of military allusion with a degree of playfulness, so too 'a perilous shot out of an elder-gun' shows a certain comfortable familiarity with new-fangled weapons, though whether that category ought properly to include 'Pistol', not recorded for the *Oxford English Dictionary* before the mid-sixteenth century, is a moot point. Siege artillery in the play, as in history, figures mainly in the earlier stages. Henry vows to turn the Dauphin's 'balls to gunstones', and Exeter repeats his king's threat to 'return your mock in second accent of his ordinance'. So the third act opens with the roars of chambers as 'the nimble gunner with linstock the devilish cannon touches, and down goes all before them'. In his harangue before the breach, Henry makes good use of a simile, comparing the eye of the determined soldier with 'the brass cannon'. He likewise finds an apt image for valiant Fluellen who is 'touched with choler, hot as gunpowder'. There is, however, no escaping the impression that though artillery, like mining, has its undoubted (and indeed historic) part to play in the campaign, especially in the early phases, such matters are better left to a rather lower class of soldier than the king and the royal dukes. Queen Isabel speaks of 'the fatal balls of murdering basilisks'. Her very language hints at a certain distancing in this recognition of the impact of new technology on the ancient art of war.

The warfare that was held in highest esteem was, in Henry's words to Williams that we should probably take quite literally, more a matter of 'the arbitrement of swords'. The campaign had been long and arduous, but was, it appears, considered to have reached its climax when, as the king puts it, 'Alençon and myself were down together'. Recording the event, Holinshed comments that 'the king that daie shewed himself a valiant knight', the appreciation being emphasized in a marginal note with the words 'a valiant king'. Though Craik's note identifies the source of the incident in the chronicle, he might have gone on to explain more exactly just what had been involved at this point. This was the ultimate combat between the king and the duke, fighting, not on their chargers, but on foot, as had come to be the style in the Hundred Years War. Here two men of blood were asserting their rank and position in the fashion that was regarded as most glorious. This was no moment to be sullied by the 'base, common and popular'.

Some further insights into the interpretation that Shakespeare gives to the battle can be gleaned from looking at Henry's speech after the French herald Mountjoy has reported on casualties. The king's enquiry whether 'prisoners of good sort' have been taken makes sense, of course, within the context of warfare in which the ransoms for distinguished prisoners made a decidedly useful contribution to the war chest. Henry V was always anxious to conduct operations at the least expense to the English treasury. The next passage, enriched with grand titles and proud names evocative of feudal France, makes a most impressive victory roll call, leading up to the magnificent epitaph, nicely balanced between regret for such losses and a proud assertion of triumph: 'Here was a royal fellowship in death'. Impressive in its brevity as in the briefer tragedy it unfolds, the king does not, however, grant that death is a great leveller when he continues in similar vein about those who have fought his battle. After mentioning a duke, an earl, a knight and even, with due condescension, Davy Gam, esquire, he concludes that there were 'none else of name, and of all other men, but five-and-twenty'. Whether the figure is totally accurate is beside the point, for Shakespeare's rhetorical purpose was plainly (and quite

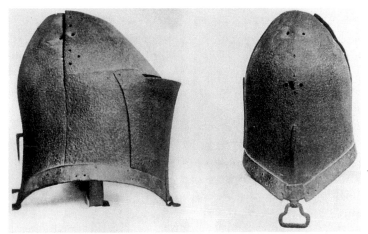

*67. A tilting helm from the chantry chapel of Henry V in Westminster Abbey. Legend has it that it was worn by the king on the battlefield of Agincourt, but this is unlikely. It formed part of his funeral achievements.*

justifiably in both historical and dramatic terms) to create the impression of an overwhelming victory. But, even if we dismiss as anachronistic any notion that in the hierarchical society of the fifteenth century there was anything especially pejorative or hard-hearted about listing the ennobled and the knighted and identifying the remainder as being without name, the fact remains that Shakespeare's Henry has not, even at this late point, allowed their due to the common soldiers who, according to all historical accounts, had had a crucial role in securing victory. The king, a monarch under God, is unhesitant in modestly ascribing his success to the deity; when it comes to humanity, he is decidedly less willing to share the credit with his soldiery.

Similar social attitudes are found in an earlier scene, though it is arguable that the handling of the matter produces an unresolved contradiction. In conversing, not to say plotting, with the bishop of Ely, the Archbishop explains how, if the church was put to contribution, the sum available would maintain to the King's honour, 'full fifteen earls and fifteen hundred knights, six thousand and two hundred good esquires'. The figures were not, of course, plucked out of the air at random; they reflect more or less the forces available to Henry, but by some alchemy the archers have been metamorphosed into 'esquires', gentlemen, as Craik reminds us and as Henry does not forget, only a little lower than knights. Well might they, in the enthusiastic words of the Chorus, 'sell the pasture now to buy the horse'.

But the question arises again: where are the archers then? For they were not 'esquires'. We can, by this point, venture the answer that they have not been allowed on scene because their presence would diminish the impact of a noble fellowship, a band of brothers, which never, of course, included any that were not already of name, that won the battle and conquered France.

And how was the battle won? Modern military historians have pored over the chronicles and paced out the land, and one certainty at least emerges. The disposition of Henry's disciplined army, and in particular that of the archers under Erpingham, was organized in such a way that the French were prevented from bringing all their large and ungainly forces into the combat at any one time with the English in numbers sufficient to crush them. They were in fact repelled piece-meal, which naturally compounded confusion. Whatever the details of the battle of Agincourt, we can be confident that under Henry V, who had studied warfare from remarkably early years, military efficiency that was modern by early fifteenth-century standards vanquished feudal chivalry under poor leadership and with only inefficient support from mercenaries. Yet – and it is important to note the fact – Shakespeare's Henry does not, in his hour of glory, see matters in this light. Far from it. Doubtless it was seemly and pious to intone *Non Nobis Domine*. But how strange it seems when Henry declares that the fight had been won 'without stratagem'. As if to emphasize the point and even to stress that no mean or ignoble advantage had been gained by outwitting his opponents, he even goes on to add that the victory with its amazingly disproportionate casualty lists has been gained 'in plain shock and even play of battle'. This, together with the suppression of the archers, constitutes quite a considerable transformation of the historical facts that were readily available in Elizabethan England to a wide public that, to all appearances, was not inclined to interpret them in the same way as Shakespeare.

Saying this is not by any means the same as complaining about it, but it does raise problems. Some might argue that the possibly questionable transformation of historical sources within a context, where the general pattern of events provides a fairly predictable framework where a number of well-known characters can be developed without too much violence to general expectations, is no more than one element in a play that had much else to offer the public – not least in rhetoric that transcended scenic limitations, bawdy humour that likewise played on words, and patriotism that could appeal to one section of the audience, while another would warm to the penetrating insights of the king's agony in the field. It would, however, be a pity just to leave the matter there. The transformation is on a scale that stirs at least curiosity. It may not be idle curiosity either, for, not long after the first performances of Shakespeare's play, Michael Drayton was to think it appropriate to revert to an historically more orthodox presentation in his 2,520 line poem, *The Battaile of Agincourt* (1627). A promising line of investigation for any history play, but especially one of Shakespeare's, is, of course, to enquire to what extent it has been made not only a reflection on the past, but a comment on its author's own age. So we may begin by noting arguments that by the end of the sixteenth century, the age of the long bow had passed. If it is, as we have seen, true that three editions of Ascham's *Taxophilus* were called for, none, it appears, was needed after 1583. Historians who make much of the fact that legislation to encourage archery was passed repeatedly might well pause to consider that when laws have to be passed more than once in a relatively short period this may be because their provisions are ineffectual, whatever the authorities happen to think about the issue in question. The whole matter was raised anew by Sir John Smythe, but only to meet with a prompt rebuttal by Humfrey Barwick. Whether or not it was the force of his arguments that tipped the scales, the Privy Council decreed in 1595 that archers should no longer be admitted as efficient soldiers in the trained bands. But, if the longbow was passing out of fashion, is there any reason for thinking that such a consideration would have carried any weight with Shakespeare? Two factors suggest that it might well have. First we have the character of Captain Fluellen. Always looking to the past, instead of to the present, he is the old-fashioned pedant of warfare, with his endless tiddle-taddle and pibble-pabble of Pompey the Great. He may have 'much care and valour', but even as the king praises him on those scores he cannot but admit that there is something, 'a little out of fashion' in his attitudes. If Fluellen is mocked, could anything smacking of Ascham's sententious scholarship escape without a smile?

Some confirmation of the view that there is reflection of later sixteenth-century military thinking in *Henry V* may be found in the comments about body protection made by the French nobles. They prattle on about their finely decorated armour, when the whole drift of the play is that even the 'best in the world' will serve them ill. As for the English, they attract the scorn of their enemies, because they wear 'such heavy headpieces'. The audience can hardly fail to realize that the French nobility have got quite the wrong end of the stick. That English headgear will serve well is made clear enough; a beaver, even a rusty one, will do its job; and though modesty forbids too much show, a bruised helmet is testimony to the protection it had provided the king. So, effectively enough, a contrast is drawn. Ostensibly it is between French and English armour, but we may arguably see that it is between the old-style full-body protection that was in vogue during the Hundred Years War and the lighter armour supplemented by a sturdy helmet that came to be preferred nearly two centuries later when firearms had replaced longbow arrows and crossbow quarrels as major hazards. All in all, it seems reasonable to conclude that Shakespeare does, to some degree, take cognizance of contemporary thinking about military equipment, on occasion either avoiding the old-fashioned or else poking fun at it while also looking to more recent developments.

According to Melchiori, some of Shakespeare's works fall into the category of what he calls Garter plays, being intended for performance as entertainment when the Noble Order forgathered. An audience formed of distinguished and active gentlemen would, it can be suggested, be alert to developments in military affairs. Dwelling on the triumph of obsolescent, if not obsolete, weaponry at Agincourt would have been no way to win its favour. What is more important, however, is that such an audience could be counted upon to warm to the emphasis on the role of the nobility in the army that served under the paragon of monarchs, who is, of course, referred to as 'this star of England'. A possible explanation could be simply that Shakespeare wished to make of the Agincourt campaign an example of the glories of chivalry, with indeed many horses to see in our mind's eye, for they are often mentioned, and, more significantly much stress on nobility. But it is hardly enough to accept this interpretation without asking why Shakespeare should have decided on it. This is why Melchiori's arguments are attractive.

To collect quotations showing the nobility in the best light is so easy as to be otiose. We may, however, note how the reverse is stressed. Before Harfleur, Henry first calls upon 'you noble English'. Then, seemingly making a distinction, he turns to address his appeal to 'you, good yeomen', supposing there is none 'so mean and base' as to lack in a neat quibble, 'noble lustre' in his eyes. Craik cannot think that anything pejorative lurks in the vocabulary Henry employs at this juncture, not even when he uses words like 'base and mean'. In fact, however, the very next scene makes it clear there ought to have been, even if the king had hoped there would not be. Scholars, like audiences, may be stirred by the king's oratory, but Nym proves himself a rascally coward immediately after, as on every other occasion. Pistol is no better. Saying so is not to deny that they add some laughter to a serious play, or to make nothing of a certain realism that has its basis in historical record.

Yet is it not remarkable that this play setting the English off against the French derives so much of its humour from the disparagement of the English common soldier? Is it not strange that we are not invited to laugh at the French soldiery too? Bates and Williams do represent something more admirable than Nym and Pistol. But do they do enough to offset the bad impression of characters who appear more often and attract more attention? The case becomes stronger still if it is admitted that the historic and amply chronicled role of the soldiery has, in effect, been passed over in silence. What applies to the lowest category of soldier is, moreover, true of what – by analogy with what was happening in public administration in Tudor times – might perhaps be called the professional middle class in the army. Erpingham, though shorn of his particular office, is preserved, conceivably because, though nothing explicit beyond the title 'Sir' is made of it in the text of the play, he was himself a knight of the Garter.

But what, for instance, of Sir Walter Hungerford? A notable warrior and servant of the crown like Erpingham, it was he who – according to the best contemporary source for the campaign, the *Gesta Henrici Quinti* – prompted Henry's inspiring response when he cried out that he wished the English army could be reinforced by ten thousand men. 'This is a foolish way to talk, because by the God in heaven upon whose grace I have relied and in whom is my firm hope of victory, I would not, even if I could, have a single man more than I do. For these I have here with me are God's people, whom he deigns to let me have at this time'. But, just as Erpingham in *The Famous Victories* had to yield pride of place as commander of the archers to the earl of Oxford, so in *Henry V* sentiments expressed in the *Gesta* by Hungerford – a knight, to be sure, but not a knight of the Garter – are allocated to the noble earl of Westmoreland. Only the four captains (Gower, Fluellen, Macmorris and Jamy) remain in Shakespeare's play to represent a lower class of officer who loyally supported the Lancastrian monarchs, and they are sadly diminished into national types with relatively lowly functions in the field. As well as enacting the triumphs abroad of a peerless king, doubtless in part at least to stir affection for the earl of Essex and his Irish mission at the end of Elizabeth's reign, *Henry V* transforms its sources, indeed history itself, as it was accepted in the sixteenth century and still is today, in order to make Agincourt a paean in praise of the great nobility gathered around the crown. To do so meant giving short shrift to those archers who had won, or at the very least made it possible to win, the field at Agincourt. By a curious quirk of reception history and in the fulfilment of a programme equally determined by contemporary motivations but in quite the opposite direction, Olivier restored the people's lustre while burnishing anew the crown imperial. That was good history as well as good politics in the context of the Second World War in a version that added technicolour spectacle to vivid rhetoric. Whether it was true to the Shakespeare of *Henry V* is quite another question.

# List of Contributors

# Further Reading

## 1 Henry V: A Life and Reign

There is an excellently rounded biography of the king: C.T. Allmand, *Henry V* (London, 1992). Also useful, not least for its illustrations, is P. Earle, *The Life and Times of Henry V* (London, 1972). A work of a rather different nature is that of J.H. Wylie and W.T. Waugh, *The Reign of Henry the Fifth* (3 vols, Cambridge, 1914-29), which provides an immensely detailed narrative. C.L. Kingsford, *Henry V. The Typical Medieval Hero* (London, 1901), is old-fashioned but interesting. A collection of essays, *Henry V. The Practice of Kingship*, ed. G.L. Harriss (Oxford, 1985), provides sharp insights into Henry's relations with his nobility and parliament amongst other matters. There is much stimulating discussion in K.B. McFarlane, *Lancastrian Kings and Lollard Knights* (Oxford, 1972), not least on the relationship between Henry and his father. See also P. McNiven, *Heresy and Politics in the Reign of Henry IV* (Woodbridge, 1987). For a rare critical view for the reign, see T.B. Pugh, *Henry V and the Southampton Plot of 1415* (Southampton Record Series, 30, 1988). E. Powell, *Kingship, Law and Society. Criminal Justice in the Reign of Henry V* (Oxford, 1989) discusses this important aspect of Henry's rule. For contemporary writings on the king, see A. Gransden, *Historical Writing in England, c. 1307 to the early sixteenth century* (London, 1982). The best overview of the period as a whole remains M.H. Keen, *England in the Later Middle Ages* (London, 1973).

## 2 The Battle

For the political background, see C.T. Allmand, *Henry V* (London, 1992), and E.F. Jacob, *Henry V and the Invasion of France* (London, 1947). The classic study of the battle remains N.H. Nicolas, *The History of the Battle of Agincourt* (2nd ed. London, 1832, reprinted 1970), which includes extracts from chronicles and other sources. It now needs to be read alongside A. Curry, *The Battle of Agincourt: Sources and Interpretations* (Woodbridge, 2000), which also presents and discusses a range of extracts from primary sources. The best primary source is printed as *Gesta Henrici Quinti: The Deeds of Henry V*, ed. F. Taylor and J.S. Roskell (Oxford, 1975).

For a summary of the campaign and battle with useful maps and plans see M. Bennett, *Agincourt, 1415: Triumph against the odds* (Osprey campaign series, London, 1991). Other useful discussions are to be found in A. Burne, *The Agincourt War* (London, 1956, reprinted 1999), C. Hibbert, *Agincourt* (London, 1964), and J. Keegan, *The Face of Battle* (London, 1976, reprinted as Penguin book

1978). For the debate in various volumes of the *English Historical Review*, see E.M. Lloyd, 'The 'Herse' of Archers at Crécy' (July, 1895), pp. 538-41; H.B. George, 'The Archers at Crécy' (October, 1895), pp. 733-38, and J.E. Morris, 'The Archers at Crécy' (July 1897), pp. 427-36. Jim Bradbury, *The Medieval Archer* (Woodbridge, 1985), covers the battle and much more. For the French battle plan see C. Phillpotts, 'The French Plan of Battle during the Agincourt Campaign', *English Historical Review* (1984). For comparison and context, see M. Bennett, 'The Development of Battle Tactics in the Hundred Years War, in *Arms, Armies and Fortifications in the Hundred Years War*, ed. A. Curry and M. Hughes (Woodbridge, 1994), P. Contamine, *War in Medieval Society*, trans. M. Jones (London, 1984), and *Medieval Warfare. A History*, ed. M. Keen (Oxford, 1999).

For editions of texts mentioned, see Jean de Bueil, *Le Jouvencel*, ed. C. Favre & L. Lecestre (2 vols, Société de l'histoire de France, Paris, 1887-9), Sir John Smythe, *Certain Discourses Military*, ed. J.R. Hale (New York, 1964), Lt.-Col. W.St.P. Bunbury, 'A Treatise on the Art of War by Thomas Audley', *Journal of the Society for Army Historical Research*, 6 (1927) pp. 65-78, 129-33. The manuscript of Audeley's treatise 'Art of War' is British Library Additional MS 23971. '*Simplex*' (3rd. edn. 1916), a First World War manual on machine gun tactics, is fascinating by way of comparison.

For reports on the Battlefields Trust Day, see The *Guardian* Monday 27 February 1995 on the outcome of the debate. *The Telegraph* covered the debate on Saturday 25, but got the opposing views the wrong way round (corrected on the Monday). *The Times* reported it on both days (also with some inaccuracies) and even made the debate an excuse for a Eurosceptical editorial. Such are the uses of History!

## 3 The Bowman and the Bow

There are two important general studies: R. Hardy, *Longbow. A Social and Military History* (Cambridge 1976, revised 1982, printed 1986, 1995), and J. Bradbury, *The Medieval Archer* (Woodbridge, 1985). Two Osprey books are also useful: E.G. Heath, *Archery. A Military History* (London, 1980), C. Bartlett and G. Embleton, *The English Longbowman* (London, 1995). C. Blair, *European Armour* (London, 1979), provides a sound overview as does M. Prestwich, *Armies and Warfare in the Middle Ages. The English Experience* (New Haven and London, 1996), and K. De Vries, *Medieval Military Technology* (Peterborough, Ontario, 1992). For Robin Hood, see J.C. Holt, *Robin Hood* (London, 1982), and J. Taylor and R.B. Dobson, *Rymes of Robyn Hood. An Introduction to the English Outlaw* (London, 1976). Many of the works recommended for Chapter Two are also useful for further information and discussion on the archers.

## 4 Sir Thomas Erpingham

### A Life in Arms

A brief biography of Erpingham is to be found in the *Dictionary of National Biography*, supplement II, pp. 189-190. On his links with the Lancastrian dukes and kings, see S. Walker, *The Lancastrian Affinity* (Oxford, 1990), T. John, 'Sir Thomas Erpingham, East Anglian Society and the Dynastic Revolution of 1399', *Norfolk Archaeology*, 35 (1970), J.D. Milner, 'Sir Simon Felbrigg, KG: the Lancastrian Revolution and Personal Fortune', *Norfolk Archaeology*, 37 (1978), and H. Castor, 'The Duchy of Lancaster and the Rule of East Anglia, 1399-1440: A Prologue to the Paston Letters', in *Crown, Government and People in the Fifteenth Century*, ed. R.E. Archer (Stroud, 1995). There is also useful material in J.H. Wylie, *History of England under Henry the Fourth* (4 vols, London, 1884-98), and J.H. Wylie and W.T. Waugh, *The Reign of Henry V* (3 vols, Cambridge, 1914-29). For a discussion of the royal household of which Erpingham was so prominent a member, see C. Given-Wilson, *The Royal Household and the King's Affinity. Service, Politics and Finance in England, 1360-1413* (Yale, 1986).

There are many useful printed primary sources in addition to the Calendars of Patent, Close and Fine rolls. *John of Gaunt's Register* is available in print with the volumes for 1371-5 edited by S. Armitage (Camden Society, third series 20-21, 1911), and those for 1379-83 edited by E.C. Lodge and R. Somerville (Camden Society, third series 56-7, 1937). For the campaigns with Bolingbroke see *Expedition to Prussia and the Holy Land made by Henry Earl of Derby (afterwards King Henry IV) in the years 1390-1 and 1392-3*, ed. L. Toulmin Smith (Camden Society, new series, 1894). Erpingham's will and a short biography is to be found in *The Register of Henry Chichele, Archbishop of Canterbury 1414-1443*, ed. E.F. Jacob (vol. 2, Canterbury and York Society, London, 1947). Letters are to be found in *Anglo-Norman Letters and Petitions*, ed. M.D. Legge (Anglo-Norman Text Society, Oxford, 1941), and *Paston Letters and Papers of the Fifteenth Century*, ed. N. Davis (2 vols, London, 1971, 1976). Also useful are the volumes of *Proceedings of the Privy Council* , edited by N.H. Nicolas (1834-7). See also *Chronique de la traison et mort de Richart II*, ed. B. Williams (London, 1846), and *The Controversy between Sir Richard Scrope and Sir Robert Grosvenor in the Court of Chivalry*, ed. N.H. Nicolas (London, 1832).

There are also some unpublished materials in addition to those in the Public Record Office which are mentioned in the text. The Norfolk Record Office holds much relevant material including the account roll of the gild of St George (NCR 8g); account rolls for some of Erpingham's manors and other materials on his landed interests (NCR 24c, and within the Phillips collection); an account roll of 1457 for his chantry dated in the Dean and Chapter records (DCN 4/7). Accounts relating to his constableship of Dover are in the British Library, Additional Charter 16,433.

On military organization in the period see J. Sherborne, 'Indentured Retinues and English Expeditions to France, 1369-1380', *English Historical Review*, 79 (1964), reprinted in his *War, Politics and Culture in Fourteenth-Century England* (London and Rio Grande,

1994), and A. Curry, 'English Armies in the Fifteenth Century', in *Arms, Armies and Fortifications in the Hundred Years War*, ed. A. Curry and M.Hughes (Woodbridge, 1994). A. Curry, *The Battle of Agincourt. Sources and Interpretations* (Woodbridge, 2000) provides a fuller discussion of the materials in the Public Record Office concerning the campaign of 1415, as well as translations of all the major chronicle sources.

### Norwich, Norfolk and Sir Thomas Erpingham

Much of the material on land- and office-holding is taken from the calendars of Chancery enrolments (the Patent rolls, Close rolls and Fine rolls). There are also some useful local histories. The best known is perhaps F. Blomefield, *An Essay Towards a Topographical History of the County of Norfolk* (11 vols, London, 1805-10), with volume 4 being particularly relevant. Four works by W. Rye are also valuable: *General History of Norfolk* (London, 1829); *Some Rough Materials for a History of the Hundred of North Erpingham* (Norwich, 1883); *Norfolk Families* (Norwich, 1913); *Some Historical Essays chiefly relating to Norfolk* (Norwich, 1926). See also T. Browne, *Repertorium; or, Some Account of the Tombs and Monuments in the Cathedral Church of Norwich in 1680*, in *Posthumous Works of the Learned Sir Thomas Browne* (London, 1712), E. Farrer, *Church Heraldry of Norfolk* (3 vols, Norwich, 1887), H. Harrod, *Gleanings among the Castles and Convents of Norfolk* (Norwich, 1857), J. Kirkpatrick, *History of the Religious Orders and Communities and the Hospitals in the County of Norfolk* (Great Yarmouth, 1845), and W.A. Smith Wynne, *St. Olaves' Priory and Bridge* (Norwich, 1914). For more recent works, see N. Tanner, *The Church in Late Medieval Norwich, 1370-1532* (Toronto, 1984), *Norwich Cathedral; Church, City and Diocese, 1096-1996* eds. I. Atherton, E. Fernie, C. Harper-Bill and H. Smith (London, 1996), J.H. Druery, 'The Erpingham House, Saint Martin's at Palace, Norwich', *Norfolk Archaeology*, 6 (1864), *Excavations at St Martin-at-Palace Plain, Norwich*, East Anglian Archaeology Report, no. 37 (Norfolk Museums Service, 1987), S. Haywood, *Digging under the Doorstep* (Norfolk Museums Service, 1983). For the records of the city of Norwich, see *Records of the City of Norwich*, vols 1 and 2, eds. W. Hudson and J.C. Tingey (Norwich, 1906). For the county context see T. John, 'Sir Thomas Erpingham, East Anglian Society and the Dynastic Revolution of 1399', *Norfolk Archaeology, 35* (1970), and H. Castor, 'The Duchy of Lancaster and the Rule of East Anglia, 1399-1440: A Prologue to the Paston Letters', in *Crown, Government and People in the Fifteenth Century*, ed. R.E. Archer (Stroud, 1995).

### The Erpingham Gate

For early references see Sir Thomas Browne, *Posthumous Works* (London, 1712), part I, *Repertorium.*, and F. Blomefield, *An Essay Towards a Topographical History of the County of Norfolk* (11 vols, London, 1805-10). There was a short article produced in 1938: E.W. Tristram, 'The Erpingham Gate', Friends of Norwich Cathedral Report. There is a fuller treatment of the gate and the whole fabric of the cathedral in *Norwich Cathedral. Church, City and Diocese, 1096-1996*, ed. I. Atherton, E, Fernie, C. Harper-Bill and H. Smith (London and Rio Grande, 1996). See also Henry Harrod, *Gleanings among the Castles and Convents of Norfolk* (Norwich, 1857); H.C. Beeching, 'The Chapels and Altars of Norwich Cathedral', *The Architect and Contract Reporter* (3, 10 December 1915), J. Shinners, 'The Veneration of Saints at Norwich Cathedral in the Fourteenth Century', *Norfolk Archaeology*, 40 (1988). For the gate's possible architect, see J. Harvey, *English Medieval Architects* (London, 1954). Also useful is an unpublished doctoral thesis, R. Fawcett, 'Later Gothic Architecture in Norfolk' (University of East Anglia, 1975).

### The Erpingham Chasuble

The chasuble is illustrated in *The Medieval Treasury. The Art of the Middle Ages in the Victoria & Albert Museum*, ed. P. Williamson (London, 1996). There is a brief notice in D. King, 'A Relic of Noble Erpingham', *Victoria and Albert Museum Bulletin*, 4 (1968). For works on English embroidery in the period, see G. Christie, *English Medieval Embroidery* (Oxford, 1938), A.F. Kendrick, *English Needlework* (London, 2nd edition, 1967), and B. Snook, *English Embroidery* (London, 1974). Similar vestments are listed in *Archdeaconry of Norwich: Inventory of Church Goods temp. Edward III*, ed. Dom Aelred Watkin, Norfolk Record Society, 19 (1947-8).

## 5  Chivalry at Agincourt

The major works on chivalry in this period are M. Keen, *Chivalry* (Yale, 1984), and M.G.A. Vale, *War and Chivalry. Warfare and Aristocratic Culture in England, France and Burgundy at the End of the Middle Ages* (London, 1981). Two useful editions of contemporary sources are *The Book of Chivalry of Geoffroi de Charny,* trans. R.W. Kaeuper and E. Kennedy (Philadelphia, 1996), and *Froissart's Chronicles*, tr. G. Brereton (Harmonsworth, 1968).

Terry Jones, *Chaucer's Knight. The Portrait of a Medieval Mercenary*, was first published in 1980 with a revised edition in 1994. Responses to his work include two articles by Maurice Keen, 'Chaucer's Knight, the English Aristocracy and the Crusade', in *English Court Culture in the Later Middle Ages*, ed. V. Scattergood and J. Sherborne (London, 1983), and 'Chaucer and Chivalry Revisited', in *Armies, Chivalry and Warfare in Medieval Britain and France*, ed. M.J. Strickland, Harlaxton Medieval Studies VII (Stamford, 1998). For the account of the sack of Vilna in 1390, see *Scriptores Rerum Prussicarum*, III, 164-7, translated by A. S. Cook, 'The Historical Background to Chaucer's Knight', *Transactions of the Connecticut Academy of Arts and Sciences*, 20 (1916).

For Henry of Derby's Prussian expeditions, see L.T. Smith, *Expeditions to Prussia and the Holy Land made by Henry Earl of Derby* (Camden Society, New Series 52, 1894), and F.R.H. Du Boulay, 'Henry of Derby's Expeditions to Prussia 1390-1 and 1392', in *The Reign of Richard II. Essays in Honour of May McKisack*, ed. F.R.H. Du Boulay and C.M. Barron (London, 1971). A.S. Cook, 'Beginning the Board in Prussia', *Journal of English and German Philology*, 14 (1915), discusses the Teutonic Knights' 'Table of

Honour', while for this order and its background, see E. Christiansen, *The Northern Crusades: The Baltic and the Catholic Frontier 1100-1525* (London 1980), and N. Houseley, *The Later Crusades, 1274-1580* (Oxford, 1992), chapters 11 and 12.

For the Order of the Garter see J. Vale, *Edward III and Chivalry* (Woodbridge, 1982), 76-91; D.J.D. Boulton, *The Knights of the Crown. The Monarchical Orders of Knighthood in Later Medieval Europe, 1325-1520* (Woodbridge, 1987).

On brasses and memorials, see B.R. Kemp, 'English Church Monuments during the Period of the Hundred Years War, in *Arms, Armies and Fortifications in the Hundred Years War*, ed. A. Curry and M. Hughes (Woodbridge, 1994). *The Age of Chivalry. Art in Plantagenet England 1200-1400*, ed. J. Alexander and P. Binski (London, 1987), provides an illustration of the Hastings brass, together with discussion and bibliography. See also A.R. Wagner and J.G. Mann, 'A Fifteenth-Century Description of the Brass of Sir Hugh Hastings at Elsing, Norfolk', *Antiquaries Journal*, 19 (1939), and A. Hartshorne, 'On the Brass of Sir Hugh Hastings in Elsing Church, Norfolk', *Archaeologia*, 60 (1906). For the armour bearing invocations, see J.G. Scott, *European Arms and Armour at Kelvingrove* (Glasgow 1980).

# 6 The Heraldry of Agincourt

## Heraldic Insights into the Battle of Agincourt

There are several useful general works on heraldry: M. Pastoreau, *Heraldry: Its Origins and Meaning* (London, 1997); T. Woodcock, *The Oxford Guide to Heraldry* (Oxford, 1990); *Boutell's Heraldry*, revised by C.W. Scott-Giles and J.P. Brooke-Little (London, 1966); T. Brighton, *Heraldry. 1. The Origin of Heraldry* (Visual Publications, 1969); C.W. Scott-Giles, *The Romance of Heraldry* (London, 1965), and C.W. Scott-Giles, *Shakespeare's Heraldry* (London, 1950, reprinted 1971). Also useful are some older works, J. and J.B. Burke, *The General Armory of England, Scotland, Ireland and Wales* (London, 1878, reprinted 1976); F. Bury Palliser, *Historic Devices, Badges and War-Cries* (London, 1870); J. Foster, *Some Feudal Coats of Arms from Heraldic Rolls 1298-1418* (London and Oxford, 1902); A.C. Fox-Davies, *Heraldic Badges* (London and New York, 1907); J. Woodward and G. Burnett, *A Treatise on Heraldry British and Foreign* (London, 1896, reprinted 1969). For flags, see C. Campbell, *Medieval Flags* (nd), and for the Norwich material, M. Rose, *The Misericords of Norwich Cathedral* (Norwich, 1994). C. Rothero, *The Armies of Crécy and Poitiers,* Osprey men-at-arms series (London, 1981, reprinted 1982), and *Crécy and Calais from the Public Records*, ed. G. Wrottesley, William Salt Archaeological Society Collections, 18, part 2 (1897), both provide information on heraldry at the battles, as does M. Bennett, *Agincourt 1415: Triumph against the odds* (London, 1994), P. Greenhill, *Heraldic Miniature Knights* (London, 1991), and *Coats of Arms of Knights at Agincourt*, a Heraldry Painting Book, produced by Achievements Ltd (nd). There are also two useful editions of rolls of arms: *English Mediaeval Rolls of Arms*, vol. 1, ed. R.W. Mitchell (Tweeddale, 1983), and *Rolls of Arms, Edward I 1272-1307*, ed. G.J. Brault, Society of Antiquaries (Woodbridge, 1997). An early fifteenth century work which includes much on heraldry is available in a modern edition: *The Essential Portions of Nicholas Upton's 'De studio militari' before 1446, translated by John Blount, Fellow of All Souls (c.1500)*, ed. F. P. Barnard (Oxford, 1931). Henry V's ordinances issued at Mantes in 1419 are given in C. Hibbert, *Agincourt* (London, 1964). R. Barber, *The Life and Campaigns of the Black Prince* (London, 1979), and J. Harvey, *The Black Prince and his Age* (London, 1976) contain much of interest. (My thanks go to two friends, Joan Hurrell in connection with heraldry and ships, and Monsieur Claude Songis for his help in connection with French coats of arms.)

## The Heralds at the Time of Agincourt

Useful starting points are A. Wagner, *Heralds and Heraldry in the Middle Ages* (London, 1956), and R. Dennys, *Heraldry and the Heralds* (London, 1982). A list of heralds and kings of arms is provided in *The College of Arms, by W.H. Godfrey, assisted by Sir Anthony Wagner, Garter King of Arms, with a complete list of the officers of arms, prepared by H.S. London, Norfolk herald Extraordinary* (London, 1963). On the institutional aspects, see also A.Wagner, *Heralds of England. A History of the Office and College of Arms* (London, 1967). For the chapter at Rouen in 1420 and further information on William Bruges, see L.S. Loudon, *The Life of William Bruges, the First Garter King of Arms*, Harleian Society, 91, 92 (London, 1959-60). On the court of chivalry, see G. Squibb, *The High Court of Chivarly: a study of the Civil Law in England* (Oxford, 1969).

# 7 Shakespeare's Agincourt

For critical editions of the play, see *King Henry V*, ed. T.W. Craik (Arden Shakespeare, Routledge, 1995), and *King Henry V*, ed. A.Gurr (New Cambridge Shakespeare, Cambridge University Press, 1992). *The Famous Victories* is printed in G. Bullough, *Narrative and Dramatic Sources of Shakespeare*, vol. 4 (London and New York, 1962), a book which contains much other useful material from Holinshed's Chronicles and other sources. *Taxophilus* is printed in Roger Ascham, *English Works,* ed. W.A. Wright (Cambridge, 1904), and Michael Drayton's *Battaile of Agincourt* in *The Works of Michael Drayton*, vol. 3, ed. J.W. Hebel (Oxford, 1932). For the ballad, 'Agincourt, or the English bowman's glory', see *Bishop Percy's Folio Manuscript. Ballads and Romances*, vol. 2, ed. J.W. Hales and F.J. Furnivall (London, 1868). For a fuller description of Shakespeare's portrayal of Sir Thomas Erpingham, see C. Smith, 'History's Sir Thomas and Shakespeare's Erpingham', *Shakespeare and History*, ed. H. Klein and R. Wymer, *Shakespeare Yearbook,* VI, (1997). For other useful studies see T.L. Berger, 'Casting *Henry V*', *Shakespeare Studies*, 20 (1988), L.B. Campbell, *Shakespeare's Histories: Mirrors of Elizabethan Policy* (San Marino, CA, 1947), T. Cranfill, 'Shakespeare's Old Heroes', *Texas Studies in Literature and Language*, 15.2 (1972), and G. Melchiori, *Shakespeare's Garter Plays* (Newark: Delaware Univeristy Press, 1994).

# Index